The Microstructure of Financial Markets

The analysis of the microstructure of financial markets has been one of the most important areas of research in finance and has allowed scholars and practitioners alike to have a much more sophisticated understanding of the dynamics of price formation in financial markets. Frank de Jong and Barbara Rindi provide an integrated graduate-level textbook treatment of the theory and empirics of the subject, starting with a detailed description of the trading systems on stock exchanges and other markets and then turning to economic theory and asset pricing models. Special attention is paid to models explaining transaction costs, with a treatment of the measurement of these costs and the implications for the return on investment. The final chapters review recent developments in the academic literature. End-of-chapter exercises and downloadable data from the book's companion website provide opportunities to revise and apply models developed in the text.

FRANK DE JONG is Professor of Financial Markets and Risk Management at Tilburg University. He is also a senior research fellow and programme coordinator at Netspar, an independent network for research and education in the field of pensions, aging and retirement.

BARBARA RINDI is Associate Professor of Economics at Bocconi University in Milan. She is also a fellow of the Innocenzo Gasparini Institute for Economic Research (IGIER) and of the Centre for Applied Research in Finance (CAREFIN).

The Microstructure of
Financial Markets

Frank de Jong

and

Barbara Rindi

CAMBRIDGE
UNIVERSITY PRESS

CAMBRIDGE UNIVERSITY PRESS
Cambridge, New York, Melbourne, Madrid, Cape Town, Singapore, São Paulo, Delhi

Cambridge University Press
The Edinburgh Building, Cambridge CB2 8RU, UK

Published in the United States of America by Cambridge University Press, New York

www.cambridge.org
Information on this title: www.cambridge.org/9780521687270

First published 2009

Printed in the United Kingdom at the University Press, Cambridge

A catalogue record for this publication is available from the British Library

ISBN 978-0-521-86784-9   hardback
ISBN 978-0-521-68727-0   paperback

Contents

Figures

Tables

Preface

This is a textbook on economic models of financial markets (market microstructure). The material is intended for PhD and Master's (MSc or MPhil) students in economics or finance. Readers are expected to have some background in microeconomic theory, basic finance and some statistics. The aim is to provide the student with the tools to be able to read and appreciate academic papers on market microstructure. The book can be used for a full semester course on financial markets and market microstructure.

The authors have been using draft versions of the book chapters in their PhD and Master's courses at Bocconi University, the University of Amsterdam and Tilburg University. We thank the students of these courses for their questions and suggestions. We would also like to thank several colleagues who provided us with invaluable feedback and comments. We thank our referees for their suggestions, and in particular Paolo Vitale for a thorough review of the manuscript. We are grateful to Roberto Battalio, Bruno Biais, Sabrina Buti, Paolo Colla, Gene Kandel, Jeremie Lefebvre, Marco LiCalzi, Angelo Ranaldo and in particular Ohad Kadan, Giovanna Nicodano and Ingrid Werner for their detailed comments. Our thanks also to Luisella Bosetti, Fabio Deotto, Luca Filippa, Martino Ghezzi, Alan Hodson, Larry Leibowitz, Enrico Mandelli, Clare McQuitty and other practitioners and regulators who gave us the opportunity to learn about the working of real financial markets.

Introduction

In the traditional approach to financial economics the price formation process is a 'black box' in which there is no explicit role for financial market structure. Aspects such as dealers, spread and the organizational structure of financial markets are ignored. In Stoll's (2000) words, 'thirty years ago friction in financial markets was largely ignored in the theory of finance'. In the last two decades a substantial literature on the process of financial price formation has developed and is generally known under the name *market microstructure*. This literature relaxes the assumptions of the traditional asset pricing models, such as the absence of transaction costs, homogeneous and symmetric information, and looks inside the 'black box' to get a better understanding of intraday price dynamics. A related objective is to formulate recommendations for the optimal design and regulation of financial markets. Market microstructure also provides new techniques for estimating transaction costs and market liquidity. This is of practical relevance for professional investors, who are interested in efficient order execution and the effect of liquidity on asset prices.

Amihud and Mendelson (1987) was one of the first papers to draw researchers' attention to the relevance of market structure. They found that the variance of the open-to-open returns was higher than that of the close-to-close returns for the hundred most liquid stocks on the New York Stock Exchange (NYSE). This suggested that, due to the different market organization of the opening and the closing, agents trading at the opening were exposed to greater volatility than traders at the close.

In the following decade a substantial empirical literature focused on the relevance of financial market microstructure to price formation in stocks, bonds, derivatives and foreign exchange order flows. One of the purposes of microstructure models is to understand the impact of the organizational structure and the design of financial markets on trading costs and asset prices. These models are then used to construct indicators of market quality, which can serve to assess the utility of regulatory interventions.

The traditional representation of price formation in financial markets is an invisible hand or a Walrasian auctioneer equating supply and demand at the equilibrium price. However, real-world examples of financial markets show that price formation is more complex since (i) traders do not arrive simultaneously at the market-place and (ii) information is asymmetric. These imperfections generate trading costs and make

1

the market protocol in which trading takes place a relevant factor. Building on these frictions, two main strands of standard theoretical microstructure literature developed, namely inventory-based and information-based models. The former assigns a primary role to market-makers as liquidity providers (professionals who undertake to supply liquidity to the market) and shows how the bid–ask spread compensates them for price risk on inventory; the latter focuses on asymmetric information among market participants and shows how market-makers set the bid–ask spread to compensate for adverse selection costs. Applications of microstructure models (for an overview, see e.g. Biais, Glosten and Spatt, 2005 and Madhavan, 2000) include estimations of transaction costs and liquidity as well as the study of the price discovery process. This illustrates how and how quickly private information is reflected in market prices.

Microstructure models can also be used to explain apparently abnormal behaviour of prices and volumes. For instance, it has been noticed that the intraday pattern of average volumes and stock returns is U-shaped (Jain and Joh, 1988; Wood, McInish and Ord, 1985): at the end and at the beginning of the trading day an increase in both volumes and volatility is observed. Microstructure models (Admati and Pfleiderer, 1988; Hong and Wang, 2000) were constructed to explain why volumes and volatility are concentrated at certain times of day and how the relationship between the two variables can be explained. Another well-known example of an abnormal price pattern, termed the 'NASDAQ controversy', is described in the adjoining box.

The NASDAQ controversy

A well-known example of abnormal price behaviour is the finding of Christie and Schultz (1994) on the distribution of price quotes for the hundred most traded stocks on the National Association of Security Dealer Automated Quotation (NASDAQ) exchange. They found a virtually total absence of odd-eighth quotes. By contrast, for a sample of a hundred stocks with similar characteristics on the NYSE, they observed that the quotes were distributed evenly over the full spectrum of the eighths. Christie, Harris and Schultz (1994) showed that the absence of odd-eighth quotes on NASDAQ produced a wider spread, suggesting collusive behaviour on the part of market-makers. Another well-known early empirical finding that questioned the effective degree of competition within and between markets was that of Huang and Stoll (1996), who showed that execution costs were twice as high for a sample of NASDAQ stocks as for a matched sample of NYSE stocks. They proposed two explanations for the lower degree of competition on the NASDAQ: the common use by NASDAQ dealers and brokers of practices such as internalization, preferencing and crossing orders (see Chapter 10); and the availability of alternative trading systems where dealers could quote non-competitive prices. The Securities and Exchange Commission (SEC) reacted to these findings in 1997 by introducing its 'order handling rules', which significantly enhanced competition, both within and between markets.

Microstructure models generally begin by observing that markets can differ in a number of respects. The differences may involve the typology of participants, their attitude towards risk, the existence of fixed entry costs, the organizational structure of trades and the degree of transparency. In the standard models, market participants are usually classified by the type of information they hold and their motive for trading.

Informed traders have access to private information about the liquidation value of the asset traded and/or the identity of the other agents in the market-place. Private information may derive from insider information on the future value of the asset, from (costly) research on the asset's value, or from knowledge of the order flow; costly information can also be obtained through analysts. In the latter cases, information can be acquired only at a cost and it is not illegal. For instance, most investment banks allocate resources to obtaining information on the flow of orders or to procuring the greatest possible number of institutional clients. This kind of privileged information is typical of secondary markets in treasury bonds and foreign exchange. Furthermore, the information available to the insiders may differ in its precision. In market microstructure models the precision of the information is defined as the inverse of the variance of the asset's liquidation value, conditional on the information available to the insiders.

Uninformed traders have no private information; usually the models make distinctions among noise traders, who are purely liquidity-motivated, hedgers, who trade to cover possible adverse fluctuations and are therefore modelled as risk-averse, and market-makers or dealers, who provide liquidity.

As far as preferences are concerned, in standard models of market microstructure, agents are generally assumed to be either risk-neutral or risk-averse. Risk-neutral agents are interested in the average (or expected) return to the asset, whether this is certain or uncertain. For example, take two assets, A and B, with A yielding \$8 or \$12 (with probability $\frac{1}{2}$) depending on the state of the world, and B yielding a certain return of \$10. Risk-neutral agents will be indifferent between these two asset returns. Risk-averse agents, however, demand a premium on the return (or a discount on the price) to hold the risky asset.

At times, the cost of acquiring information is modelled in order to make the number of agents with privileged information endogenous. It may be useful, in fact, to evaluate the possible effect of changes in regulations or market organizational structure, bearing in mind that these changes can modify the insiders' incentive to trade.

Outline of the book

A road-map for this book is suggested in Figure Intro.1. Chapter 1 provides a detailed overview of the organizational structure of financial markets around the world, plus an in-depth description of the working of the limit order book, which is an increasingly important market structure. It also describes the trading protocol on the New York Stock Exchange.

Chapters 2 to 5 present the basic models of market microstructure, based on asymmetric information and inventory control. Chapter 2 starts with rational expectations

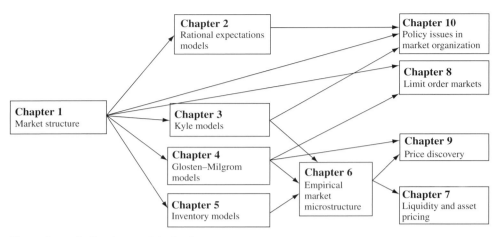

Figure Intro.1. Road-map of the book.

models for financial market equilibrium. Strictly speaking, these are not models of the workings of a financial market but illustrations of the equilibrium outcome that the trading process may produce. This chapter also introduces several useful tools, such as Bayesian updating and the rational expectations equilibrium. Chapter 3 discusses the Kyle (1985) model with an informed trader who maximizes trading profits by strategically choosing the size of his order. This model is the workhorse of theoretical market microstructure, and also indeed of many models in corporate finance. The model implies that order flow moves prices: buy orders drive prices up, sell orders down. Chapter 4 presents Glosten and Milgrom's (1985) model, which instead of Kyle's order-driven market considers a dealership market, showing that differences in information between traders create an adverse selection problem for the dealer. The dealers respond by driving a wedge between buying and selling prices, the bid–ask spread. Chapter 5 provides an alternative explanation for the bid–ask spread. Even if all traders have the same information, a spread may arise endogenously in the market. If traders come to the market randomly, a counterparty cannot be found immediately. The dealer absorbs the temporary imbalances in supply and demand, but if he is risk-averse, he has to be compensated for the risk of price fluctuations on the inventory: this compensation is provided by the bid–ask spread.

These chapters form the core of the market microstructure theory. The subsequent chapters build on these theories and develop empirical methods (Chapters 6 and 7) and offer more advanced, recent applications of market microstructure (Chapters 8 to 10).

Chapter 6 deals with empirical models and the estimation of transaction costs. First it discusses Roll's (1984) estimator; this model shows that transaction costs induce negative serial correlation in returns and provides a method to estimate bid–ask spreads using return data alone. The chapter then presents the Glosten and Harris (1988) model for estimating transaction costs from intraday price and trade data. The chapter also discusses several sources of intraday data and methods for estimating liquidity in the absence of high-frequency data. Chapter 7 establishes the relevance of liquidity and transaction costs for asset pricing. This chapter builds a bridge between market microstructure and asset pricing.

The last three chapters contain more advanced and recent material. Chapter 8 focuses on developments of models that describe the working of the open limit order book (OLOB), the most common type of financial trading system. Chapter 9 is devoted to time-series models for price discovery, i.e. the empirical modelling of the convergence to the equilibrium price. It presents the econometric tools for the analysis of price and trade data, from one or several markets. Finally, Chapter 10 applies the theoretical models to the analysis of various policy issues in the organization of financial markets, with sections on transparency, dual capacity trading, and the debate on consolidation or fragmentation of trading.

The book can be used for a full semester course on financial markets and market microstructure. For a shorter course, we suggest taking Chapter 1 (market organization), Chapters 2–5 (theory), and Chapters 6–7 (empirical models and asset pricing).

Several other textbooks on market microstructure are available. O'Hara (1995) was the first, and it is chiefly theoretical in nature. More recent, and compared to the present book more specialized texts, are the following. Lyons (2001) focuses on the microstructure of the foreign exchange market. Harris (2003) gives a very detailed introduction to markets and trading structures. Hasbrouck (2007) gives a comprehensive overview of empirical methods in microstructure.

References

Admati, A. and P. Pfleiderer, 1988, 'A theory of intraday patterns: volume and price variability', *Review of Financial Studies,* 1, 3–40.

Amihud, Y. and H. Mendelson, 1987, 'Trading mechanism and stock returns: an empirical investigation', *Journal of Finance*, 42, 533–55.

Biais, B., L. Glosten and C. Spatt, 2005, 'Market microstructure: a survey of microfoundations, empirical results, and policy implications', *Journal of Financial Markets,* 8, 217–64.

Christie, W. and P. Schultz, 1994, 'Why do NASDAQ market makers avoid odd-eighth quotes?', *Journal of Finance*, 49, 1813–40.

Christie, W., J. Harris and P. Schultz, 1994, 'Why did NASDAQ market makers stop avoiding odd-eighth quotes?', *Journal of Finance*, 49, 1841–60.

Glosten L. and E. Harris, 1988, 'Estimating the component of the bid/ask spread', *Journal of Financial Economics*, 21, 123–42.

Glosten L. and J. Milgrom, 1985, 'Bid, ask and transaction prices in a specialist market with heterogeneously informed traders', *Journal of Financial Economics*, 14, 71–100.

Harris, L. 2003, *Trading and Exchange*, Oxford University Press.

Hasbrouck, J. 2007, *Empirical Market Microstructure*, Oxford University Press.

Hong, H. and J. Wang, 2000, 'Trading and returns under periodic market closures', *Journal of Finance,* 55, 297–354.

Huang, R, and H. Stoll, 1996, 'Dealer versus auction markets: a paired comparison of execution costs on NASDAQ and the NYSE', *Journal of Financial Economics,* 41, 313–57.

Jain, O and G. Joh, 1988, 'The dependence between hourly prices and trading volume', *Journal of Financial and Quantitative Analysis,* 23, 269–83.

Kyle, A. 1985, 'Continuous auctions and insider trading', *Econometrica*, 53, 1315–35.

Lyons, R. 2001, *The Microstructure Approach to Exchange Rates*, Cambridge, Mass.: MIT Press.

Madhavan, A. 2000, 'Market microstructure: a survey', *Journal of Financial Markets,* 3, 205–58.

O'Hara, M. 1995, *Market Microstructure Theory*, Oxford: Blackwell.

Roll, R. 1984, 'A simple implicit measure of the bid–ask spread in an efficient market', *Journal of Finance*, 39, 1127–39.

Stoll, H. 2000, 'Friction', *Journal of Finance*, 55, 1479–1514.

Wood, R., T. McInish and J. Ord, 1985, 'An investigation of transactions data for NYSE Stocks', *Journal of Finance*, 40, 723–39.

1 Institutions and market structure

This chapter sets out the basics of institutions and market organization, concentrating on those elements which are most useful in discussing the theory. The book by Harris (2003) provides an excellent reference manual and where further clarification is required or if more in-depth examination is desired, we refer the student to that text.

1.1 Trading protocol

The organizational structure of a financial market comprises the rules that regulate trading and the trading procedures. The market structure indicates who can access the trading venue, which instruments can be traded, the location of the trading sessions and the order routing systems. The market structure also spells out the rules governing the access of market participants to public and private information and so affects the degree of pre- and post-trade transparency decisively. It follows that the market structure has an impact on agents' trading strategies and therefore on market quality.

This chapter discusses how different market structures can be classified, according to both the order execution systems and to the type of trading sessions. As far as execution systems are concerned, markets can be classified as either order-driven or quote-driven. Markets based on the direct interaction of agents' orders are commonly called order-driven, whilst those where contracts must be fulfilled through intermediaries are called quote-driven; markets where both systems are in use are called hybrid. As will be discussed later in this chapter, most financial markets today have a hybrid protocol, as it is quite flexible in accommodating the liquidity needs of different instruments.

1.1.1 Order-driven markets

In order-driven markets the prices at which contracts are executed may be determined either at the same time the orders are transmitted to the market-place or afterwards. Investors' buy and sell orders are matched directly, without intermediaries. Liquidity is guaranteed by a constant flow of orders from market participants. There are no designated market-makers. The only intermediary on the market is the broker, who transmits clients' orders, but does not take own positions in the asset traded. All order-driven

Order-driven markets

   Auction markets

   Order matching rules: order precedence rules and trade pricing rules

      ➤ *Call (or batch) markets*

      ○ *Oral auction (open-outcry in floors or pits)*

      ○ *Electronic auction*

      ➤ *Continuous market (limit order book)*

   Crossing networks

   Order matching rules: order precedence rules and derivative pricing rules

Quote-driven markets

      ➤ *Screen-based markets – dealer markets*

      ➤ *Continuous auction markets*

      ➤ *Brokered markets*

Hybrid markets

Figure 1.1. Market structures.

markets are based on order precedence rules that rank and match orders for execution, but they do not all use the same pricing rule. As shown in Figure 1.1, these markets can be organized either as auctions or as crossing networks. Auction markets are based on specific trade pricing rules, while crossing networks use prices determined in other markets.

Auction markets   The prevailing type of market in the leading financial centres at present is the auction. Auction markets can take two forms: call markets or continuous auctions. In call (or batch) auctions, orders are submitted simultaneously, whereas in continuous auctions agents can submit orders at any time during the *trading phase*.

In auction markets, there are two basic types of order – *limit orders* and *market orders*. A limit order specifies both a quantity and a maximum price or minimum price for execution depending on whether it is a buy or a sell order. A market order only specifies a quantity and will be executed at the best price available. A market order will always be executed as long as there is sufficient supply or demand, but the price may be unfavourable. Limit orders have a guaranteed price, but immediate execution is not guaranteed unless there are matching orders on the opposite side of the market. If immediate execution is not possible, the limit order will be placed in the *limit order book* and remain there until it is either executed against a new incoming order or cancelled. Limit orders are valuable for patient traders who wait for favourable prices, but they carry the risk of non-execution. Market orders are more suitable for impatient traders who want to execute the order immediately and are less sensitive to price.

In *call markets,* orders entered for the call can be publicized either orally or electronically. Call markets are characterized by a high degree of pre-trade transparency since traders can observe each other's orders during the auction.

In *oral call auctions*, also termed open-outcry auctions, agents cry their offers to buy or sell face-to-face on a trading floor. The rules governing oral auctions are quite simple. Firstly, it is compulsory for traders to communicate both prices and executions publicly. Secondly, traders with the highest bid and lowest ask gain precedence for order execution (*price priority*). Thirdly, traders who bid the best prices earlier gain precedence over those who bid the same prices later (*time priority*). Order matching rules are hierarchical, with price priority primary and time priority secondary. There exist other secondary precedence rules that discriminate in favour of certain classes of agents, for example, the public versus the specialists on the floor of the NYSE (*class priority* or *public order precedence*). Equilibrium trade prices in oral auctions are determined either by an auctioneer who minimizes net demand imbalances, or by brokers on the floor who match orders for different investors. The trade price rule in oral auctions is therefore quite simple, with orders executed at the best quoted prices. The most prominent example of an open-outcry auction is the futures market organized by the Chicago Board of Trade.

In *electronic call auctions,* orders are submitted to a computerized system during a predetermined period of time, and all trades in a stock take place at the same time and at the same equilibrium price under the uniform pricing rule (see Figure 1.2).

The price rule governing *electronic continuous auctions* is, instead, discriminatory. Prices are formed over time as traders observe the order flows, and orders are executed one by one as submitted, at the available prices. Market participants observe past transactions before submitting an order. This kind of market is generally automatic and is

Oral auction (open-outcry auction)
    Rules of pre-trade transparency
    Order precedence rules (time and price priority, public precedence)
    Trade pricing rules governed by the best quoted prices
Electronic call auction, continuous auction and crossing networks
    Order precedence rules
        Time priority
        Price priority
        Visibility and size restriction
    Trade pricing rules
        Uniform price (electronic call)
        Discriminatory price (continuous call)
        Derivative price (crossing network)

Figure 1.2. Trading rules.

the most frequent mode of trading derivatives and stocks.[1] This is currently the most common form of order-driven market, and is structured as an open limit order book (OLOB). The first characteristic of a platform organized as an OLOB is the accumulation of orders in an electronic book. A limit order is registered in the book and executed when an order of opposite sign and identical or better price is entered. An 'at best' order is carried out at the best price available in the order book. Price and time priority rules govern the order book. The limit orders executed first are those with the best price (price priority). If there are several orders for a given price, the first one to be executed can be selected in a number of ways. The most common rule is time priority: first submitted, first executed. There are also other rules. Size priority considers the number of shares in the order. Another type of priority rule is based on origin; for instance, at the NYSE orders from the public are filled first, those from specialists only afterwards.

Continuous and batch markets each have their own specific advantages. Continuous markets provide immediacy, enhance intraday price discovery and allow for easy enforcement of priority rules. Batch markets should reduce execution costs and settlement noise and thus provide better price stabilization, especially for thinly traded stocks.

Electronic communication networks (ECN) also work as open limit order books. These are forms of the Alternative Trading System (ATS) and describe trading systems that bring buyers and sellers together for the electronic execution of trades. They are registered under the Securities and Exchange Commission regulation which governs special purpose trading facilities that are not exchanges. The Commission has defined an ECN as *any electronic system that widely disseminates orders entered into it by the subscribers to third parties, and permits such orders to be executed in whole or in part.* Subscribers to ECNs can be retail investors, institutional investors, market-makers and other broker-dealers. The definition specifically excludes internal broker-dealer order-routing systems and crossing systems. Examples of ECNs are INET, Archipelago, BRUT and ATTN.

Opening and closing auctions   Batch auctions can be used at the opening, at the closing and during intraday trading halts. The way in which the opening and closing auctions function in the European exchanges is almost identical, whereas some differences characterize the American markets. The US markets are discussed in section 1.1.3. Here we outline the functioning of the European auctions.

The opening auction has three phases. The first is the pre-opening phase, where all agents submit proposals to a centralized body that acts as the auctioneer. During the pre-opening there are no trades, only order submissions. Investors can observe the orders submitted and the tentative clearing price, which the algorithm computes continuously. This process of price formation follows order matching and trade pricing

---

[1] Examples of derivative markets are MATIF and MONEP for France, EUREX for Switzerland and Germany and IDEM for Italy; examples of stock markets are Euronext, Deutsche Börse (XETRA) for Germany, MTA for Italy, LSE (SETS) for the UK and TSE (STP) for Japan.

rules. The computer initially ranks and matches orders according to the primary and secondary order precedence rules. The primary rule, as in the case of the oral auction, is price priority, while time priority is the most prevalent secondary rule. Once the orders are ranked according to the precedence rules, the system selects a single equilibrium price that satisfies the relevant pricing rules; these rules differ from market to market, but all aim to maximize trading volume and to minimize excess demand. Both of these objectives demand a guarantee that all the orders submitted at prices higher (lower) than the market-clearing price for buy (sell) orders are satisfied; orders submitted at the marginal price are instead rationed according to various rules. The problem is that if the first two pricing principles cannot determine a market-clearing price, other rules are necessary. Each exchange imposes different rules that drive the algorithm at the end of the pricing process. An example of price determination in the opening or closing auctions of European exchanges is given in section 1.3.

The process of price discovery ends with the determination of the equilibrium price during the validation phase. The actual opening phase follows, with the system simultaneously clearing orders by crossing the trade proposals that are compatible according to time and price priority. In this phase, contracts are concluded. For example, the SETS (Stock Exchange Electronic Trading Service) opening auction lasts ten minutes from 7.50 a.m. to 8.00 a.m., when limit orders and market orders can be entered, modified and deleted. Matching will normally run at 8.00 a.m. plus a random time (0–30 seconds). At Euronext the opening phase lasts from 7.15 a.m. to 9.00 a.m. A similar opening procedure is used in Germany at the Xetra and in Italy at the Borsa Italiana. The closing auction, which was introduced in most European exchanges in 2000 or 2001, has an analogous structure. Some exchanges, such as Deutsche Börse and Borsa Italiana (which, in 2008, merged with the London Stock Exchange), also introduced a random close for all calling auctions. The random close comes during a one-minute period in which the closure of the auction is announced; the main purpose of the procedure is to discourage manipulation of the final price.

Crossing networks Crossing networks are call systems that cross orders at a number of predetermined times during the day. Orders are submitted without price indication and are then ranked according to time priority. Price priority does not exist, since crossing networks use derivative pricing rules. The price at which all orders are crossed is in fact derived from the stocks' primary markets. It follows that crossing networks differ crucially from auction markets in that they do not produce an equilibrium price, but rather use derivative pricing rules. The actual crossing networks differ depending on the asset traded and the derivative rule used. For example, Posit crosses US equities eight times a day and the average bid–ask price used to settle contracts is chosen randomly from the stock's primary market during the seven minutes following the end of the call. Regulators should be concerned about the problems that may arise from the use of derivative pricing rules, such as higher adverse selection costs and the incentive to manipulate the primary market prices.

1.1.2   Quote-driven markets

A market is quote-driven when its contracts are defined on the basis of the prices previously quoted by designated liquidity suppliers (often called market-makers or dealers). These liquidity suppliers have a monopoly on trading and market-making, which means that every trader has to deal with these liquidity suppliers. They trade on their own account, but sometimes also act as brokers for client (limit) orders. In a quote-driven market (or dealer market), investors transmit orders to a dealer, who continuously displays bid and ask prices. At these prices the dealer guarantees market liquidity by filling customers' buy and sell orders. In a pure quote-driven market investors cannot submit limit orders and attempt to compete with the dealer's prices.[2] It is possible sometimes to negotiate better prices with the dealer than the quoted prices. This may be particularly interesting for large traders who go to the market frequently, such as institutional investors. These investors can build a relationship with the dealers and bargain for better prices. Markets where liquidity is provided by market-makers' quotes, are generally characterized by low ex-post transparency, which allows dealers to offset the risk of excessive inventory positions.

1.1.3   Hybrid markets

Market structures often combine elements from both order- and quote-driven protocols, and so are called hybrid. In the United States, such markets as the NYSE, AMEX (American Stock Exchange), and the regional stock exchanges are organized by specialists who play a dual role, namely ensuring liquidity and managing the order book. Both an automated sorting system (SuperDot – designated order turnaround –) and brokers on the floor can transmit these orders to the specialist. The orders exhibited by the specialist are therefore not necessarily the same as his/her price quotes but may come from the limit orders transmitted by the final investors or by brokers. In this system liquidity is ensured not only by specialists, but also by limit orders submitted by market participants.

Recently, the NASDAQ also took on some characteristics of a hybrid structure, namely that of a quote-driven market, where, however, the dealers have the option of transmitting their clients' limit orders to the electronic trading system. Similarly, with the launch of SETS in 1997, the London Stock Exchange (LSE) became a hybrid market. The LSE now provides a variety of market structures, as illustrated in Table 1.1. It comprises SETS, a purely order-driven open limit order book for trading the most liquid domestic stocks; a SETS market supported by specialists, for the next most liquid stocks; the SEAQ service, a two-way continuous market-maker quoting system for the majority of small to mid-cap stocks; and the SEATs Plus, which combines an order-driven service with competing quotes for trading a less liquid official list and some

---

[2] Examples of these markets are EuroMTS, London SEAQ International and most secondary government bond markets, i.e. MTS Italy, Amsterdam ATM, inter-dealer bond markets in the USA, Paris Bourse (SVT, Prominnofi SCOPE OCT), MTS Greece and MTS Japan. Others are such derivatives markets as the Chicago Mercantile Exchange and the Electronic Broking System (EBS) platform for foreign exchange trading.

Table 1.1. *Market structure of the London Stock Exchange*

Trading service	Trading structures	Securities traded	
United Kingdom			
SETS	Order book (order-driven)	Most liquid securities including FTSE100 and liquid FTSE250	↑ Liquidity
SETSmm	Order book with market-makers (hybrid)	Next most liquid securities including FTSE250 not on SETS, ETFs, some small cap and some leading Irish securities, liquid AIM	
SEAQ	Competing quotes (quote-driven)	All other domestic securities (including AIM) with at least two market-makers	
SEATS plus	Competing quotes and order book (hybrid)	Domestic securities (including AIM) with less than two market makers	
Covered warrants	Order book	All covered warrants	
International			
Dutch Trading Service	Order book	Liquid Dutch equities	↑ Liquidity
International Order Book (IOB)	Order book	Liquid international depository receipts	
International Retail Service (IRS)	Competing quotes	European and US blue chips	
International Bulletin Board (IBB)	Order book	International equities	

Source: LSE Guide to Trading Services.

AIM[3] company equities, whose liquidity is less than those securities listed on SEAQ or SETS. Finally, it includes an order-driven segment for covered warrants. Different degrees of liquidity also characterize the LSE segments dedicated to international equity trading.

In the same vein, the Hybrid NYSE Market proposal (2006) sought to enhance the competition between specialists and off-floor investors through a more flexible order routing system (Direct+). Furthermore, in the vast majority of stock markets there are segments dedicated to less liquid assets, with a specialist ensuring liquidity (e.g. AIM at LSE and the STAR segment at Borsa Italiana). Euronext has voluntary market-makers known as 'animateurs' for small stocks (Euronext, 2007).

Finally, there are markets, such as those for illiquid instruments or for large blocks, where the role of brokers is central to the provision of liquidity. Brokers are important in opaque markets, where they engage to find a counterparty and bilaterally negotiate most of the preliminary trade conditions. Brokers can exploit economies of scale in the search process by developing relations with potential liquidity traders. These markets are sometimes termed brokered markets (Harris, 2003). Examples are the markets in corporate bonds, off-the-run treasury bonds and stocks with very low capitalization.

1.1.4   Transparency

An important aspect of markets is *transparency*. This is defined as the capability of market participants to obtain information regarding the trading process. As illustrated in Figure 1.3, information can be either *pre-trade* or *post-trade*.

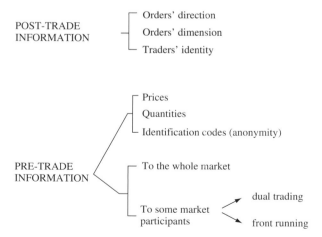

Figure 1.3. Post- and pre-trade transparency.

---

[3] AIM stands for Alternative Investment Market, the London Stock Exchange's international market for smaller growing companies.

Post-trade transparency refers to the rules of disclosure on the size and direction of the orders executed and the identity of the traders. Pre-trade transparency refers to the quoted prices and quantities and/or to the market participants' identities, and may be directed either to all the agents present in the market or to some only (i.e. brokers/dealers). Analysing the level of transparency is relevant because it influences traders' strategies and consequently the pricing process; for instance, dual trading and front running can derive from dealers' privileged information about customers' identities. In Chapter 10, we model transparency and its consequences for price formation in greater detail, using several models of reference.

1.2 Market structure

This section provides an overview of the trading structures used in actual financial markets. We discuss the market structure of the NYSE, the world's largest stock market, in more detail.

1.2.1 Market structures around the world

Table 1.2 summarizes the main features of the major financial markets related to organizational structure and transparency. First of all, it distinguishes between order- and quote-driven markets, and also between automated and screen-based systems. Euronext, the London Stock Exchange (SETS), Borsa Italiana, the Swiss Exchange (SWX), the Tokyo Stock Exchange (STP) and the US platforms are automated order-driven (AOD) markets. The London Stock Exchange (SEAQ-International) is screen-based quote-driven (SBQD), while the traditional NYSE is floor-based quote-driven (FBQD). Table 1.2 also shows that the NYSE, the Frankfurt Stock Exchange (XETRA/Floor) and the Toronto Stock Exchange (TOREX) are hybrid systems where order- and quote-driven features co-exist and that the US exchanges have recently introduced automated platforms such as the Integrated Single Book at the NASDAQ, and the Hybrid Market (SuperDot – Direct+) at the NYSE. With the exception of SEAQ-I, all these markets have both an opening and a closing auction. In many markets intraday call auctions are also present, to manage the so-called trading halts.

While post-trade information is regulated uniformly in most financial markets, the degree of pre-trade transparency of the limit order book has not yet been harmonized. With the exception of the Tokyo Stock Exchange and the London SEAQ-I, market members generally observe the entire order book, but investors other than members can see the depth of the whole book (full book) only on the London Stock Exchange, the Toronto Stock Exchange and, after the adoption of OpenBook, the NYSE SuperDot. And on XETRA, the Swiss Exchange and the London SEAQ-I investors observe only the best bid/ask prices. An intermediate level of pre-trade transparency, where investors observe the five best bid/ask prices, is present on Euronext, Borsa Italiana, the NASDAQ and the Tokyo Stock Exchange. With the introduction of the Euronext platform, anonymity is now pervasive among financial systems; finally, most exchanges, with the exception of the Tokyo Stock Exchange, allow the submission of incompletely disclosed orders ('hidden' or 'iceberg' orders).

Table 1.2. *Overview of Market Structures around the world*

Stock exchange	Structure	Call market, Market on close (MoC), Cross (Cr)			Pre-trade transparency					
		Mkt opening	Mkt closing	Intraday (trading halts)	Limit order book		Identities of liquidity providers		Hidden orders	Anonymity
					Members	Investors	Members	Investors		
Borsa Italiana (Bit)	AOD	yes	yes	yes	Full Book	5 Best B/A	no	no	yes	yes
Euro next	AOD	yes	yes	yes	Full Book	5 Best B/A	no	no	yes	yes
Frankfurt Stock Exchange (XETRA and Floor)	AOD/AQD	yes	yes	yes	Full Book	Best B/A	no	no	yes	yes
London Stock Exchange (SETs)	AOD	yes	yes	yes	Full Book	Full Book	no	no	yes	yes
London Stock Exchange (SEAQ-I)	SBQD	no	yes (Cr)	yes (2 Cr)	Best B/A	Best B/A	yes	no	no	no
NASDAQ (Integrated Single Book)	AOD	yes (Cr)	yes (Cr)	yes	Full Book	5 Best B/A	no	no	yes	yes
NYSE Hybrid Market (SuperDot)	AOD	yes	yes	yes	Full Book	Full Book	no	no	yes	yes
NYSE (Floor)	FBQD	yes (MoC)	yes (MoC)	yes	Full Book	Full Book	yes	no	yes	yes
Swiss Exchange (SWX)	AOD	yes	yes	yes	Full Book	Best B/A	no	no	yes	yes
Tokyo Stock Exchange (STP)	AOD	yes	yes	yes	5 Best B/A	5 Best B/A	no	no	no	yes
Toronto Stock Exchange (TOREX)	AOD/AQD	yes	no	yes	Full Book	Full Book	no	no	yes	yes

Note: AOD = Automated order-driven; AQD = Automated quote-driven; SBQD = Screen-based quote-driven; FBQD = Floor-based quote-driven; B/A = Bid/ask.

1.2.2   The market structure of the NYSE

The New York Stock Exchange (NYSE) is characterized by a mixed market structure where the electronic limit order book competes with professional market-makers to supply liquidity. On the floor of the NYSE a number of trading posts with panels exist (Figure 1.4a), where the specialists manage the limit order book and interact with brokers who form the crowd; trading in each stock is concentrated in the assigned trading post.[4] Around the trading floor, there are also a number of posts, called booths, where brokers receive orders from their member firms. For each stock, there is one designated specialist.

The investors' orders can reach a specialist's trading post either directly through the SuperDot Direct+[5] or through floor brokers. Order size usually determines how an order goes to the floor. Smaller orders, requiring less special handling, are typically sent to the specialist through SuperDot, regardless of whether the source is retail or institutional, while larger orders typically go to floor brokers. With the advent of algorithmic trading for institutions, however, technology slices large orders into many smaller orders according to a pre-selected algorithm, and then executes them through SuperDot. When instead the order is sent by the trading desk of a member firm to the floor's booth, the broker who receives it brings it to the post, where it can be either offered by auction to other brokers forming the crowd or left with the specialist, who

Figure 1.4a. Trading posts on the New York Stock Exchange trading floor.

[4] Each post has an average of twenty panels and each panel presents an average of eight issues.
[5] The Super Designated Order Turnaround System is the NYSE order routing system introduced in 1976; the Direct+ is an electronic connection that executes marketable orders against the published NYSE quotes, which are offered by both the specialist and the crowd.

in turn may either fill it out of his own portfolio, or place it in the limit order book waiting for a counterparty.

Rules of price and time priority, as well as precedence and parity rules regulate trading on the floor. Price priority is absolute, as an offer of 90 always has priority over an offer of 91. As for the precedence rules, orders that are transmitted by floor brokers and by the SuperDot to the market hold precedence over the specialist's orders if they all carry the same price. Strict time priority only applies to the first order submitted to the market; if this execution clears the first order having time priority, all the remaining orders at the same price are considered on an equal basis to subsequent orders (i.e. they will split the following orders equally); if, instead, the first execution alone does not clear the floor[6] the residual part of the order is offered to the other counterparties according to the original time priority. There is finally a size precedence rule governing orders that are otherwise at parity: priority is given to the order(s) that can satisfy the whole incoming quantity offered to the market.

Opening and closing prices are determined by the specialist, who gathers the market open/close orders transmitted both electronically via the Opening Automated Report System (OARS) and by brokers from the floor of the exchange. The OARS computes the aggregate demand and supply and identifies trading volume and imbalances for each price. To set the clearing price, the specialist seeks to minimize the market imbalances by matching buy and sell orders; he can either submit his own order, or in the case of abnormal price change (with respect to the previous day's closing price) he can halt trading and disseminate the imbalance information to attract new order flows.

Since the merger with Archipelago, the NYSE Arca opening and closing auctions, at 9.30 a.m. and 4.00 p.m., also set prices. Here the principles governing the price formation algorithm are such that the opening/closing prices are those that maximize trading volume. If two or more prices can maximize executable volume, then the system will choose the one closest to the previous closing price.

In the traditional NYSE market, orders could never be executed automatically, but had first to be evaluated by the specialist, who had to publicize the orders among floor brokers to obtain price improvement.[7] If the order was of no interest to brokers, the specialist could either act as a counterparty to that trade, or 'stop' the order and search for price improvement.[8] After at most thirty minutes the order had to be executed at least at the 'stop price'. This stopping procedure was available by default for orders arriving from the SuperDot.

If a broker instead wanted to match two orders, the specialist had to publicize them among the other brokers by offering a price equal to the crossing price proposed by the broker plus the minimum tick size (Rule 75, NYSE). Once an order was executed, a report was immediately sent both to the NYSE member brokerage firm that had submitted the order and to the Consolidated Trade Reporting System for publicizing the

---

[6] See the NYSE Floor Official Manual.
[7] Limit orders with the 'NX' identifier, however, have direct execution on the book.
[8] If the prevailing spread was equal to the tick size, the specialist could stop orders larger than 2,000 shares only if authorized by an NYSE official.

order, and to the Clearing and Settlement System. As discussed in the next paragraph, some of these rules have been changed with the advent of the Hybrid Market protocol.

Trading at the NYSE is conducted from 9.30 a.m. (opening auction) to 4.00 p.m. (closing auction). As noted above, the opening and closing prices are set by the specialist who tries to minimize the market imbalances after observing the orders received both electronically from the OARS and from the floor brokers. The order book is managed by the specialist, who can enter his own orders as well. The specialist is also assigned 'to maintain a fair and orderly market' and hence has certain positive and negative obligations;[9] to this end he constantly monitors the book and where necessary intervenes to manage transient mismatches. Traditionally, only the specialist could observe the orders in the book, but since the inception of NYSE OpenBook in 2002, investors off the exchange floor have been allowed to observe the book electronically (Boehmer, Saar and Yu 2005).

The NYSE offers brokers the options of either sending orders to the limit order book, or interacting with the specialist on the floor where they can conclude contracts. Brokers can build long-term relationships with the specialists in order to mitigate the adverse selection costs due to asymmetric information. Up until 2006, within this system the book would attract roughly 12% of total volume and the specialist 9%, while 79% went to the floor.[10] However, direct access to the electronic system was limited to orders smaller than 1,099 shares, and was also limited to one order per thirty seconds.

1.2.3 The Hybrid Market model

In March 2006 the SEC approved the Hybrid Market initiative, which introduced a number of innovations to the traditional NYSE structure. It changed the organization of the electronic limit order book by enhancing both Direct+ and the trading tools used by floor brokers and specialists to access the order book. Figure 1.4b shows the traditional NYSE structure and the changes introduced by the Hybrid Market model.

The size and time restrictions on automatic execution of orders were removed, and new orders were introduced both for the public and for floor brokers and specialists. At the same time, however, a maximum order size (3 million shares) was introduced. Limit orders now enjoy direct and immediate execution, whereas the automated execution (AutoEx) of market orders needs to be specified. By default, market orders are treated as auction market (AM) orders and are offered by specialists to the floor brokers at a price equal to the best bid offer (BBO) plus one tick; after fifteen seconds, if not executed, they are submitted to the book as standard NX market orders. Notice that the same facility is now offered to auction limit (AL) orders, which are marketable limit orders. Market and marketable limit orders are also allowed to search for price improvement and liquidity by 'sweeping' the limit order book. In practice, they can

---

[9] According to the NYSE Floor Official Manual, the specialist has to offer a narrow spread and to monitor transaction prices in order to avoid price jumps; he also has to give precedence to public orders and avoid destabilizing trades.

[10] See Hendershott (2005) and the NYSE website for further details and updates.

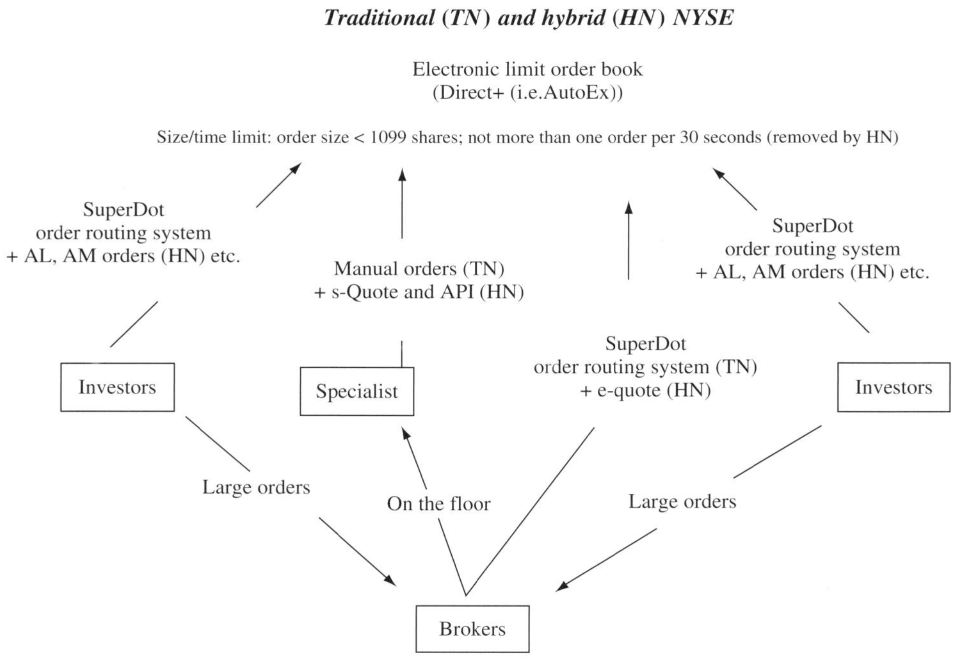

Traditional (TN) and hybrid (HN) NYSE

Electronic limit order book
(Direct+ (i.e.AutoEx))

Size/time limit: order size < 1099 shares; not more than one order per 30 seconds (removed by HN)

SuperDot
order routing system
+ AL, AM orders (HN) etc.

Manual orders (TN)
+ s-Quote and API (HN)

SuperDot
order routing system
+ AL, AM orders (HN) etc.

Investors

Specialist

SuperDot
order routing system (TN)
+ e-quote (HN)

Investors

Large orders

On the floor

Large orders

Brokers

Figure 1.4b. Trading system at the New York Stock Exchange.

walk up or down the book and be executed according to the price, parity and time priority rules; however, if they reach a sweep liquidity replenishment point (SLRP) or a momentum liquidity replenishment point (MLRP), they are stopped by the specialist and auctioned to the floor brokers to elicit liquidity supply.[11] Trading will restart after at most ten seconds, or as soon as an order is executed in the auction or the specialist has submitted an order. The LRPs were introduced in order to dampen the potential volatility induced by automatic executions or by temporary imbalances, but they are open to the criticism that they grant the specialists permission to execute orders with larger adverse selection costs against the book.

Market and marketable orders are also offered price improvement by quotes publicized by other markets, as they can sweep to intermarket trading systems (ITS) when these offer better execution.

As for the new trading tools that the Hybrid NYSE offers to liquidity suppliers, both the floor brokers and the specialists are now allowed to submit electronic orders (e-Quote and s-Quote), which are hidden from the public; however, the specialists' franchises are preserved as they alone can observe the orders submitted by the floor brokers in the aggregate. The NYSE Hybrid also permits the specialists to use a new

---

[11] An SLRP is hit if an individual order moves the stock price by more than 9 cents; an MLRP is hit if the (absolute) stock price moves more than 25 cents or 1% of prices in the last thirty seconds.

algorithm (Application Programming Interface, API) to fulfil obligations and automate much of what they used to do manually in the traditional NYSE.

1.3   Orders and order properties

This section analyses orders in more detail, describing the working of the limit order book and showing how liquidity is provided and consumed in an order-driven market. Orders are traders' statements of their intention to trade. Orders stipulate the terms of the contract offered by market participants. They specify the agents' willingness to trade and the modality of execution. In bilateral negotiations, trading conditions are defined by the client and intermediary, and are often the result of a complicated bargaining process. In centralized electronic markets organized as an open limit order book, orders are standardized in order to enhance immediacy and price discovery. The minimum information in the instructions is type of instrument, sign (i.e. the buy/sell indicator) and the size of the trade. In addition, orders may contain more detailed information (see Table 1.3) regarding their execution conditions, such as price- and quantity-related instructions, duration of commitment, time of expiration, visibility and the terms of any principal–agent obligation. All these instructions affect orders' precedence and show whether market participants provide or take up liquidity. There are two broad categories of order, market orders and limit orders.

Market orders are 'at best' orders and are usually submitted by impatient traders who care about minimizing execution time more than the price at which the contract is executed. These orders take liquidity from the book and then disappear.

Limit orders are submitted by patient traders, who care about price terms and add an indication of the limit price to the order. Limit sell orders can only be executed at or above the price specified in the order, buy orders at or below it. Limit orders therefore supply liquidity and increase the depth of the limit order book. Some authors

Table 1.3. *Common order types*

Price instructions
Limit order (marketable if at or beyond the best bid offer (BBO))
Market order
Order at the auction price
Maturity instructions
Day order (valid for the day)
Good-till-cancel (valid until cancelled)
Market-on-open and market-on-close (valid at the opening or closing auction)
Quantity instructions
Fill or kill = All-or-nothing (valid if completely filled at submission)
Minimum-or-none (valid if filled for a minimum specified quantity)
Fill & Kill (valid only for the quantity filled at submission)
Hidden (valid for a disclosed and an undiscloded quantity)

have also considered them as free put or call options (Copeland and Galai, 1983), which are 'in the money' when the market price hits the limit price. These options are free since the writer does not get any explicit premium, but rather receives an implicit gain if the limit price is hit and his contract is executed on better terms. Limit order submitters are usually patient traders who are more concerned with price risk than execution risk. The former is the risk a trader runs when his order is executed at unfavourable prices; this risk is maximized when a trader submits a market order. The latter is the risk a trader runs when his order is not executed; the larger the price premium or discount required by the limit order price, the greater the execution risk. Clearly, there is a trade-off between execution risk and price risk. Aggressive traders require immediacy and submit market orders or marketable limit orders, whereas patient traders submit limit orders on their own side of the book. Marketable limit orders, however, are submitted at prices above the best price on the opposite side of the book and are executable upon submission, like market orders. The only difference between market and marketable limit orders is that the latter limit the eventual losses in terms of price risk as they specify a limit price.

Table 1.4 provides a more detailed order classification similar to that introduced by Biais, Hillion and Spatt (1995), which distinguishes orders by their aggressiveness: the most aggressive orders consume liquidity, the least aggressive orders provide liquidity to the book.

Example 1: Batch opening and closing auction

Opening auctions usually start with a pre-opening period, when traders submit proposals, and finish with a phase in which the system computes the equilibrium price and contracts are concluded. The matching algorithm used to set the auction price differs slightly across various markets. There are four principal rules that the matching system follows. The first maximizes trading volume and the second minimizes order imbalances; these rules drive the algorithm used by the majority of today's order-driven markets.[12] If more than one price satisfies the first two principles, additional rules come into play. A third rule may be based on price pressure, while a fourth may select the reference price (generally the previous closing auction price) as the equilibrium opening price. Under the price pressure rule, if both prices selected with the previous rules exhibit surplus buy (sell) volume, then the system chooses the highest (lowest) price as the equilibrium call price. If the previous selected prices instead exhibit equal buy and sell imbalances, then the fourth rule is invoked, using the reference price to set the equilibrium price. According to this final principle, the algorithm sets the equilibrium price equal to the reference price only if the reference price lies between the highest and lowest potential limit prices, whereas the algorithm selects the highest

---

[12] These are the London Stock Exchange, Euronext, the Toronto Stock Exchange, the Australian Stock Exchange, the Deutsche Börse, the Hong Kong Exchange and the Borsa Italiana.

Table 1.4. *Order classification*

This table reports different types of orders classified from the most to the least aggressive; examples refer to the state of the limit order book shown in Table 1.8

Aggressive orders

Type 1a. Market order that can walk up the book for a size greater than the cumulative quantity at the best price on the opposite side of the order book, e.g. *Market buy 20.*

Type 1b. Limit orders improving on the best price on the opposite side of the order book with associated size greater than the cumulative quantity at the best price on the opposite side of the order book, e.g. *Limit buy 70 @ 51.00.*

Type 2. Market order for a size equal to the cumulative quantity at the best price on the opposite side of the order book, e.g. *Market buy 5.*

Type 3a. Market order that cannot walk up the book for a size greater than the cumulative quantity at the best price on the opposite side of the order book, e.g. *Market buy 20.*

Type 3b. Limit order with price improving on the best price on the opposite side of the order book and for a size smaller than the cumulative quantity at the best price on the opposite side of the order book or market order for a size smaller than the cumulative quantity at the best price on the opposite side of the order book, e.g. *Limit buy 4 @ 50.50 or Market buy 4.*

Patient orders

Type 4a. Limit orders with price strictly inside the BBO, better than best price on its own side, but worse than the best price on the opposite side of the order book, e.g. *Limit buy 10 @ 49.50.*

Type 4b. Limit orders with price equal to the best price on its own side. The order stays on the BBO: best bid if it is a buy order, best offer if it is a sell order, e.g. *Limit buy 10 @ 49.00.*

Type 4c. Limit orders with price worse than the best price of its own side of the order book; if it is a buy (sell) order, the price is below (above) the best bid (ask), e.g. *Limit buy 20 @ 48.50.*

(lowest) limit price as the market-clearing price when the reference price is higher (lower) than that limit price.

Let us see how the call auction in electronic markets works, using an example. Assume that traders have submitted the orders shown in Table 1.5 during the pre-opening phase, when the system collects and matches orders according to the price and time priority rules. We assume that the pre-opening period lasts sixty minutes from 8.00 a.m. to 9.00 a.m. At the end of the pre-opening phase, the system selects the equilibrium price using the rules. Table 1.6 shows how orders are ranked according to the price and time priority rules in a hypothetical limit order book. Buy orders are ranked in decreasing order of price, sell orders in increasing order. In this way, the best buy orders are shown at the top left of the book, the best sell orders are shown at the bottom right. Thus, Rob's buy market order has the highest price precedence on the buy side, and Luke's sell market order on the sell side. Once orders are ranked by precedence rules, the system begins to compute the possible trades, matching the highest-ranking buy and sell orders. Table 1.7 shows how the matching algorithm selects the equilibrium price according to the four pricing rules. Columns 2 and 3 show the cumulated buy and sell orders. Column 4 shows trading volume at each possible price, column 5 ranks the order imbalance on the demand side, and column 6 shows the sign of the

Table 1.5. *Order Submission*

This table shows a list of proposals submitted to the pre-auction phase

Time	Trader	Orders	Size	Price
8.01	Alan	Buy	20	48.00
8.02	Fred	Sell	20	47.50
8.04	Art	Buy	30	47.50
8.06	Tom	Sell	40	51.00
8.09	Mike	Buy	40	46.00
8.15	Lucy	Sell	30	51.50
8.30	James	Buy	15	49.00
8.34	Guy	Sell	20	49.50
8.37	Larry	Buy	40	51.00
8.38	Pete	Sell	25	48.50
8.40	Phil	Sell	10	50.00
8.42	Nick	Sell	10	50.00
8.43	Rob	Buy	30	Market
8.44	Gene	Sell	15	50.00
8.45	Andrew	Buy	20	48.50
8.50	Luke	Sell	40	Market
8.55	Frank	Buy	20	50.50
8.56	Chris	Buy	20	50.00
8.57	Tito	Sell	15	50.50
8.58	Ingrid	Buy	40	50.00
8.59	Ale	Sell	15	49.00

Table 1.6. *Pre-auction order book*

This table shows the order book, where orders have been organized according to the price and time priority rules.

Buyers			Sellers	
Trader	Size	Order price	Size	Trader
Rob	30	Market buy		
		51.50	30	Lucy
Larry	40	51.00	40	Tom
Frank	20	50.50	15	Tito
Chris	20	50.00	15	Gene
Ingrid	40	50.00	10	Nick
		50.00	10	Phil
		49.50	20	Guy
James	15	49.00	15	Ale
Andrew	20	48.50	25	Pete
Alan	20	48.00		
Art	30	47.50	20	Fred
Mike	40	46.00		
		Market sell	40	Luke

Table 1.7. *Equilibrium price selection*

This table shows how the equilibrium price is selected in a call market.

Price	Aggregate demand schedule	Aggregate supply schedule	Trading volume	Excess demand order imbalance	Market pressure
51.50	30	240	30	−210	Sell
51.00	70	210	70	−140	Sell
50.50	90	170	90	−80	Sell
50.00	150	155	150	−5	Sell
49.50	150	120	120	30	Buy
49.00	165	100	100	65	Buy
48.50	185	85	85	100	Buy
48.00	205	60	60	145	Buy
47.50	235	60	60	175	Buy
46.00	275	40	40	235	Buy

imbalance (market pressure). Trading volume is maximized at 50.00, since 150 shares can be traded at this price. It follows that here the volume maximization principle is sufficient to determine the equilibrium auction price. But if 150 shares would trade at two different prices, say at both 50.00 and 49.50, then the volume maximization principle would not be sufficient to select the equilibrium price. Moreover, if there was an equal excess demand at both these prices, the second principle would not be of help either. Using the third rule, the algorithm would therefore apply the price pressure principle, which considers the sign of the imbalance in reference to the possible equilibrium price. If, for instance, both prices would guarantee the same maximum trading volume and the minimum order imbalance would display excess demand, the equilibrium auction price would be the highest price i.e. 50.00. If, however, there were no market pressure (e.g. with excess demand at 50.00 and excess supply at 49.50) the last principle would apply and the algorithm would look at the reference price.

Going back to the initial example, Table 1.8 shows that, after the call, the order book exhibits a bid–ask spread of 1.00. Notice that at the equilibrium price (50.00) there is an excess supply of five shares, which is moved to the continuous auction on the ask side at the same price; this is part of Gene's order. Clearly, after the opening call all buy/sell orders submitted at prices below/above the call auction equilibrium price are moved to the continuous auction with their original price and time priority.

The opening and closing auction at NASDAQ[13]   The NASDAQ opening and closing prices are determined within the NASDAQ Market Center, which is a fully integrated order display and execution system for all NASDAQ securities as well as for other exchange-listed securities. In 2004, both an opening and a closing cross (OC

---

[13] See NASDAQ Stock Market (2006).

Table 1.8. *Limit order book after opening auction*

This table gives a snapshot of the state of the order book after the call auction during the continuous trading phase.

	Bid		Ask		
Q (no. shares)	Price (euro)		Price (euro)	Q (no. shares)	
			51.50	30	Least aggressive sell orders
			51.00	40	
			50.50	15	
			50.00	5	Best offer
		⇔			inside spread
15	49.00				Best bid
20	48.50				Least aggressive buy orders
20	48.00				Most aggressive sell orders (marketable)
30	47.50				
40	48.00				

Most aggressive buy orders (marketable)

and CC) were introduced. The opening and closing NASDAQ crosses are price discovery mechanisms that cross orders at a single price at 9.30 a.m. local time for the
opening and at 4.00 p.m. for the closing. The designs of the two crosses are very similar. NASDAQ accepts different on-open (on-close) orders that are executable only
during the OC/CC. If these orders are market on-open/close (MOO/C) and limit on-
open/close (LOO/C), they are accepted from 7.30 a.m. and 9.30 a.m. for the opening
and closing crosses respectively; if instead they are imbalance-only (IO) orders, they
are accepted from 7.30 a.m. (OC) and from 3.30 p.m. (CC) and they can only be executed at or above/below the NASDAQ Market Center offer/bid at 9.30 a.m./4.00 p.m..
Leading up to the open (close) NASDAQ disseminates information with increasing
frequency starting from 9.28 a.m. (OC) and 3.50 p.m. (CC). The information released
(NASDAQ Crossing Network) concerns the following items (NASDAQ Stock Market,
2006):

- Near Clearing Price: the crossing price at which orders in the NASDAQ open-
  ing/closing book and continuous book would clear against each other;
- Far Clearing Price: the crossing price at which orders in the NASDAQ open-
  ing/closing book would clear against each other;
- Current Reference Price: a price within the NASDAQ inside quotes at which paired
  shares are maximized, the imbalance is minimized and the distance from the bid–ask
  midpoint is minimized, in that order;
- Number of Paired Shares: the number of opening/closing shares that NASDAQ is
  able to pair off at the current reference price;
- Imbalance Quantity: the number of opening/closing shares that would remain
  unexecuted at the current inside price, and the sign of the imbalance.

Notice that the system in use at the NASDAQ for the closing cross differs from
the European one. The main difference is that while in Europe trading on the continuous auction ends as soon as the pre-auction period starts, at NASDAQ there is a
period of ten minutes during which traders can choose either to send orders that are
executable at the closing cross, or to submit to the continuous auction. In this way the
pre-auction period and the continuous trading session overlap. Notice also that the first
two principles that govern the price formation algorithm at the NASDAQ crosses are
the same as those used in the European trading platforms, but the third, i.e. the distance
minimization from the bid–ask midpoint, differs.

Example 2: Limit order book (LOB)
In a continuous electronic auction market, orders are ranked in the book according
to the precedence rules set out above. Buy and sell orders are first ranked by their
precedence and then filled according to the discriminatory pricing rule as outlined
previously. The buy and sell orders with the highest precedence are ranked at the top
of the book and form the inside spread.

According to their type and priority, incoming orders are filled completely or partially by one or more of the limit orders standing on the book. Market orders and marketable limit orders are filled immediately at the best bid and offer. Other limit orders stay on the book, waiting for better price conditions.

The following example illustrates how a limit order book works and how orders can be classified according to their degree of aggressiveness (Biais, Hillion and Spatt, 1995). A final example will also show the mechanisms generally used by exchanges to stabilize price volatility. For ease of reference, we start from the book presented in Table 1.8 and evaluate the effects on the inside spread and market depth (i.e. the number of shares available at the prices at the top of the book) of the orders shown in Table 1.4. Orders in this table are ranked by degree of aggressiveness; the market orders that are allowed to walk up the book are the most aggressive, as in the Euronext platform.

Given the state of the book as shown in Table 1.8, a market buy order for twenty shares will absorb five shares from the top of the ask side at 50.00 and will match the fifteen shares at 50.50 on the next level, leaving the book with a wider spread $(51.00 - 49.00 = 2.00)$ and an associated depth equal to fifty-five. The change of depth at the top of the book depends on the state of the book itself. In this particular case the depth increases on the top of the ask side after the market order is filled (see Table 1.9).

We can now say more about the order classification presented in Table 1.4. The type 1b order is a marketable limit order for seventy shares at 51.00. Because of the limit price (51.00), it can be executed for only sixty shares (Table 1.8), widening the spread to 2.50 $(51.50 - 49.00)$. The type 2 order is a market order that widens the spread but leaves the depth on the second level of the book unchanged. The type 3a order is a market order that is not allowed to walk up the book; in this case the amount in excess of the depth available on the opposite side of the book forms a limit order on its own side at the price that filled the first part. Here, a market buy of twenty shares is filled at 50.00 for five shares, leaving the remaining fifteen shares as a limit buy order at 50.00 on the top of the bid side. This is the only type of order that can decrease rather than increase the spread. A type 3b order can only reduce the depth at the inside spread. With the exception of a type 3a order, aggressive orders reduce liquidity, widen the spread and/or decrease depth. A type 4 order, however, is a patient order that either narrows the spread (type 4a) or increases depth at the top of the book (type 4b) and at lower levels (type 4c).

Example 3: LOB and excess volatility price ranges

In order to prevent excess volatility, exchanges usually set static and dynamic price ranges for both limit order submissions and contract executions. The price range changes with the instrument and the trading phase. Typically it is narrower for more liquid securities than for less liquid ones. On European trading platforms, there are typically two types of price range: a static one limiting order submissions and a dynamic one governing contract executions. For instance, for the Italian most liquid blue chips

Table 1.9. *Limit order book after aggressive order*

This table gives a snapshot of the limit order book during the continuous trading phase and shows the effect of a Type 1a order on the state of the limit order book presented in Table 1.8.

	Bid		Ask		
	Q (no. shares)	Price (euro)	Price (euro)	Q (no. shares)	
Most aggressive buy orders (marketable)			51.50	30	Least aggressive sell orders
			51.00	40	Best offer
		⇕			inside spread
Best bid	15	49.00			
Least aggressive buy orders	20	48.50			Most aggressive sell orders (marketable)
	20	48.00			
	20	48.00			
	30	47.50			
	40	48.00			

traded on MTA (now merged with LSE's TradElect), the equilibrium opening price cannot be validated unless it is within ±10% of the reference price.[14] Moreover, during continuous trading, contracts cannot be executed at prices exceeding ±5% of the reference price, whereas during the after-hours phase this price range is tighter, ±3.5%. These are called static parameter ranges. During the continuous auction there is also a dynamic price range, so that contracts cannot be executed if the price exceeds ±2.5% of the previous execution price (Euronext, 2007). Orders exceeding the static parameters are automatically cancelled, whereas orders exceeding the dynamic price range also cause a five-minute halt in trading (or more, at the exchange's discretion).

For example, given the state of the book in Table 1.8, if the reference price was equal to 50.00, contracts could not be executed at prices above 55.00 or below 45.00, nor at prices that exceed the dynamic price range of ±2.5% of the price associated with the last contract executed.

These price ranges can be adjusted by the regulators, depending on market conditions.

References

Admati, A. and P. Pfleiderer, 1988, 'A theory of intraday patterns: volume and price variability', *Review of Financial Studies,* 1, 3–40.

Amihud, Y. and H. Mendelson, 1987, 'Trading mechanism and stock returns: an empirical investigation', *Journal of Finance*, 42, 533–55.

Biais, B., L. Glosten and C. Spatt, 2005, 'Market microstructure: a survey of microfoundations, empirical results, and policy implications', *Journal of Financial Markets,* 8, 217–64.

Biais, B., P. Hillion and C. Spatt, 1995, 'An empirical analysis of the limit order book and the order flow in the Paris Bourse', *Journal of Finance,* 50, 1655–89.

Boehmer, E., G. Saar and L.Yu, 2005, 'Lifting the veil: an analysis of pre-trade transparency at the NYSE', *Journal of Finance,* 60, 783–815.

Christie, W. and P. Schultz, 1994, 'Why do NASDAQ market makers avoid odd-eighth quotes?', *Journal of Finance*, 49, 1813–40.

Christie, W., J. Harris and P. Schultz, 1994, 'Why did NASDAQ market makers stop avoiding odd-eighth quotes?', *Journal of Finance*, 49, 1841–60.

Copeland, T. and D. Galai, 1983, 'Information effects on the bid–ask spread', *Journal of Finance*, 38, 1457–69.

Euronext, 2007, 'Euronext cash market trading manual'.

Glosten L. and E. Harris, 1988, 'Estimating the component of the bid/ask spread', *Journal of Financial Economics*, 21, 123–42.

Glosten L. and J. Milgrom, 1985, 'Bid, ask and transaction prices in a specialist market with heterogeneously informed traders', *Journal of Financial Economics*, 14, 71–100.

Harris, L. 2003, *Trading and Exchanges*, Oxford University Press.

Hasbrouck, J. 2007, *Empirical Market Microstructure*, Oxford University Press.

Hendershott, T. 2005, 'Merger and hybrid market at the NYSE', Equity and Currency Market Microstructure Conference, Oslo.

---

[14] For those platforms with both opening and closing auctions and with an after-hours trading phase, the reference price is generally determined as follows: during the opening auction it is equal to the previous day's closing auction price; during continuous trading it is set equal to the opening price until the beginning of the closing auction. The closing auction price is also used as the reference price during the after-hours trading phase.

Hong, H. and J. Wang, 2000, 'Trading and returns under periodic market closures', *Journal of Finance,* 55, 297–354.

Huang, R, and H. Stoll, 1996, 'Dealer versus auction markets: a paired comparison of execution costs on NASDAQ and the NYSE', *Journal of Financial Economics,* 41, 313–57.

Jain, O and G. Joh, 1988, 'The dependence between hourly prices and trading volume', *Journal of Financial and Quantitative Analysis,* 23, 269–83.

Kyle, A. 1985, 'Continuous auctions and insider trading', *Econometrica,* 53, 1315–35.

Lyons, R. 2001, *The Microstructure Approach to Exchange Rates,* Cambridge, Mass.: MIT Press.

Madhavan, A. 2000, 'Market microstructure: a survey', *Journal of Financial Markets,* 3, 205–58.

NASDAQ Stock Market, 2006, 'NASDAQ Cross. A truly innovative single-priced open/close', www.nasdaqtrader.com/trader/openclose/openclose.stm.

O'Hara, M. 1995, *Market Microstructure Theory,* Oxford: Blackwell.

Roll, R. 1984, 'A simple implicit measure of the bid–ask spread in an efficient market', *Journal of Finance,* 39, 1127–39.

Stoll, H. 2000, 'Friction', *Journal of Finance,* 55, 1479–1514.

Wood, R., T. McInish and J. Ord, 1985, 'An investigation of transactions data for NYSE Stocks', *Journal of Finance,* 40, 723–39.

2   Financial market equilibrium

As we observed in the Introduction, the purpose of this book is to discuss models of price formation that discard some of the assumptions of the traditional asset pricing approach. We shall start by removing the hypothesis of symmetric information and assess the relevance of adverse selection costs in asset pricing theory. To this end, after a brief introductory discussion of the importance of asymmetric information and the related new concept of rational expectations equilibrium, we start from a very simple model of asset pricing with symmetric information and then introduce models with asymmetric information, where prices are vehicles of information and where this role of prices is central to the analysis.

When traders use market prices to learn about the future value of an asset, by trading they affect the informational efficiency of the market, which ultimately depends on traders' preferences and the number and types of agents.

This chapter starts with a simple general framework in which a representative risk-averse agent allocates his wealth between a risk-free and a risky asset. The model is then extended to the case where the representative agent can choose to distribute his wealth among N risky assets; this will allow us to obtain the equilibrium asset prices that are consistent with the capital asset pricing model (CAPM) approach. Finally, we will introduce asymmetric information and show how equilibrium asset prices reflect public as well as private information. This model will be solved under the assumptions of both naïve and rational expectations. On the assumption of rational expectations we will present a model in the spirit of Grossman and Stiglitz (1980). Finally, we will discard the hypothesis that agents do not take the effect of their own trading strategies on the market price into account, assuming instead that agents behave strategically. To this end, we will present a simplified version of Kyle's (1989) model.

We start by presenting models that embed rational expectations equilibrium prices both because they are easily derived from the basic framework of the traditional asset pricing theory and because, even if they do not explicitly describe the mechanism of convergence to the rational expectations equilibrium, they have been extensively used to discuss issues of market design and regulations. For example, rational expectations models with agents behaving competitively have been used to show the effect of asymmetric information and market design on equilibrium asset prices (e.g. Admati, 1985;

Admati and Pfleiderer, 1991; Brown and Zhang, 1997; Hellwig, 1980); in the same vein, rational expectations models with strategic traders have been the main precept of a vast area of microstructure research, which is widely discussed in O'Hara (1995). Chapters 3, 5 and 10 of the present book also comment extensively on this literature.

2.1   Introduction

In traditional economics, the function of prices is to allocate scarce resources, but this is not their only function: they also serve as the vehicle of information on the future value of the asset being exchanged.

The information content of prices was considered by economists as early as the 1940s. In 'The use of knowledge in society' Hayek (1945) writes: 'We must look at the price system as such a mechanism for communicating information if we want to understand its real function . . . The most significant fact about this system is the economy of knowledge with which it operates, or how little the individual participants need to know in order to be able to take the right action.' This clearly states the relationship between information, prices, individuals' decisions and market equilibrium; in other words, it underscores the fact that market prices can play two roles: allocation mechanism and information signal.

2.1.1   Allocating scarce resources

Prices serve to co-ordinate consumption and production decisions. Consider, for instance, active agents' behaviour in the grain market. Each individual comes with his/her own demand or supply function, and the equilibrium price reflects the production technology and consumers' preferences.

The sums of the individual supplies and demands give the aggregate supply and demand curves S and D (Figure 2.1). The equilibrium price p^* is the price at which consumers' and enterprises' decisions are co-ordinated.

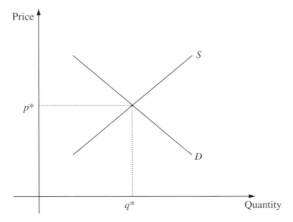

Figure 2.1. Walrasian equilibrium.

In this example the equilibrium price p^* represents the Walrasian equilibrium, since it allocates scarce resources efficiently. There is no uncertainty as to the value of the goods exchanged, and information is exogenous; that is, the individuals do not use knowledge of the equilibrium price to modify their consumption or production decisions. Finally, information is implicitly assumed to be homogeneous, in that all market participants receive the same information.

2.1.2 Transmitting information

When the hypothesis of asymmetric information is introduced, prices become a vehicle of information. Consider, for example, the auction at the opening of a financial market.[1] Suppose that investor i has received information, y_i, indicating that the future value of the security will be high, and has accordingly placed a buy order, $x(y_i)$. Meanwhile, investor i observes the demands of the other investors in the market-place and sees that the new equilibrium price is lower than he had expected; he thus infers that the information available to the other agents is not as promising as his own and revises his investment decision accordingly. His new market demand becomes $x\left\{y_i,\ p^*\left(y_{-i}\right)\right\}$, which is a function of both his information y_i and the equilibrium price $p^*\left(y_{-i}\right)$, the latter being a function of the information available to the other agents, y_{-i}. In this example, the information available to traders is not uniform. Some agents hold better information than others. The information influences investment decisions, and this is at least partly reflected in market prices. Thus prices become a vehicle of information, and the observation of prices leads the less informed to revise their expenditure decisions in accordance with the new information acquired. This is an example of endogenous information.

The problem now is to show how at one and the same time prices can clear the market and also be efficient information signals. To this end a new definition of equilibrium, the *rational expectations equilibrium*, is necessary: *if the price is a vehicle of information, the equilibrium price is such that, once agents have observed it, they do not wish to trade again, or in other words, they no longer wish to alter their investment decisions.*

This new definition of equilibrium leads to conclusions that may differ from the Walrasian paradigm.

(1) The market demand function may not be decreasing: if the price is a vehicle of information, its reduction may signal a lower value of the security and cause a decline rather than an increase in trading demand. It follows that the quality of the goods traded, as perceived by the agents, depends on the market price.

(2) There may be interdependence between the demand and supply functions. If the price acts as a vehicle of information, then an increase in supply can drive both the price of the security and the demand for it down. 'An increase of supply leads to the reduction of the price. Moreover, given that lower prices correspond on average

---

[1] See Chapter 1 for a detailed explanation of the working of an opening auction.

to states where the value of the securities is lower, the price decrease leads to a worse valuation of the security on behalf of the uninformed individuals and, consequently, to the negotiations of their demand' (Grossman and Stiglitz, 1976).

(3) There may be no equilibrium. According to Grossman and Stiglitz's (1980) paradox, if it is possible to obtain all the available information from the observation of market prices, agents no longer have an incentive to acquire information, if this entails a cost. However, if fewer agents acquire information, then prices lose informational content, creating a new incentive to acquire information. But prices then regain their informational content, which again diminishes the incentive to acquire information. To solve this paradox, Grossman and Stiglitz introduce the concept of 'noise traders'[2] so as to make the price not perfectly informative (in their terminology, *not fully revealing*). This noise prevents agents who have no private information from acquiring its equivalent simply by observing the market price. If there are three types of agent – informed, uninformed and noise traders – rather than just informed and uninformed, then the uninformed agents cannot isolate the insiders' signal simply by looking at the price, because prices now reflect noise traders' net demand as well. An analogous result is obtained if we assume that the insiders are subject to an endowment shock[3] at the start of the trading game. As we shall see, because of the existence of noise, it is possible to determine an equilibrium price, p. This equilibrium, however, has two limitations: firstly, it is not very robust when agents are nearly risk-neutral, or when there is too little noise in the market-place. In either case, the equilibrium price tends to be *fully revealing*, as it may reveal all the available information. In fact, quasi-risk-neutral agents transmit their information to the market very aggressively. The second limitation is that agents react in a paradoxical manner. Under the assumption of competitive behaviour, traders do not consider the effect of their own demand on the equilibrium price; it follows that they know that the market price is influenced by their net demand but do not internalize this knowledge in their investment decisions, and trade without taking the price impact of their own trades into account. This is a paradox that may characterize the concept of competitive equilibrium.

To overcome these limitations, Kyle (1989) introduces *imperfect competition*, positing that agents do factor in the effects of their own investment strategies. In this case, on average agents will submit less aggressive orders. On this basis, Kyle shows both that prices cannot reveal more than half the information available to insiders and that the information revealed under imperfect competition is always less than under competitive behaviour. Thus with imperfect competition, an equilibrium always exists, even in the presence of informed risk-neutral agents. This conclusion justifies the literature's broad use of models allowing for strategic interaction.

---

[2] The presence of agents who submit casual orders reduces the information content of the equilibrium price.

[3] This is tantamount to assuming implicitly that the insiders trade not only in order to speculate on their own information, but also to hedge their endowment of risky assets.

2.2   Financial market equilibrium with symmetric information

This section briefly reviews the pricing of assets in a market with symmetric information. After deriving the equilibrium price for a single risky asset, we turn to the multiple
asset model. For this latter case, we also derive the capital asset pricing model.

2.2.1   A single risky asset

Consider a one-period model: before transactions take place, the representative risk-
neutral agent receives an endowment of both the risky asset, I, and the risk-free asset,
I_f. At the end of the trading game, the risk-free asset pays $1 + r_f$ and the risky asset
pays $\widetilde{F}$. Since $\widetilde{F}$ is a normal random variable, so is the final cash flow of the risky
asset.

The agent's objective function is to maximize the expected utility of his end-of-
period welfare:

$$\underset{X}{\text{Max}}\ E[U(\widetilde{w})], \quad \widetilde{w} = (I + X)\widetilde{F} + (I_f - Xp)(1 + r_f) \tag{2.1}$$

where X is the agent's demand for the risky asset and p is the price he pays for each
unit of it. The price of the risk-free asset is normalized to 1. In addition, the market-
clearing condition in this simple economy dictates that, in equilibrium, the single agent
holds his own endowment of the risky asset, I.

From the first-order conditions (f.o.c.), we obtain:

$$E[u'(\widetilde{w})(\widetilde{F} - p(1 + r_f))] = 0 \tag{2.2}$$

Using the formula for covariance, we can compute:

$$E[u'(\widetilde{w})(\widetilde{F} - p(1 + r_f))] = E[u'(\widetilde{w})]E[\widetilde{F} - p(1 + r_f)] + Cov[u'(\widetilde{w}), (\widetilde{F} - p(1 + r_f))] \tag{2.3}$$

The covariance term on the right-hand side can be evaluated using Stein's lemma[4] as:

$$Cov[u'(\widetilde{w}), (\widetilde{F} - p\,(1 + r_f))] = E[u''(\widetilde{w})]Cov[\widetilde{w}, (\widetilde{F} - p\,(1 + r_f))]$$
$$= E[u''(\widetilde{w})]Cov[\widetilde{w}, \widetilde{F}] \tag{2.4}$$

Now substituting $\widetilde{w} = (I + X)\widetilde{F} + (I_f - Xp)(1 + r_f)$ we obtain $Cov[\widetilde{w}, \widetilde{F}] = (I + X)Var(\widetilde{F})$ and hence the first-order condition (2.3) implies:

$$E[u'(\widetilde{w})]\,E[\widetilde{F} - p\,(1 + r_f)] + E[u''(\widetilde{w})]\,(I + X)Var(\widetilde{F}) = 0 \tag{2.5}$$

From this equation, the equilibrium price follows immediately as:

$$p = \frac{1}{1 + r_f}\left[E(\widetilde{F}) + \frac{E[u''(\widetilde{w})]}{E[u'(\widetilde{w})]}(I + X)Var(\widetilde{F})\right] \tag{2.6}$$

---

[4] Given two random variables, x_1 and x_2, that are both continuous, differentiable and jointly normal, Stein's
lemma can be applied to compute $Cov[g(x_1), x_2] = E[g'(x_1)]Cov(x_1, x_2)$.

As a special case, consider the CARA utility function $u(\widetilde{w}) = -\exp(-A\widetilde{w})$. In this case, $E[u''(\widetilde{w})]/E[u'(\widetilde{w})] = -A$ and the pricing equation reads:

$$p = \frac{1}{1+r_f}\left[E(\widetilde{F}) - A(I+X)Var(\widetilde{F})\right] \tag{2.7}$$

This interpretation is quite nice: the price of the asset is its discounted expected cash flow less a discount for risk. The risk discount depends on (i) the variance of the payoff, (ii) the endowment of the risky asset and (iii) the risk aversion as measured by the coefficient of absolute risk aversion A.

From the pricing equation (2.6), the expected return on this asset is:

$$E(\widetilde{r}) = \frac{E(\widetilde{F})-p}{p} = r_f - \frac{E[u''(\widetilde{w})]}{E[u'(\widetilde{w})]}(I+X)Var(\widetilde{F})/p \tag{2.8}$$

and in the special case with CARA utility:

$$E(\widetilde{r}) = \frac{E(\widetilde{F})-p}{p} = r_f + A(I+X)Var[\widetilde{F}]/p \tag{2.9}$$

The expected return on the asset equals the risk-free rate plus a risk premium. The risk premium depends on the total supply of the asset, the agent's risk aversion and the variance of the asset's payoff.

2.2.2 Multiple risky assets and the CAPM

If we now consider the more general case with N risky assets, the representative agent will maximize:

$$E[U(\widetilde{\underset{\rightarrow}{w}})] = E[U((\underset{\rightarrow}{I} + \underset{\rightarrow}{X})\widetilde{\underset{\rightarrow}{F}} + (I_f - \underset{\rightarrow}{X}'\underset{\rightarrow}{p})(1+r_f))]$$

with $\underset{\rightarrow}{p} = [p_1...p_N]'$, $\widetilde{\underset{\rightarrow}{F}} = [\widetilde{F}_1...\widetilde{F}_N]'$ and $\underset{\rightarrow}{I} = [I_1...I_N]'$ with respect to the vector $\underset{\rightarrow}{X} = [X_1...X_N]'$, and from the f.o.c. we obtain that for each of the N assets, condition (2.2) still holds. It follows that, using the formula for the covariance, we can compute:

$$E[u'(\widetilde{w})(\widetilde{F}_i - p_i(1+r_f))] = E[u'(\widetilde{w})]E[\widetilde{F}_i - p_i(1+r_f)] + Cov[u'(\widetilde{w}),$$
$$(\widetilde{F}_i - p_i(1+r_f))] \tag{2.10}$$

Again using Stein's lemma to evaluate the covariance term on the right-hand side, we find:

$$Cov[u'(\widetilde{w}), (\widetilde{F}_i - p_i(1+r_f))] = E[u''(\widetilde{w})]Cov[\widetilde{w}, \widetilde{F}_i] \tag{2.11}$$

Substituting this result into equation (2.10) we obtain:

$$E[u'(\widetilde{w})]E(\widetilde{F}_i - p_i(1+r_f)) + E[u''(\widetilde{w})]Cov[\widetilde{w}, \widetilde{F}_i] = 0 \tag{2.12}$$

and:

$$p_i = \frac{1}{1+r_f}\left[E(\widetilde{F}_i) + \frac{E[u''(\widetilde{w})]}{E[u'(\widetilde{w})]}Cov[\widetilde{w}, \widetilde{F}_i]\right] \tag{2.13}$$

The price of the asset is equal to the sum of the agent's expected cash flow plus a risk premium term, which depends on the covariance between the asset's cash flow and total wealth. The expected return follows immediately as:

$$E(\tilde{r}_i) = r_f + \left[-\frac{E[u''(\tilde{w})]}{E[u'(\tilde{w})]} \right] Cov[\tilde{w}, \tilde{r}_i] \qquad (2.14)$$

where $\tilde{r}_i = (\tilde{F}_i - p_i)/p_i$ is the return on asset i.

Let us now introduce the market portfolio, $\tilde{F}_m$, as the cash flow generated by the final quantity invested in the risky assets $\tilde{F}_m = \sum_{i=1}^{N} X_i \tilde{F}_i$, and the price of the market portfolio as $p_m = \sum_{i=1}^{N} X_i p_i$, where the number of shares of each asset i held in the market portfolio is equal to $\mu_i = X_i p_i / \sum_{i=1}^{N} X_i p_i$. The return on asset i and on the market portfolio are equal to: $\tilde{r}_i = (\tilde{F}_i - p_i)/p_i$ and $\tilde{r}_m = (\tilde{F}_m - p_m)/p_m$ respectively. It follows that in equilibrium the total wealth of the economy will be equal to the market portfolio plus the initial endowment of risk-free asset: $\tilde{W} = \tilde{F}_m + I_f(1 + r_f)$.

In algebraic terms, it is now possible to show that equation (2.14) is consistent with the CAPM. Multiply both terms of equation (2.14) by μ_i / p_m and sum across the N assets to obtain:

$$E(\tilde{r}_m) - r_f = \left[-\frac{E[u''(\tilde{W})]}{E[u'(\tilde{W})]} \right] Cov[\tilde{W}, \tilde{r}_m] \qquad (2.15)$$

Notice that $Cov[\tilde{W}/p_m, \tilde{r}_m] \, p_m = Var(\tilde{r}_m) \, p_m$, and hence:

$$-\frac{E[u''(\tilde{W})]}{E[u'(\tilde{W})]} = \frac{E(\tilde{r}_m) - r_f}{Var(\tilde{r}_m) \, p_m} \qquad (2.16)$$

Consider now that for an individual asset, equation (2.15) reads:

$$E(\tilde{r}_i) - r_f = \left[-\frac{E[u''(\tilde{W})]}{E[u'(\tilde{W})]} \right] Cov[\tilde{W}, \tilde{r}_i] \qquad (2.17)$$

Substitute expression (2.16) into (2.17) and use $Cov[\tilde{W}/p_m, \tilde{r}_i]$ and $p_m = Cov[\tilde{r}_m, \tilde{r}_i] p_m$ to obtain:

$$E(\tilde{r}_i) - r_f = \frac{Cov[\tilde{r}_m, \tilde{r}_i]}{Var(\tilde{r}_m)} [E(\tilde{r}_m) - r_f] = \beta_i [E(\tilde{r}_m) - r_f] \qquad (2.18)$$

which is equivalent to:

$$p_i = \frac{E(\tilde{F}_i)}{1 + r_f + \beta_i [E(\tilde{r}_m) - r_f]} \qquad (2.19)$$

These are exactly the expected return and the pricing equations of the CAPM.

2.3   Financial market equilibrium with asymmetric information

We now introduce asymmetric information and assume that the market is formed by two groups of risk-averse agents, N informed and M uninformed, as well as Z noise traders. Each agent in these groups has, respectively, the demand functions X_I, X and $\tilde{x}$ with:

$$\tilde{x} \sim N(0, \sigma_x^2) \tag{2.20}$$

To keep the model tractable, we consider the case with a single risky asset and for the moment assume that traders receive no endowment at the beginning of the game. We also normalize r_f to zero and assume that agents hold a prior distribution on the future value of the asset, $\tilde{F}$ which is normally distributed with mean $\overline{F}$ and variance σ_F^2:

$$\tilde{F} \sim N(\overline{F}, \sigma_F^2) \tag{2.21}$$

We assume that agents do not behave strategically and thus do not take into account the effects of their investment strategies either on prices or on the other traders' behaviour.[5] The time sequence of the events is the following: at time $t = 0$ the insiders receive a signal $\tilde{S}$ on the future value of the asset that is independently and identically distributed and drawn from the distribution:

$$\tilde{S}|F \sim N(F, \sigma_S^2) \tag{2.22}$$

with mean F and variance σ_S^2.

Given the prior and the signal, it is straightforward to show that the posterior distribution of the asset value is also normal and equal to:[6]

$$\tilde{F}|S \sim N \left(\frac{\frac{1}{\sigma_S^2}}{\frac{1}{\sigma_F^2} + \frac{1}{\sigma_S^2}} S + \frac{\frac{1}{\sigma_F^2}}{\frac{1}{\sigma_F^2} + \frac{1}{\sigma_S^2}} \overline{F}, \frac{1}{\frac{1}{\sigma_F^2} + \frac{1}{\sigma_S^2}} \right) \tag{2.23}$$

or:

$$\tilde{F}|S \sim N \left(\beta S + (1 - \beta)\overline{F}, (1 - \beta)\sigma_F^2 \right) \tag{2.24}$$

where:

$$\beta = \frac{\tau_S}{\tau_F + \tau_S}, \quad \tau_S = \frac{1}{\sigma_S^2}, \quad \tau_F = \frac{1}{\sigma_F^2}$$

The parameters τ_S and τ_F are the precision of $\tilde{S}$ and $\tilde{F}$, respectively.[7]

---

[5] In a later section we will extend this model to strategic agents, albeit considering only the case with one risky asset and thus simplifying Kyle's (1989) model.

[6] To prove this result, one should consider the prior distribution for F:

$$g(\tilde{F}) = \frac{1}{\sqrt{2\pi}\sigma_F} \exp\left[-\frac{1}{2\sigma_F^2}(\tilde{F} - \overline{F})^2 \right]$$

and the conditional distribution of the signal:

$$f(\tilde{S}|F) = \frac{1}{\sqrt{2\pi}\sigma_S} \exp\left[-\frac{1}{2\sigma_S^2}(\tilde{S} - F)^2 \right]$$

and apply Bayes' rule to compute the posterior density function for $\tilde{F}$ given S:

$$g(\tilde{F}|S) = \frac{f(\tilde{S}|F) \, g(\tilde{F})}{\int f(\tilde{S}|F) \, g(\tilde{F}) \, dF}$$

[7] Notice that the conditional mean of $\tilde{F}|S$ is the average of the prior mean $\overline{F}$ and the signal S, weighted by their respective precision, τ_F and τ_S. Notice also that in the case of two random variables $\tilde{F}$ and $\tilde{S}$, the conditional

At time $t = 1$, trading takes place as the risk-averse agents submit limit orders and the noise traders submit market orders. Finally, at time $t = 2$, the value of the asset becomes public information.

Since agents are risk-averse, let us assume that they have a negative exponential utility function with constant absolute risk aversion coefficient (CARA) and maximize:

$$E[U(\widetilde{\pi})] = E[-e^{-A\widetilde{\pi}}] \qquad (2.25)$$

where A is the coefficient of risk aversion and $\widetilde{\pi}$ is the end-of-period profit:

$$\widetilde{\pi} = X(\widetilde{F} - p) \qquad (2.26)$$

As $\widetilde{F}$ is normally distributed, $\widetilde{\pi}$ is also normal:

$$\widetilde{\pi} \sim N\left(X(E(\widetilde{F}) - p),\ X^2 Var(\widetilde{F})\right) \qquad (2.27)$$

Exploiting the property of the moment generating function for a normal random variable,[8] it is straightforward to show that:

$$\underset{X}{\text{Argmax}}\ E[-e^{-A\widetilde{\pi}}] = \underset{X}{\text{Argmax}}\ \left\{E(\widetilde{\pi}) - \frac{A}{2} Var(\widetilde{\pi})\right\} \qquad (2.29)$$

It follows that in this CARA world, traders' demand can be obtained from first-order conditions:

$$X = \frac{E(\widetilde{F}) - p}{A\ Var(\widetilde{F})} \qquad (2.30)$$

Equation (2.30) shows the demand for a trader who does not hold private information and simply uses his prior to formulate investment decisions. The demand function of an informed trader, instead, is equal to:

$$X_I = \frac{E(\widetilde{F}|S) - p}{A\ Var(\widetilde{F}|S)} \qquad (2.31)$$

where $E(\widetilde{F}|S)$ and $Var(\widetilde{F}|S)$ are given by (2.24).

---

mean and variance could be computed using the Theorem of Projection for Normal Distributions according to which:

$$E\left(\widetilde{F}|S\right) = E\left(\widetilde{F}\right) + \frac{Cov\left(\widetilde{F}, \widetilde{S}\right)}{Var\left(\widetilde{S}\right)}\left[\widetilde{S} - E\left(\widetilde{S}\right)\right]$$

and:

$$Var\left(\widetilde{F}|S\right) = Var\left(\widetilde{F}\right) - \frac{\left[Cov\left(\widetilde{F}, \widetilde{S}\right)\right]^2}{Var\left(\widetilde{S}\right)}$$

[8] Given normality of $\widetilde{\pi}$, the property of the moment generating function for a normal random variable, $G(.)$, allows us to write:

$$G(-A) = E_\pi[-e^{-A\widetilde{\pi}}] = -e^{-A[E(\widetilde{\pi}) - \frac{A}{2} Var(\widetilde{\pi})]} \qquad (2.28)$$

Clearly, to maximize $G(-A)$, one can simply maximize $E(\widetilde{\pi}) - \frac{A}{2} Var(\widetilde{\pi})$.

2.3.1 Naïve expectations

Having defined traders' strategies, we are now in a position to solve the model for the equilibrium price function p, by plugging X, X_I and x into the market-clearing condition:

$$N X_I + M X + Z \tilde{x} = 0 \tag{2.32}$$

$$N \left(\frac{E(\tilde{F}|S) - p}{A \, Var(\tilde{F}|S)} \right) + M \left(\frac{E(\tilde{F}) - p}{A \, Var(\tilde{F})} \right) + Z\tilde{x} = 0 \tag{2.33}$$

In this way, we have assumed that three groups of traders come to the market and submit their demand to a Walrasian auctioneer, who ensures that the market clears. Notice that each of the Z liquidity traders simply submits a market order $\tilde{x}$, while each of the N insiders conditions his demand on the signal received, and the M uninformed traders only use $E(\tilde{F})$ to formulate their demand function. Solving for p, we obtain:

$$p = \mu_1 \, E(\tilde{F}|S) + (1 - \mu_1) \, E(\tilde{F}) + \mu_2 \, \tilde{x} \tag{2.34}$$

with $\mu_1 = N \, Var(\tilde{F})/[N \, Var(\tilde{F}) + M \, Var(\tilde{F}|S)]$ and $\mu_2 = A \, Z \, Var(\tilde{F})Var(\tilde{F}|S)/ [N \, Var(\tilde{F}) + M \, Var(\tilde{F}|S)]$. Equation (2.34) shows that the equilibrium price is a combination of the weighted average of the expected cash flow of insiders ($E(\tilde{F}|S)$) and uninformed traders ($E(\tilde{F})$) plus a risk premium $\beta\tilde{x}$. Moreover, substituting $E(\tilde{F}|S)$ from (2.24) into (2.34), we can see that the equilibrium price is a noisy version of the signal $\tilde{S}$:

$$p = E(\tilde{F}) + \mu_1 \frac{Cov\left(\tilde{F}, \tilde{S}\right)}{Var\left(\tilde{S}\right)}(\tilde{S} - E(\tilde{S})) + \mu_2 \, \tilde{x} \tag{2.35}$$

The problem with this equilibrium, however, is that uninformed traders only use their prior to update expectations on the liquidation value of the asset; in other words, they form *naïve expectations*. If they were rational, they would also use the information contained in prices to update their beliefs on $\tilde{F}$. For this reason, let us solve the model assuming that both informed and uninformed traders use the information they can extract from the market price to update their beliefs.

2.3.2 Rational expectations

Assume for the sake of simplicity that the signal is such that the future value of the risky asset is equal to:

$$\tilde{F} = \tilde{S} + \tilde{\varepsilon} \tag{2.36}$$

with:

$$\tilde{S} \sim N(0, \sigma_S^2) \qquad \tilde{\varepsilon} \sim N(0, \sigma_\varepsilon^2) \qquad \tilde{S} \perp \tilde{\varepsilon} \tag{2.37}$$

As a result, the distribution of the asset payoff can be written as:

$$\tilde{F} \sim N(0, \sigma_S^2 + \sigma_\varepsilon^2) \tag{2.38}$$

Now, if insiders observe the signal S, their conditional expectation and variance of $\widetilde{F}$ become:

$$E(\widetilde{F}|S) = S \quad \text{and} \quad Var(\widetilde{F}|S) = \sigma_\varepsilon^2 \tag{2.39}$$

Considering that traders now use the market price to update their beliefs, the respective demands of uninformed and informed traders are equal to:

$$\widetilde{X} = \frac{E(\widetilde{F}|p) - p}{A \ Var\left(\widetilde{F}|p\right)} \tag{2.40}$$

$$\widetilde{X}_I = \frac{E(\widetilde{F}|S, p) - p}{A \ Var\left(\widetilde{F}|S, p\right)} = \frac{E(\widetilde{F}|S) - p}{A \ Var\left(\widetilde{F}|S\right)} \tag{2.41}$$

Notice that the insiders' signal is a sufficient statistic for the market price, i.e. $E(\widetilde{F}|S, p) = E(\widetilde{F}|S)$ and $Var\left(\widetilde{F}|S, p\right) = Var\left(\widetilde{F}|S\right)$. Essentially, the market price that insiders observe reflects both public information and all private signals; since for simplicity it has been assumed that all insiders acquire the same signal, they cannot learn anything new from the market price, so their demand is conditioned only on their private signal, S.

To solve the model, we must use the concept of *rational expectations equilibrium (REE)*. This equilibrium can be obtained where agents perceive that the price contains information. Taking this into consideration, they realize that others do the same and that this behaviour has an impact on the price function. As a consequence, the price is correlated with the insider's signal, which in turn is correlated with the liquidation value of the security.

If the following assumptions hold, we have a *linear rational expectations equilibrium*:

(1) The uninformed agents make a conjecture on the equilibrium price function equal to:

$$\widetilde{p} = \alpha_1 \widetilde{S} + \alpha_2 \widetilde{x} \tag{2.42}$$

(2) They use this conjecture to estimate $E\left(\widetilde{F}|p\right)$ and $Var\left(\widetilde{F}|p\right)$ so as to determine X.

(3) Equilibrium is attained when the price that meets the *market-clearing condition*:

$$N \ X_I + M \ X + Z \ \widetilde{x} = 0, \tag{2.43}$$

is a linear combination of S and x or, indeed, is equal to (2.42). In other words, in equilibrium the agents' conjectures coincide with realizations.

In order to prove the existence of a rational expectations equilibrium, we must consider that insiders and uninformed agents make investment decisions on the basis of all the available information, and first specify their demand functions. As noted earlier, the insiders use the signal S so that their demand is simply equal to:

$$X_I = \frac{S - p}{A \, \sigma_\varepsilon^2} \tag{2.44}$$

Uninformed agents extract information from the market price and hence we have to compute the conditional mean and variance of $\widetilde{F}$:

$$E\left(\widetilde{F}|p = \alpha_1 S + \alpha_2 x\right) = \frac{\alpha_1 \sigma_S^2}{\alpha_1^2 \sigma_S^2 + \alpha_2^2 \sigma_x^2} p = \vartheta \, p \tag{2.45}$$

$$Var(\widetilde{F}|p = \alpha_1 S + \alpha_2 x) = \sigma_S^2 + \sigma_\varepsilon^2 - \frac{\alpha_1^2 \sigma_S^4}{\alpha_1^2 \sigma_S^2 + \alpha_2^2 \sigma_x^2} \tag{2.46}$$

and plug them back into (2.40). To obtain p, simply substitute X_I and X into the market-clearing condition (2.43) and solve for p:

$$\widetilde{p} = \varphi_1 \{\alpha_1, \alpha_2\} \, \widetilde{S} + \varphi_2 \{\alpha_1, \alpha_2\} \, \widetilde{x} \tag{2.47}$$

with:

$$\varphi_1 \{\alpha_1, \alpha_2\} = \frac{N \, Var(\widetilde{F}|p)}{M \, \sigma_\varepsilon^2 (1 - \vartheta) + N \, Var(\widetilde{F}|p)}$$

and:

$$\varphi_2 \{\alpha_1, \alpha_2\} = \frac{A \, Var(\widetilde{F}|p)\sigma_\varepsilon^2 Z}{M \, \sigma_\varepsilon^2 (1 - \vartheta) + N \, Var(\widetilde{F}|p)}$$

Now, to find a REE price for the stock, we need to make sure that the actual price rule (2.47) is equivalent to the expected price rule (2.42), and hence solve the following system in two equations and two unknowns, α_1 and α_2:

$$\begin{cases} \alpha_1 = \varphi_1 \{\alpha_1, \alpha_2\} \\ \alpha_2 = \varphi_2 \{\alpha_1, \alpha_2\} \end{cases} \tag{2.48}$$

The solution to this system is a pair of α_1^* and α_2^* such that we have the REE price function:

$$\widetilde{p}^* = \alpha_1^* \widetilde{S} + \alpha_2^* \widetilde{x} \tag{2.49}$$

with $\alpha_1^* = f_1 \{A, M, N, Z, \sigma_S^2, \sigma_\varepsilon^2, \sigma_x^2\}$ and $\alpha_2^* = f_2 \{A, M, N, Z, \sigma_S^2, \sigma_\varepsilon^2, \sigma_x^2\}$. We now show how to calculate this equilibrium. First, we describe the case with a deterministic supply, x. We then discuss the more complicated case with random noise trade $\widetilde{x}$.

Fully revealing equilibrium   Here it is shown that in the case of an exogenously given, non-random supply x, the equilibrium is very easily calculated. The naïve equilibrium price (2.34) is given by:

$$p = \mu_1 \, E(\widetilde{F}|S) + (1 - \mu_1) \, E(\widetilde{F}) + \mu_2 \, x$$

$$= \mu_1 \left(\frac{\frac{1}{\sigma_S^2}}{\frac{1}{\sigma_F^2} + \frac{1}{\sigma_S^2}} S + \frac{\frac{1}{\sigma_F^2}}{\frac{1}{\sigma_F^2} + \frac{1}{\sigma_S^2}} \overline{F} \right) + (1 - \mu_1)\overline{F} + \mu_2 x \qquad (2.50)$$

In this equation, the only unknown is the informed trader's signal S. Hence, the uninformed trader can infer the signal perfectly, from the price p, and update his beliefs (expectation and variance) conditional on the price. In this case, this is equivalent to conditioning on the signal; it follows that the uninformed demand becomes:

$$X = X_I = \frac{E(\widetilde{F}|S) - p}{A \, Var(\widetilde{F}|S)} \qquad (2.51)$$

and the REE equilibrium price is given by:

$$p = E(\widetilde{F}|S) - A \, Var(\widetilde{F}|S) \, Z \, x/(N + M) \qquad (2.52)$$

where $E(\widetilde{F}|S)$ is given in equation (2.23).

The equilibrium price equals the expected payoff less a discount for aggregate risk aversion. Notice that the expectation is conditional on the informed trader's signal. This equilibrium is thus fully revealing (the signal S can be inferred perfectly from the equilibrium price) and prices are strong-form efficient, because they fully incorporate public and private information.

Noisy rational expectations equilibrium   In the fully revealing REE, uninformed traders learn the informed trader's signal at zero cost from the market equilibrium price. This inspired Grossman and Stiglitz (1980) in their critique of the rational expectations equilibrium. A possible way to address this criticism is to replace the fixed supply x with a random noise trade $\tilde{x}$.

In this case, the solution for the equilibrium price (2.49) can be obtained by solving the system of two equations (2.48) and two unknowns to obtain α_1^* and α_2^*; but this procedure, which involves some laborious algebra, can be simplified by exploiting the assumptions of REE.[9] To extract information from the market price, uninformed agents form a conjecture on the equilibrium price, which is based on the price being formed. Under the model's assumptions, this is tantamount to a conjecture on the demand function of the informed agents and to the solution of the market-clearing condition. More precisely, when uninformed traders make conjectures on the equilibrium price, they also make a conjecture on the demand function both for insiders and for the other uninformed traders. We exploit this property to show that an REE can be obtained if the conjectures of uninformed traders on the others' demand functions

---

[9] See Rindi (2008) for this version of Grossman and Stiglitz's (1980) model.

match their realizations. Now, uninformed traders are in a position to guess from the beginning that the insiders' demand is equal to (2.44); this is because insiders do not get information from the market price and so do not reformulate their demand function in the process of convergence to the REE. Conversely, conjectures on the uninformed traders' demand must converge on the rational equilibrium, since they adjust over time. Now let us assume that each uninformed trader conjectures that the other $(M - 1)$ uninformed traders submit a downward-sloping demand function of the type:

$$X = -Hp \tag{2.53}$$

Substituting (2.44) and (2.53) into the market-clearing condition:

$$N \left(\frac{\widetilde{S} - p}{A\sigma_\varepsilon^2} \right) - (M - 1) Hp + X + Z \widetilde{x} = 0 \tag{2.54}$$

and solving for the price, the uninformed trader gets:

$$p = \lambda \left[\frac{N\widetilde{S}}{A\sigma_\varepsilon^2} + X + Z \widetilde{x} \right] \quad \text{with} \quad \lambda = \left[\frac{N}{A\sigma_\varepsilon^2} + (M - 1) H \right]^{-1} \tag{2.55}$$

which he uses to update his expectations of the future value of the asset, $\widetilde{F}$.

Let us now show how one can simplify the problem of signal extraction from the market price, p. Notice that the expression for p given by (2.55) contains X, a term that is known to the uninformed trader. So, it is reasonable to assume that, in updating their expectations, uninformed agents use the residual signal $\widetilde{\Theta}$ extracted from the price:

$$\widetilde{\Theta} = \widetilde{S} + \frac{A\sigma_\varepsilon^2 Z}{N} \widetilde{x} = \gamma_1 p - \gamma_2 X = \Theta \tag{2.56}$$

$$\text{with} \quad \gamma_1 = \frac{N + A\sigma_\varepsilon^2 (M - 1) H}{N} \quad \text{and} \quad \gamma_2 = \frac{A\sigma_\varepsilon^2}{N} \tag{2.57}$$

It is in fact straightforward to show that:

$$E\left(\widetilde{F}|p\right) = E\left(\widetilde{F}|\Theta\right) \quad \text{and} \quad Var\left(\widetilde{F}|p\right) = Var\left(\widetilde{F}|\Theta\right) \tag{2.58}$$

By using the projection theorem, we compute:

$$E\left(\widetilde{F}|\Theta\right) = \left(\frac{\sigma_S^2}{\sigma_S^2 + \dfrac{A^2\sigma_\varepsilon^4 Z^2}{N^2}\sigma_x^2} \right) (\gamma_1 p - \gamma_2 X) \tag{2.59}$$

and:

$$Var\left(\widetilde{F}|\Theta\right) = \sigma_S^2 + \sigma_\varepsilon^2 - \frac{\sigma_S^4}{\sigma_S^2 + \dfrac{A^2\sigma_\varepsilon^4 Z^2}{N^2}\sigma_x^2} \tag{2.60}$$

Substituting the former values into the uninformed agents' demand function and solving for X we obtain:

$$X = - \left[\frac{1 - \dfrac{Cov(\widetilde{F}, \widetilde{\Theta})}{Var(\widetilde{\Theta})} \gamma_1}{A \, Var\,(\widetilde{F}|\Theta) + \dfrac{Cov(\widetilde{F}, \widetilde{\Theta})}{Var(\widetilde{\Theta})} \gamma_2} \right] p \qquad (2.61)$$

As mentioned above, the existence of a linear REE requires that both the conjectures on the price that solves the *market-clearing* condition and those on the demand function of market participants coincide with the realizations.

Since we have assumed that the conjecture on each uninformed agent's demand is equal to $X_U = -Hp$, in equilibrium we have:

$$\left[\frac{1 - \dfrac{Cov\left(\widetilde{F}, \widetilde{\Theta}\right)}{Var\left(\widetilde{\Theta}\right)} \gamma_1}{A \, Var\,(\widetilde{F}|\Theta) + \dfrac{Cov(\widetilde{F}, \widetilde{\Theta})}{Var(\widetilde{\Theta})} \gamma_2} \right] = H \qquad (2.62)$$

Explicating the values of γ_1 and γ_2 and solving for H, we obtain:

$$H^* = \left[\frac{1 - \dfrac{Cov(\widetilde{F}, \widetilde{\Theta})}{Var(\widetilde{\Theta})}}{A \, Var\,(\widetilde{F}|\Theta) + \dfrac{Cov(\widetilde{F}, \widetilde{\Theta})}{Var(\widetilde{\Theta})} \dfrac{M \, A\sigma_\varepsilon^2}{N}} \right] \qquad (2.63)$$

In this way, we have determined all the values that we need to solve the *market-clearing* condition (2.43) for the *equilibrium price*:

$$p^* = \left[\frac{N}{A\sigma_\varepsilon^2} + MH^* \right]^{-1} \left[\frac{N}{A\sigma_\varepsilon^2} \widetilde{S} + Z\widetilde{x} \right] \qquad (2.64)$$

In the end, expectations coincide with the true realization (rational expectations). This result is relevant in the sense that, as in real-world markets, agents' expectations influence the real value of prices. Notice that if all the parameters (mean, variance, risk aversion and aggregate supply) are known, the signal value S can be inferred exactly from the market price p^*, and prices are strong-form efficient. Notice also that this is a competitive equilibrium, in the sense that agents are non-strategic. As the next section shows, this model can easily be extended to include strategic agents without substantially altering the results (see Kyle, 1989).

Once the equilibrium price is determined, it is possible to compute some indicators of market quality (liquidity, volatility and informational efficiency) and use them to discuss the effects of possible changes in market design. The following are standard indicators of liquidity (L), volatility $(Var(p^*))$ and informational efficiency (IE):

$$L = \left| \frac{dp}{dx} \right|^{-1} = \left[\frac{N}{A\sigma_\varepsilon^2} + MH^* \right] = \left(\frac{N}{A\sigma_\varepsilon^2} + \frac{M \left(1 - \dfrac{Cov(F, \widetilde{\Theta})}{Var(\widetilde{\Theta})} \right)}{A\, Var(\widetilde{F}|\Theta) + \dfrac{Cov(F, \widetilde{\Theta}) A\sigma_\varepsilon^2 M}{Var(\widetilde{\Theta})N}} \right) \tag{2.65}$$

$$Var\left(p^*\right) = (L)^{-2} \left[\frac{N^2}{A^2\sigma_\varepsilon^4}\sigma_S^2 + Z^2\sigma_x^2 \right] \tag{2.66}$$

$$IE = Var\left(\widetilde{F} \mid \Theta\right)^{-1} = \left(\sigma_S^2 + \sigma_\varepsilon^2 - \frac{\sigma_S^4}{\sigma_S^2 + \dfrac{A^2\sigma_\varepsilon^4 Z^2}{N^2}\sigma_x^2} \right)^{-1} \tag{2.67}$$

Note that L measures the inverse of the price impact of each noise trader's order; clearly, the smaller the price impact, the greater the depth of the market, and hence the greater the liquidity. Note also that IE is an indicator of informational efficiency as it measures the inverse of the residual variance of the fundamental value of the asset; and this residual variance measures what is left once agents have conditioned on the random signal extracted from the equilibrium price: the lower the conditional volatility, the better the equilibrium price as a vehicle of information on $\widetilde{F}$.

2.4 Financial market equilibrium with asymmetric information and strategic agents

Up to this point we have assumed that risk-averse agents are price-takers. We now posit that agents act strategically and factor in the effects of their own orders on the equilibrium price. If they do so, agents will scale back their orders accordingly and be less aggressive than when they act competitively. Let us further assume that prior to trading informed traders receive an endowment shock equal to $\widetilde{I} \sim N(0, \sigma_I^2)$. This assumption will be necessary to find a non-fully-revealing equilibrium price when the model is used to study pre-trade transparency (Chapter 10). Clearly, both the informed traders' signal and their endowment shock are unknown to the uninformed.

Under these new assumptions, each informed trader submits a linear demand equal to:

$$X_I^S = \frac{\widetilde{S} - p^S - A\sigma_\varepsilon^2 \widetilde{I}}{A\sigma_\varepsilon^2 + \lambda_I} = D(\widetilde{S} - p^S) - G\widetilde{I} \tag{2.68}$$

$$\text{with } D = \frac{1}{A\sigma_\varepsilon^2 + \lambda_I} \quad \text{and} \quad G = \frac{A\sigma_\varepsilon^2}{A\sigma_\varepsilon^2 + \lambda_I} \tag{2.69}$$

which can be easily derived from the first-order condition:

$$\widetilde{S} - p^S - \frac{\partial p^S}{\partial X_I} X_I^S - \frac{A}{2}\left[2\left(X_I^S + \widetilde{I}\right)\right]\sigma_\varepsilon^2 = 0, \quad \text{with} \quad \lambda_I = \frac{\partial p^S}{\partial X_I^S} \quad (2.70)$$

What is new in this version of the model is the parameter λ_I, which measures the price impact of the informed trader's order X_I^S. This price elasticity can be computed by each informed trader by solving for p the conjectured market-clearing condition:

$$(N - 1)(D(S - p^S) - GI) - MH^S p^S + Z\widetilde{x} + X_I^S = 0 \quad (2.71)$$

Similarly, each uninformed trader extracts the following signal from the market price:

$$\begin{aligned}
\Theta_S &= \widetilde{S} - A\sigma_\varepsilon^2\widetilde{I} + \frac{(A\sigma_\varepsilon^2 + \lambda_I)Z}{N}\widetilde{x} \\
&= -\frac{(A\sigma_\varepsilon^2 + \lambda_I)}{N}X_U^S + \frac{N + (A\sigma_\varepsilon^2 + \lambda_I)(M - 1)H^S}{N}p^S \\
&= \gamma_1^S p^S - \gamma_2^S X_U^S
\end{aligned}$$

and uses it to update expectations on $\widetilde{F}$ and to formulate a limit order equal to:

$$X^S = \frac{E\left[\widetilde{F}|\Theta_S\right] - p^S}{A \, Var\left[\widetilde{F}|\Theta_S\right] + \lambda_U} = -H^S p^S \quad (2.72)$$

with:[10]

$$H^{S*} = \left[\frac{1 - \dfrac{Cov(\widetilde{F}, \widetilde{\Theta})}{Var(\widetilde{\Theta})}}{\lambda_U + A \, Var\left(\widetilde{F}|\Theta\right) + \dfrac{Cov(\widetilde{F}, \widetilde{\Theta})}{Var(\widetilde{\Theta})} \dfrac{M(A\sigma_\varepsilon^2 + \lambda_I)}{N}}\right] \quad (2.73)$$

and:

$$\lambda_I = [(N - 1)D + MH^S]^{-1} \quad (2.74)$$

$$\lambda_U = [ND + (M - 1)H^S]^{-1} \quad (2.75)$$

The equilibrium value for H^S is obtained by equating the parameter from the solution of each uninformed trader's first-order condition to the previous conjecture for that parameter value, while λ_U can be derived as before, solving for p the conjectured market-clearing conditions: $N(D(\widetilde{S} - p^S) - G\widetilde{I}) - (M - 1)H^S p^S + Z\widetilde{x} + X^S = 0$.

Substituting D into H^S, λ_U and λ_I, we get the solution to the model with strategic traders by solving the system with three equations and three unknowns (2.73)–(2.75):

$$p^S = [LSA]^{-1}[ND\widetilde{S} - NG\widetilde{I} + Z\widetilde{x}] \quad (2.76)$$

---

[10] For ease of exposition, but without loss of generality, it is assumed here that uninformed traders have zero endowment shock.

$$LSA = \left| \frac{dp}{dx} \right|^{-1} = [ND + MH^{S*}] \tag{2.77}$$

$$= \frac{N}{A\sigma_\varepsilon^2 + \lambda_I} + M \frac{1 - \dfrac{Cov(\widetilde{F}, \widetilde{\Theta}_S)}{Var(\widetilde{\Theta}_S)}}{A \, Var \, (\widetilde{F}|\Theta_S) + \lambda_U + \dfrac{Cov(\widetilde{F}, \widetilde{\Theta}_S)M}{Var(\widetilde{\Theta}_S)N}(A\sigma_\varepsilon^2 + \lambda_I)}$$

Comparing the results for both the equilibrium price and the price impact of a noise trader's order under the two models, i.e. that with competitive and that with strategic agents (equations (2.64) and (2.65) for the competitive model, and (2.76) and (2.77) for the model with strategic agents), it can be noticed that when agents behave competitively liquidity is higher; in fact, when they ignore the price impact of their demand, they trade more aggressively and are more willing to accommodate a noise trader's order.

Table 2.1 reports numerical simulations for the values of the parameters λ_I, λ_U, H^S and D, which show that liquidity (LS) is greater when agents behave competitively. Both H^S and D, which measure uninformed and informed traders' price reactivity, are higher when traders behave competitively. What drives the results, though, is the assumption on the behaviour of the informed traders, not of the uninformed. Take Panel I as an example: when agents act competitively, liquidity is equal to 6.775, but when they behave strategically it falls to 5.736. However, when only uninformed traders are strategic ($\lambda_I = 0$), L is 6.513, and when only informed traders are strategic ($\lambda_U = 0$), L falls to 5.876. This result holds regardless of the relative number of N, M and Z (Panels II and III). Notice also that when the number of informed traders is four times greater than that of uninformed ($N = 20$ in Panel II) liquidity is more than three times greater, whereas when M is increased to 20, liquidity increases by only 30 per cent (Panel III).

This simple exercise yields the conclusion that traders' strategic behaviour diminishes their willingness to supply liquidity; it also suggests that informed traders should be considered as the best liquidity suppliers: in fact, they face the lowest adverse selection costs.

Exercise

Exercise 1

Assume that traders form naïve expectations about the future value of the asset, and that public information is characterized by $\widetilde{F} \sim N(\overline{F}, \sigma_F^2)$, with $\overline{F} = 100$ and $\sigma_F = 20$. The informed trader receives a signal drawn from the distribution $S|F \sim N(F, \sigma_S^2)$ with $\sigma_S = 20$. The actual value of the signal is $S = 180$. Traders have a CARA utility function with risk-aversion parameter $A = 0.02$. Consider two values for the net demand of liquidity traders, $x = 0$ and $x = -1$. First compute the equilibrium price in a market without private information and two uninformed traders. Then compute the

Table 2.1. *Equilibrium parameter values and liquidity for the model with strategic traders* $(A = 2, \sigma_x^2 = \sigma_\varepsilon^2 = \sigma_s^2 = \sigma_I^2 = .5)$

Panel I: N = 5, M = 5, Z = 5

	λ_I	λ_U	H^S	D	LS
Strategic	.204	.185	.316	.831	5.736
$\lambda_I = 0$	0	.160	.309	1	6.513
$\lambda_U = 0$	.198	0	.344	.835	5.876
Competitive	0	0	.333	1	6.775

Panel II: N = 20, M = 5, Z = 5

	λ_I	λ_U	H^S	D	LS
Strategic	.051	.049	.305	.951	20.555
$\lambda_I = 0$	0	.047	.306	1	21.529
$\lambda_U = 0$	.051	0	.314	.952	20.603
Competitive	0	0	.314	1	21.578

Panel III: N = 5, M = 20, Z = 5

	λ_I	λ_U	H^S	D	LS
Strategic	.127	.117	.218	.888	8.791
$\lambda_I = 0$	0	.110	.214	1	9.250
$\lambda_U = 0$	.124	0	.226	.890	8.965
Competitive	0	0	.315	1	9.751

Informed (X_I^S) and uninformed (X^S) traders' demand
$$X_I^S = D(S - p^S) - GI \qquad X^S = -H^S p^S$$

equilibrium price with private information and show that prices convey information about the signal.

Solution

Market equilibrium with no private information: the demand schedule for a trader without private information is $X = [E(F) - p]/A\sigma_F^2 = \frac{1}{8}(100 - p)$. When the net liquidity demand is equal to zero, the equilibrium price is 100, i.e. the security's expected value. With two uninformed traders and an aggregate liquidity demand equal to -1, $x = -1$, the equilibrium price is $p = 96$, and each trader's demand is 0.5. These prices conform to the equilibrium price rule (2.34). Prices in this equilibrium are semi-strong form efficient as they embody all publicly available information.

Market equilibrium with private information: the demand schedule for an informed trader depends on the posterior distribution. Using (2.23) and substituting the values of σ_F and σ_S into β, we have: $E(F|S = 180) = 0.5 * 180 + 0.5 * 100 = 140$

and $Var(F|S) = (1 - \beta)\sigma_F^2 = 0.5 * 400 = 200$. The posterior distribution (after observing the signal) has a higher mean than the prior distribution (because of the high signal) and a lower variance. The demand schedule for the informed trader is: $X_I = [E(F|S) - p]/A \ Var(F|S) = \frac{1}{4}(140 - p)$. The table below collects the optimizing traders' individual demands and the aggregate demand $D = X + X_I$ for a few values of p (the demand schedule for the uninformed trader is the same as before). We find

p		92	100	124	126.66	140
X		1	0	-3	-3.33	-5
X_I		12	10	4	3.33	0
$D = X + X_I$		13	10	1	0	-5

that for a liquidity demand of $x = -1$, $p = 124$ is an equilibrium price. For zero net liquidity demand, $p = 126.66$ is an equilibrium price. Letting $N = M = Z = 1$, these prices conform to the Walrasian equilibrium price rule (2.34). If we now compare the prices obtained for $x = -1$ and $x = 0$ (i.e. $p = 124$ and $p = 126.66$) with those derived without private information ($p = 100$ and $p = 96$), we notice that the equilibrium price has moved in the direction of the signal (i.e. upwards). Hence, the price conveys information about the signal.

References

Admati, A. 1985, 'A noisy rational expectations equilibrium for multi-asset securities markets', *Econometrica*, 53, 629–57.

Admati, A. and P. Pfleiderer, 1991, 'Sunshine trading and financial market equilibrium', *Review of Financial Studies*, 4, 443–81.

Brown, D. P. and Z. M. Zhang, 1997, 'Market orders and market efficiency', *Journal of Finance*, 52, 277–308.

Grossman, S. and J. Stiglitz, 1976, 'Information and competitive price system', *American Economic Review*, Papers and Proceedings, 66, 246–53.

1980, 'On the impossibility of informationally efficient markets', *American Economic Review*, 70, 393–408.

Hayek, F. A. 1945, 'The use of knowledge in society', *American Economic Review*, 35, 519–30.

Hellwig, M. 1980, 'The aggregation of information in competitive markets', *Journal of Economic Theory*, 22, 477–98.

Kyle, A. 1989, 'Informed speculation with imperfect competition', *Review of Economic Studies*, 56, 317–56.

O'Hara, M. 1995, *Market Microstructure Theory*, Oxford: Blackwell.

Rindi, B. 2008, 'Informed traders as liquidity providers: anonymity, liquidity and price formation'. *Review of Finance*, 12, 497–532.

3 Batch markets with strategic informed traders

3.1 Introduction

There are three principal determinants of the bid–ask spread: fixed costs, adverse selection costs and inventory costs. Fixed costs are order processing costs, such as administrative costs and compensation for the market-maker's time. Adverse selection costs stem from asymmetric information. Finally, dealers must sustain the inventory costs of holding undesired portfolios of risky assets. By nature, only risk-averse dealers will be concerned with inventory costs, so the models that include them assume that liquidity providers are risk-averse. This assumption, which complicates the algebra, can be dispensed with in models with adverse selection.

The next two chapters are dedicated to models that focus on the adverse selection component of the bid–ask spread. Chapter 5 will also discuss inventory and fixed costs.

The model presented in this chapter draws on the work of Kyle (1985), who posits a group of risk-neutral market-makers facing insiders and liquidity traders. In fact, Kyle models the strategic interaction between an insider who chooses to trade in order to maximize his profits and a group of market-makers who take the insider's strategy into account in updating their beliefs on the future value of the asset and setting the equilibrium price. In this way, Kyle shows how information is incorporated into prices and how the latter reflect both the trading protocol where market-makers set prices and the strategic behaviour of the informed trader.

Even if the final outcome is a single equilibrium price, Kyle's model differs from the rational expectations protocol discussed in Chapter 2 in three ways. Firstly, in Grossman and Stiglitz's (1980) model all the agents, informed, uninformed and noise traders, submit their orders to the market concurrently, acting as liquidity suppliers. Secondly, in Grossman and Stiglitz, all market participants except for noise traders are risk-averse and non-strategic. Their model could be modified to incorporate strategic behaviour without altering the microstructure substantially; the assumption of risk neutrality, by contrast, would modify that market protocol significantly. In fact, if the uninformed agents were risk-neutral, they would have no incentive to trade with the informed agents, and would therefore leave the market. To give uninformed risk-neutral agents an incentive to trade, one should assume that they have some privileged information such as, for example, exclusive access to the order flow; but this assumption would turn them into market-makers, and the Grossman and Stiglitz model would collapse into Kyle's protocol.

Thirdly, the rational expectations model can be viewed as an auction in which the price formation process is not explicitly modelled; Kyle's model retains the auction structure and the rational expectations pricing rule but makes the price formation process more explicit.

A comparison with Glosten and Milgrom's (1985) model, which will be presented in Chapter 4, is needed here. Like that of Kyle, this model assumes that a group of risk-neutral market-makers faces insiders and liquidity traders. In Glosten and Milgrom's model, dealers post bid and ask quotes which are subsequently chosen by their customers, who are asymmetrically informed and arrive sequentially at the market-place. The assumption of asymmetric information generates adverse selection costs, which force dealers to open the bid–ask spread. Such spread is the premium that dealers demand for trading with agents with superior information. The novelty in Kyle's model is that these traders do not arrive sequentially as in the Glosten and Milgrom quote-driven market. Kyle's protocol is order-driven and resembles a batch auction where risk-neutral Bertrand competitive dealers set a single equilibrium price after observing the aggregate order flow. Thus, the market described here is order-driven and, since dealers do not observe each single order's direction and quantity, the learning process embedded in the semi-strong efficient pricing rule is also different. Furthermore, in Kyle's batch auction informed traders act strategically and choose the size of their orders to exploit private information and maximize their expected end-of-period profits. It follows that the equilibrium process embeds a strategic interaction between market-makers and insiders, and turns out to be more complex than in Glosten and Milgrom (1985).

In section 3.2 we discuss Kyle's seminal model with one informed trader who trades in only one period. In section 3.3 this model is extended to multiple traders.

3.2   The Kyle model

This section presents Kyle's (1985) model. This model assumes asymmetric information and imperfect competition and has become the benchmark of theoretical modelling for markets with informed traders. It is therefore worth presenting in detail. We start from the simplest setting, with one insider who receives a perfect signal about the value of the asset. We then present some extensions to settings with multiple insiders and imperfect signals.

3.2.1   One insider and a perfect signal

As in Kyle (1985), we consider a one-period, one-asset economy in which a group of risk-neutral market-makers faces one monopolistic risk-neutral insider and a group of liquidity traders. At time $t = 0$ the insider receives a perfect signal δ on the future value of the risky asset which is equal to:[1]

$$\widetilde{F} = \overline{F} + \widetilde{\delta} \quad \text{with} \quad \widetilde{\delta} \sim N(0, \sigma_F^2) \tag{3.1}$$

and submits the net demand $x(F)$. Thus the insider knows the future value of the asset in advance. Liquidity traders are uninformed and submit a random net demand equal to $\widetilde{z} \sim N(0, \sigma_{\widetilde{z}}^2)$ at time $t = 1$. Their reasons for trading may be a sudden need for consumption or idiosyncratic shocks to wealth, or needs relating to the life cycle. It follows that at time $t = 1$, market-makers receive a net order flow equal to $\widetilde{w} = x(\widetilde{F}) + \widetilde{z}$, which they can only observe in the aggregate. Holding this information, they compete on prices, offering a price function:

$$p(\widetilde{w}) = E(\widetilde{F}|\widetilde{w}) \tag{3.2}$$

Bertrand competition drives market-makers' expected profits to zero:

$$E(\widetilde{\pi}_{MM}|w) = E((p(\widetilde{w}) - \widetilde{F})\widetilde{w}|\widetilde{w}) = E((p(\widetilde{w}) - E(\widetilde{F}|\widetilde{w}))\widetilde{w}) = 0 \tag{3.3}$$

Notice that the market-makers' pricing function depends on the informed agent's demand function, $x(F)$. If there were no insiders, the aggregate order flow observed by market-makers would be equal to the noise traders' net demand, $\widetilde{w} = \widetilde{z}$. The pricing function that results would reduce to $p(\widetilde{w}) = E(\widetilde{F}|z) = \overline{F}$ and the market would be infinitely deep (see Figure 3.1).

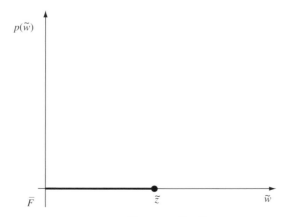

Figure 3.1. Infinitely deep market, $\widetilde{x} = 0$ and $\widetilde{w} = \widetilde{z}$.

---

[1] All random variables are independent and jointly normally distributed, with strictly positive standard deviations.

The informed trader's strategy depends on the market-makers' pricing function. Actually, the informed trader's problem is choosing the demand function, $x(F)$, that maximizes his expected end-of-period profits:[2]

$$\widetilde{\pi} = E[x(\widetilde{F} - p(\widetilde{w}))|\widetilde{F}] \tag{3.4}$$

This optimal strategy depends on the market-makers' pricing function, $p(\widetilde{w})$.

In order to compute the equilibrium solution for this strategic game, we use a concept of equilibrium that embodies the strategic interaction of traders with incomplete information. More precisely, under the model's assumptions, an equilibrium[3] can be obtained by considering that market-makers maximize their expected profits given their rational Bayesian interpretation of the information content of the aggregate order flow, and that the insider sets his own demand function to maximize expected profits given his rational expectations of the impact of his order, $x(F)$, on the market price.

Kyle proves that there is a linear equilibrium for this strategic game, such that the market-makers' pricing rule is:

$$p^*(\widetilde{w}) = E(\widetilde{F}|w = x^*(F) + \widetilde{z}) = \overline{F} + \lambda^*\widetilde{w} \tag{3.5}$$

and the insider's trading strategy is:

$$x^*(F) = \beta^*(\delta) = \beta^*(F - \overline{F}) \tag{3.6}$$

where:

$$\lambda^* = \frac{1}{2}\sqrt{\frac{\sigma_F^2}{\sigma_z^2}} = \frac{1}{2}\frac{\sigma_F}{\sigma_z} \quad \text{and} \quad \beta^* = \sqrt{\frac{\sigma_z^2}{\sigma_F^2}} = \frac{\sigma_z}{\sigma_F} \tag{3.7}$$

Computation of the equilibrium   To show that (3.5) and (3.6) form an equilibrium, we need to prove that if players hold conjectures equal to (3.5) and (3.6) on the other traders' strategies, these conjectures actually are the best response to one another's strategies.

First we prove that (3.6) is the best response to (3.5). Assume that the insider's conjecture on the market-makers' pricing rule is (3.5), i.e. $p(\widetilde{w}) = \overline{F} + \lambda\widetilde{w}$, with $\lambda > 0$; the insider's problem is therefore the following:

$$\underset{x}{\text{Max}}\ E[x(\widetilde{F} - p(\widetilde{w}))|F] = \underset{x}{\text{Max}}\ E[x(\widetilde{F} - (\overline{F} + \lambda(x + \widetilde{z})))|F]$$

From the first-order conditions we obtain:

$$\frac{\partial E[x(\widetilde{F} - p(\widetilde{w}))|F]}{\partial x} = \frac{\partial E[x(\widetilde{F} - (\overline{F} + \lambda(x + \widetilde{z})))|F]}{\partial x} = 0$$

---

[2] Under the assumption of risk neutrality, the expected utility of the end-of-period profits is simply equal to expected end-of-period profits. In fact, with an exponential utility function, we obtain: $\underset{\pi_i}{\text{Max}}\ E[U(\widetilde{\pi}_i)] = \underset{\pi_i}{\text{Max}}[E(\widetilde{\pi}_i) - (A/2)Var(\widetilde{\pi}_i)]$. Adding risk neutrality ($A = 0$), maximization of expected utility simplifies to maximization of expected profits.

[3] In game theory, this equilibrium is known as perfect Bayesian equilibrium, where 'Bayesian' indicates market-makers' use of Bayes' rule to update their beliefs. This updating model was discussed in Chapter 2.

or:

$$F - \overline{F} - 2x\lambda = 0 \qquad (3.8)$$

Notice that the term $\lambda = \partial E[p(\widetilde{w})|F]/\partial x$ in (3.8) is the price impact factor, which shows that in his decision the informed trader internalizes the price impact of his own demand; that is, he behaves strategically. It follows that the insider's demand is equal to:

$$x^*(F) = \beta(F - \overline{F}), \quad \text{with} \quad \beta = \frac{1}{2\lambda} \qquad (3.9)$$

Notice that the insider will buy, $x^*(F) > 0$, if and only if $F - \overline{F} > 0$. Notice also that the informed trader holds a monopsonist position and his profits depend on both the 'size' of his private information and the depth of the market (Figure 3.2). We leave it as an exercise to show that the expected profit for the insider is equal to $E(\widetilde{\pi}) = \sigma_F^2/4\lambda$.

We can now demonstrate that market-makers' best response to the insider's trading strategy (3.6) is indeed (3.5). The market-makers anticipate that the informed agent will play (3.6) and use their information on the aggregate order flow, $\widetilde{w}(\widetilde{F})$, to update their beliefs. It follows that, competing à la Bertrand, they set prices equal to their best estimate of the future value of the asset:[4]

$$p(\widetilde{w}) = E(\widetilde{F}|w)$$

$$= E(\widetilde{F}) + \frac{Cov(\widetilde{F}, \widetilde{w})}{Var(\widetilde{w})}(\widetilde{w} - E(\widetilde{w}))$$

$$= \overline{F} + \frac{\beta\sigma_F^2}{\beta^2\sigma_F^2 + \sigma_z^2}\widetilde{w}$$

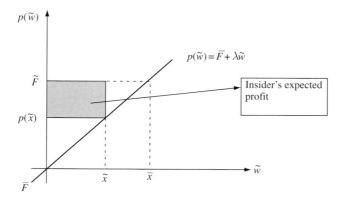

Figure 3.2. The insider's monopsonist position. The value of λ influences the size of the insider's order. Note that if the insider trades $\overline{x}$, he obtains no profits.

---

[4] Recall that for two normally distributed random variables $\widetilde{x}$ and $\widetilde{y}$, the following result obtains: $E(\widetilde{y}|x) = E(\widetilde{y}) + (Cov(\widetilde{y}, \widetilde{x})/Var(\widetilde{x}))(\widetilde{x} - E(\widetilde{x}))$. Recall also that $Cov(\widetilde{x}, \widetilde{y}) = E(\widetilde{x}\widetilde{y}) - E(\widetilde{x})E(\widetilde{y})$.

Thus, the price function is $p(\widetilde{w}) = \overline{F} + \lambda \widetilde{w}$ with $\lambda = \beta \sigma_F^2 / (\beta^2 \sigma_F^2 + \sigma_z^2)$.

The equilibrium solutions for λ^* and β^* are obtained by solving the following system of two equations and two unknowns:

$$\begin{cases} \lambda = \dfrac{\beta \sigma_F^2}{\beta^2 \sigma_F^2 + \sigma_z^2} \\ \beta = \dfrac{1}{2\lambda}. \end{cases}$$

which gives:

$$\begin{cases} \lambda^* = \dfrac{1}{2} \dfrac{\sigma_F}{\sigma_z} \\ \beta^* = \dfrac{\sigma_z}{\sigma_F} \end{cases}$$

This verifies that the equilibrium values of β and λ are those shown in (3.7).

Interpretation of the equilibrium The market liquidity, $1/\lambda$, is equal to the inverse of the price impact of an uninformed order and is a proxy for market depth (Figure 3.3). Equation (3.7) shows that in equilibrium, the illiquidity parameter λ increases in σ_F^2 and decreases in σ_z^2. As λ is a positive function of σ_F^2, the greater the variance of $\widetilde{F}$, the less deep the market. This result can be explained by considering that σ_F^2 measures the insider's informational advantage, which is positively related to the adverse selection costs. An increase in the volume of uninformed trading, σ_z^2, however, increases liquidity, since the variance of the noise traders' net demand, σ_z^2, proxies the size of their orders ($\sigma_z^2 = E(\widetilde{z}^2)$). Clearly, the greater the latter, the greater the liquidity.

The parameter for trading aggressiveness β is a positive function of σ_z; this is because the insider can conceal his strategy behind the demand of the noise traders. And it is a negative function of σ_F, because an increase in the variance of $\widetilde{F}$

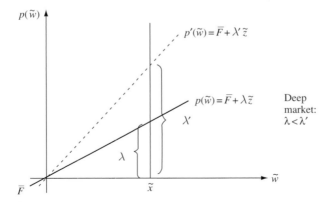

Figure 3.3. Market depth. Market depth depends on the value of λ; the lower λ, the deeper the market.

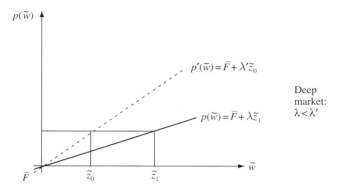

Figure 3.4. Market liquidity. Market liquidity depends on the size of the noise traders' net demand, $\widetilde{z}$. Notice that, since $\sigma_{\widetilde{z}_0}^2 < \sigma_{\widetilde{z}_1}^2$, it follows that $\lambda_0 > \lambda_1$.

increases λ. In equilibrium, with $\beta = \sigma_z / \sigma_F$, the informed traders' expected profit is $E(\widetilde{\pi}) = \sigma_F^2 / 4\lambda = \frac{1}{2}\sigma_z \sigma_F$.

Expected transaction costs for liquidity traders are given by:

$$E(\widetilde{CT}) = E[(p - \widetilde{F})\widetilde{z}] = \lambda E(\widetilde{z}^2) = \lambda \sigma_z^2 \tag{3.10}$$

Equation (3.10) shows that the lower the value of λ, the lower the trading costs of liquidity traders. However, since λ is decreasing in σ_z^2, the greater the noise traders' demand, the lower the trading costs (Figure 3.4). In equilibrium, with $\lambda = \sigma_F / 2\sigma_z$, the expected trading costs equal $E(\widetilde{CT}) = \lambda \sigma_z^2 = \sigma_z \sigma_F / 2$, which is exactly equal to the insiders' expected profit. The market-makers' expected trading profits are zero.

3.2.2 Noisy signal

So far it has been assumed that the informed trader receives a perfect signal about the value of the asset. A more realistic model would posit a noisy signal, i.e. one that is not perfectly correlated with the future value of the asset and leaves some uncertainty over the payoff, $\widetilde{F}$. Assume now that the signal corresponds to the true value $\widetilde{F}$ plus an independent noise component, $\widetilde{u}$:

$$\widetilde{F} + \widetilde{u} = \overline{F} + \widetilde{\delta} + \widetilde{u} \tag{3.11}$$

with $\widetilde{F} = \overline{F} + \widetilde{\delta}, \widetilde{\delta} \sim N(0, \sigma_F^2)$ and $\widetilde{u} \sim N(0, \sigma_u^2)$. For analytical convenience, we redefine the signal (by removing the known mean $\overline{F}$) as:

$$\widetilde{\delta} + \widetilde{u} \sim N(0, \sigma_F^2 + \sigma_u^2) \tag{3.12}$$

Thus $1/\sigma_u^2$ indicates the precision of the signal. This is the definition of the signal used in the exposition below.

As before, on the basis of the signal received, the informed agent maximizes his end-of-period profits:

$$E[\widetilde{\pi}|\delta + u] = E[x(\widetilde{F} - p)|\delta + u]$$

and submits a market order of size x. To find the optimal order size, notice that the conditional expectation of the value given the signal is:

$$E[\widetilde{F}|\delta + u] = \overline{F} + \frac{Cov(\widetilde{F}, \widetilde{\delta} + \widetilde{u})}{Var(\widetilde{\delta} + \widetilde{u})}(\widetilde{\delta} + \widetilde{u}) = \overline{F} + \frac{\sigma_F^2}{\sigma_F^2 + \sigma_u^2}(\widetilde{\delta} + \widetilde{u}) \quad (3.13)$$

Hence we can write $E[\widetilde{F}|\delta + u] = \overline{F} + \varphi(\widetilde{\delta} + \widetilde{u})$ where $\varphi \equiv \sigma_F^2/(\sigma_F^2 + \sigma_u^2) < 1$ is the weight attached to the signal in forming expectations. Facing the price schedule $p = \overline{F} + \lambda\widetilde{w}$, the informed trader's profit-maximizing demand is:

$$x = \beta(\widetilde{\delta} + \widetilde{u}), \quad \text{with} \quad \beta = \frac{\varphi}{2\lambda} \quad (3.14)$$

Uninformed traders, however, are non-strategic and only turn to the market to meet liquidity requirements. These agents submit random orders equal to:

$$\widetilde{z} \sim N(0, \sigma_z^2)$$

where σ_z^2 proxies their aggregate net demand. Finally, market-makers set prices such that the semi-strong efficiency condition obtains:

$$p = E[\widetilde{F}|w] = \overline{F} + \lambda\widetilde{w} \quad \text{with} \quad \widetilde{w} = \beta(\widetilde{\delta} + \widetilde{u}) + \widetilde{z},$$

and $\widetilde{w}$ is the net flow of orders that the market-makers receive. The solution is:

$$\lambda = \frac{Cov(\widetilde{F}, \widetilde{w})}{Var(\widetilde{w})} = \frac{\beta\sigma_F^2}{\beta^2(\sigma_F^2 + \sigma_u^2) + \sigma_z^2}$$

It is now straightforward to compute the equilibrium strategies that characterize this extension to the basic model:

$$\beta = \frac{\sigma_z}{\sqrt{\sigma_F^2 + \sigma_u^2}} = \frac{\sigma_z}{\sigma_F}\sqrt{\varphi} \quad (3.15)$$

and:

$$\lambda = \frac{\sigma_F^2}{2\sigma_z\sqrt{\sigma_F^2 + \sigma_u^2}} = \frac{\sigma_F}{2\sigma_z}\sqrt{\varphi} \quad (3.16)$$

Notice that as the precision of the signal $1/\sigma_u^2$ increases, φ is closer to 1; β increases and the insiders become more aggressive. At the same time, λ increases and depth decreases. The informed traders' expected profit is $E(\widetilde{\pi}) = \beta\sigma_F^2/2$ while the uninformed traders' expected trading costs are $E(\widetilde{CT}) = \lambda\sigma_z^2$. As before, the two numbers are equal since the market-maker is expected to just break even. Notice that both trading profits and costs are lower with noisy signals ($\varphi < 1$) than with a perfect signal ($\varphi = 1$).

It is now fairly easy to compute the informational efficiency of the equilibrium price, which is defined as the inverse of the conditional variance of the true value $\widetilde{F}$, given the price $\widetilde{p}$. From Bayes' rule and the projection theorem we know that:

$$Var(\widetilde{F}|p) = Var(\widetilde{F}) - Cov(\widetilde{F}, p)^2/Var(p) \quad (3.17)$$

From the true value $\widetilde{F} = \overline{F} + \widetilde{\delta}$ and the pricing rule $\widetilde{p} = \overline{F} + \lambda\widetilde{w}$ with $\widetilde{w} = \beta(\widetilde{\delta} + \widetilde{u})$ $+ \widetilde{z}$, it immediately follows that:

$$Var(\widetilde{F}|p) = \sigma_F^2\left(1 - \frac{1}{2}\varphi\right) \tag{3.18}$$

In the limiting case with perfect information, $\varphi = 1$, price efficiency is $0.5\,\sigma_F^2$, i.e. the informed trader gives away half of his information.

3.3   The Kyle model with multiple insiders

Let us now relax the hypothesis that market-makers face just one monopolistic insider and assume that there are k informed traders. In this section we show how competition between these traders affects the information content of trades and liquidity.

3.3.1   Perfect signals

For simplicity, we start with informed traders observing a perfect signal on the future value of the asset. Let the conjectures on the market-makers' pricing rule and on the insiders' trading strategies be:

$$p_k(\widetilde{w}) = \overline{F} + \lambda_k\widetilde{w}$$
$$x_i(\widetilde{F}) = \beta_k(\widetilde{F} - \overline{F}) \quad \forall i = 1, \ldots, K$$

with $\widetilde{w} = \sum_{i=1}^K x_i(\widetilde{F}) + \widetilde{z}$. The strategy of each insider depends on the demand of the other informed traders, $\sum_{j\neq i}^K x_j^*(\widetilde{F})$. This can be seen from the insiders' best response to the market-makers' pricing rule. In fact, insiders have the following objective function:

$$\underset{x}{\text{Max}}\ E[x_i(\widetilde{F} - p_k(\widetilde{w}))|F] = \underset{x}{\text{Max}}\ E[x_i(\widetilde{F} - (\overline{F} + \lambda_k(x_i + \sum_{j\neq i}^k x_j^*(\widetilde{F}) + \widetilde{z})))|F]$$

$$= \underset{x}{\text{Max}}\ E[x_i(\widetilde{F} - \overline{F} - \lambda_k(k-1)x^* - \lambda_k x_i - \lambda_k\widetilde{z})|F]$$

and from the first-order conditions we obtain:

$$x_i^*(\widetilde{F}) = \frac{(\widetilde{F} - \overline{F})}{2\lambda_k} - \frac{(k-1)x^*}{2}$$

Notice that for $k = 1$, the insiders' best response equals the previous solution (3.9). Conversely, when the number of insiders is $k > 1$, each insider takes the others' strategy into account and reduces his demand by $\frac{(k-1)x^*}{2}$.

  In equilibrium we must have $x_i^*(\widetilde{F}) = x^*$, hence:

$$x_i^*(\widetilde{F}) = \frac{(\widetilde{F} - \overline{F})}{\lambda_k(k+1)} \quad \text{with} \quad \beta_k = \frac{1}{\lambda_k(k+1)} \tag{3.19}$$

As before, the equilibrium value of λ_k can be obtained by considering the market-makers' pricing rule:

$$p(\widetilde{w}) = E(\widetilde{F}|w) = E(\widetilde{F}|w = kx^*(\widetilde{F}) + \widetilde{z})$$

$$= E(\widetilde{F}) + \frac{Cov(\widetilde{F}, \widetilde{w})}{Var(\widetilde{w})}[\widetilde{w} - E(\widetilde{w})]$$

$$= \overline{F} + \frac{k\,\beta_k\sigma_F^2}{\sigma_z^2 + k^2\beta_k^2\sigma_F^2}\,\widetilde{w}$$

Substituting for β_k from (3.19) we obtain:

$$\lambda_k^* = \frac{1}{(k+1)}\frac{\sigma_F\sqrt{k}}{\sigma_z} \tag{3.20}$$

and consequently:

$$\beta_k^* = \frac{\sigma_z}{\sigma_F\sqrt{k}} \tag{3.21}$$

Note that the value of β_k^* indicates how aggressively the informed traders exploit their information; clearly, the higher the number of informed traders, the lower the value of the information each insider holds, hence the smaller β_k^* $\left(\partial\beta_k^*/\partial k < 0\right)$. Notice also that since insiders' competition for the signal intensifies with their number, market depth increases with k as $\partial\lambda_k^*/\partial k < 0$. It will be clear, below, how this result can change if informed traders are assumed to be risk-averse (Figure 3.5).

3.3.2 Noisy signals

This extension of the model includes the proposals of Subrahmanyam (1991) for constructing indicators of market quality and agents' welfare. These measures are useful, for example, to assess the effects of changes in regulations and financial market design.

As in Kyle (1985) and its extensions, it is assumed that competitive risk-neutral market-makers face k insiders and a group of liquidity traders. It is also assumed that insiders get a noisy signal, the same for all insiders and equal to:

$$\widetilde{\delta} + \widetilde{u} \sim N(0, 1 + \sigma_u^2) \tag{3.22}$$

where, for the sake of simplicity, we normalize σ_F^2 to 1 and assume that $\widetilde{\delta}$ and $\widetilde{u}$ are normally distributed with mean zero and variance equal to 1 and σ_u^2 respectively ($\widetilde{\delta} \sim N(0, 1)$; $\widetilde{u} \sim N(0, \sigma_u^2)$). Notice that because $Var(\widetilde{u}) = \sigma_u^2 \neq 0$, the informed agents observe the security's future value with a disturbance equal to $\widetilde{u}$ and the amount of noise relative to the signal increases along with σ_u^2; thus $1/\sigma_u^2$ indicates the precision of the signal. As before, on the basis of the signal received, each strategic informed agent maximizes his end-of-period profits:

$$E[\widetilde{\pi}_i|\delta + u] = E[x_i(\widetilde{F} - p)|\delta + u]$$

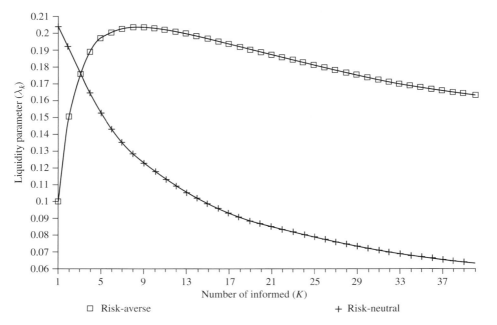

Figure 3.5. Equilibrium liquidity parameter. Equilibrium liquidity parameter, λ_k, as a function of the number of informed traders, k, under risk neutrality and risk aversion of informed traders. It is assumed that $\sigma_z^2 = 2$ and the variance of the noise in the informed traders' signal is $\sigma_u^2 = 2$. (*Source*: Subrahmanyam, 1991.)

by submitting market orders of size:

$$\widetilde{x_i} = \beta_k(\widetilde{\delta} + \widetilde{u}) \quad \forall i = 1, \dots, K$$

As in the previous example, uninformed traders are non-strategic and turn to the market to meet liquidity requirements. These agents submit random orders equal to:

$$\widetilde{z} \sim N(0, \sigma_z^2)$$

where σ_z^2 proxies the size of their aggregate net demand. Being uninformed, liquidity traders make, on average, negative profits.

Finally, market-makers set prices such that the semi-strong efficiency condition obtains:

$$\widetilde{p} = E[\widetilde{F}|w] \quad \text{with} \quad \widetilde{w} = k\,\beta_k(\widetilde{\delta} + \widetilde{u}) + \widetilde{z}$$

where $\widetilde{w}$ is the net flow of orders that they receive.

To summarize, the time structure of the model is unchanged. At $t = 0$, the informed agents observe the noisy signals and, together with noise traders, choose the quantity they wish to trade. At the moment when the informed agents submit their market orders, their information consists only of the signal on the security's liquidation value and the market-makers' price schedule, not the noise traders' net demand. At $t = 1$, market-makers observe the aggregate order flow, determine a price and trade the quantity that balances demand and supply. Market-makers have no additional information, so changes in the equilibrium price are due exclusively to the order flow. As the market is anonymous, market-makers cannot distinguish insiders from noise traders, so that the latter thus constitute a cover for the insiders' profits. Insiders use the uninformed order quantity to conceal their own trades. At $t = 2$, the liquidation value of the security becomes known.

It is now straightforward to compute the equilibrium strategies that characterize this extension of the basic model:

$$\widetilde{p} = \overline{F} + \lambda_k \widetilde{w} \quad \text{and} \quad x = \beta_k (\widetilde{\delta} + \widetilde{u}) \qquad (3.23)$$

with:

$$\lambda_k = \frac{\sqrt{k}}{(k+1)\sqrt{1+\sigma_u^2}\,\sigma_z} \quad \text{and} \quad \beta_k = \frac{\sigma_z}{\sqrt{(1+\sigma_u^2)\,k}} \qquad (3.24)$$

where (3.24) are solutions to the system of equations:

$$\begin{cases} \lambda_k = \frac{k\beta_k}{k^2\beta_k^2(1+\sigma_u^2)+\sigma_z^2} \\ \beta_k = \frac{1}{(1+\sigma_u^2)\lambda_k(k+1)} \end{cases}$$

Notice that as λ_k, k or σ_u^2 decrease, β_k increases and insiders become more aggressive. In fact, as λ_k declines, depth increases; as k declines, the number of informed agents diminishes, making private information more valuable and, similarly, as σ_u^2 declines, the precision of the signal increases and so accordingly does traders' incentive to exploit private information.

Finally, the equilibrium value of λ_k is decreasing in k, σ_z and σ_u^2. This means that as k (the number of insiders) increases, so does competition among them, and λ_k diminishes. As σ_z^2 increases, so does liquidity, given that market-makers' adverse selection costs are spread over a greater liquidity demand; finally, as σ_u^2 increases, the precision of the insiders' signal diminishes, and so do adverse selection costs, which increases liquidity. Subrahmanyam (1991) shows that if insiders are risk-neutral, λ_k is monotonically decreasing in k; if instead insiders are risk-averse, λ_k does not possess this property and, plotted as a function of k, is hump-shaped, increasing for low values of k and decreasing for higher ones (Figure 3.5). Under the assumption of risk aversion, when the number of insiders is small, increasing k increases adverse selection costs, whereas for large values of k, insiders' competition for the signal dominates and λ_k decreases (liquidity increases).

Price efficiency   In this model, traders get information on the future value, $\widetilde{F}$, from the equilibrium price. Clearly, the smaller the residual conditional variance of $\widetilde{F}$, the more efficient the price discovery process. It follows that the model's implications for informational efficiency can be derived using the indicator:

$$Q = Var\left[(\widetilde{\delta}|p)\right]^{-1} = 1 + \frac{1}{\sigma_u^2 + \frac{\sigma_z^2}{k^2\beta_k^2}} \tag{3.25}$$

Substituting for the value of β_k, we obtain:

$$Q = 1 + \frac{k}{1 + (1+k)\sigma_u^2} \tag{3.26}$$

Notice that informational efficiency does not change with the noise variance, σ_z^2, since under risk-neutrality an increase in noise has two mutually offsetting effects: a reduction in informational efficiency and an increase in the informed traders' aggressiveness that augments the information content of the aggregate order flow.

Also, notice that, as expected, an increase in k (the number of informed agents) increases Q, while an increase in σ_u^2 (the signal's variance) diminishes information efficiency.

Volatility   The following indicator of volatility may also be useful in evaluating the effects of structural changes on market quality:

$$Var(p) = \lambda_k^2 k^2 \beta_k^2 (1 + \sigma_u^2) + \lambda_k^2 \sigma_z^2 = \left[(1+\sigma_u^2)\left(1+\frac{1}{k}\right)\right]^{-1} \tag{3.27}$$

Notice that an increase in the number of insiders, k, increases volatility, as it increases the number of the informative shocks. This happens even though an increase in k reduces both the price impact, λ_k, and the informed traders' aggressiveness, β_k. Furthermore, when the precision of the insiders' signal, $1/\sigma_u^2$, increases, insiders become more aggressive and volatility increases.

Welfare of market participants   Finally, the effects on the welfare of market participants can be gauged by computing the unconditional expected profits of insiders:

$$E(\widetilde{\pi}_i) = \frac{\sigma_z}{(k+1)\sqrt{k}\sqrt{1+\sigma_u^2}} \tag{3.28}$$

and of liquidity traders:[5]

$$E(\widetilde{\pi}_i) = -\lambda_k \sigma_z^2 = -\frac{\sigma_z \sqrt{k}}{(k+1)\sqrt{1+\sigma_u^2}} \tag{3.29}$$

As expected, an increase in σ_z increases insiders' expected profits, whereas an increase in k and σ_u^2 reduces it. The explanation is that this model can be viewed

---

[5] Notice that, even if liquidity traders are not optimizing agents, it is quite standard in the literature to compute their costs and welfare in this way (e.g. Admati and Pfleiderer, 1988).

Table 3.1. *Main results from the model with k informed traders and noisy signal*

	Liquidity $(1/\lambda)$	Informational efficiency	Volatility $Var(p)$	Informed traders' welfare	Liquidity traders' welfare
$\Uparrow k$	$\uparrow$	$\uparrow$	$\uparrow$	$\downarrow$	$\uparrow$
$\Uparrow \sigma_z^2$	$\uparrow$	$=$	$=$	$\uparrow$	$\downarrow$
$\Uparrow \sigma_u^2$	$\uparrow$	$\downarrow$	$\downarrow$	$\downarrow$	$\uparrow$

as a zero-sum game, in which market-makers get zero profits while the insiders' profits are the liquidity traders' losses. On the contrary, an increase in σ_z^2 diminishes the expected profits of liquidity traders and an increase in k and σ_u^2 augments it. As we have already seen, although market depth increases with the net demand of liquidity traders, an increase in the noise traders' order size increases their losses, and this effect overwhelms the increase in market depth. Table 3.1 summarizes the results from the model with k informed traders who observe a noisy signal.

3.3.3   Fixed entry costs
In evaluating the effects of a regulatory change or a modification of architecture on the quality of financial markets, one must factor in the possibility of traders leaving or entering the market following the change. So far, the model has been solved for a given number of informed traders. Clearly, when the equilibrium number of insiders changes, results may change too. For this reason let us now introduce fixed entry costs and make the number of informed agents endogenous.

Suppose that the agents who are willing to buy a signal pay the price C. An agent decides to buy the signal and trade the stock up to the point where the expected profit from trading is greater than the cost of the signal.

For simplicity, we normalize the expected profits of the agent who does not trade to zero; so agents will acquire information to the point where:

$$E[x_i(F - p) - C] = 0 \tag{3.30}$$

Given that:

$$E\left[x_i(\widetilde{F} - p)\right] = \beta_k \left[1 - \lambda_k \, k \, \beta_k \, (1 + \sigma_u^2)\right]$$

agents enter the market as long as:

$$\beta_k \left[1 - \lambda_k \, k \, \beta_k \, (1 + \sigma_u^2)\right] = C$$

Substituting for the equilibrium values of λ_k and β_k we obtain:

$$\frac{\sigma_z}{\sqrt{k}(k+1)\sqrt{1+\sigma_u^2}} - C = 0$$

As we shall see later on, this result can be used to discuss the effects of a variation in σ_z on market quality. According to the Implicit Function Theorem, we obtain:

$$\frac{\partial k}{\partial \sigma_z} = 2\frac{k\,(k+1)}{\sigma_z(3k+1)} > 0$$

Since the expected utility from trading on private information increases together with the variance of the noise, the number of informed agents also increases.

3.3.4 Heterogeneous signals

So far we have assumed that all the insiders receive the same signal. Let us now assume that they get different signals, such as:

$$\tilde{\delta} + \tilde{u}_k \neq \tilde{\delta} + \tilde{u}_j \quad \text{for all } k \neq j \tag{3.31}$$

The objective function of the ith agent is thus:

$$E\left[\tilde{\pi}_i | \delta + u_i\right] = x_i\,E\left[\tilde{\delta} | \delta + u_i\right] - x_i \lambda_k E\left[\tilde{w} | \delta + u_i\right]$$

$$= x_i\frac{\left(\tilde{\delta} + \tilde{u}_i\right)}{1+\sigma_u^2}\left[1 - \lambda_k \beta_k\,(k-1)\right] - \lambda x_i^2$$

where:

$$\tilde{w} = \sum_{p\neq i}^{k}\beta\left(\tilde{\delta} + \tilde{u}_p\right) + \tilde{z} + x_i$$

Solving for x_i from the first-order condition, we obtain:

$$x_i = \frac{1 - \lambda_k \beta_k(k-1)}{2\lambda_k\left(1+\sigma_u^2\right)}\left(\tilde{\delta} + \tilde{u}_i\right)$$

As before, solving for β_k we obtain:

$$\beta_k = \frac{1}{\lambda_k\left(k + 2\sigma_u^2 + 1\right)} \tag{3.32}$$

In this case, competition among market-makers also leads to the semi-strong efficiency condition:

$$P = E(\tilde{F}|w) = \overline{F} + \frac{k\,\beta_k}{k\,\beta_k^2(k+\sigma_u^2) + \sigma_z^2}\,\tilde{w}$$

with:

$$\lambda_k = \frac{k\,\beta_k}{k\,\beta_k^2(k+\sigma_u^2) + \sigma_z^2} \tag{3.33}$$

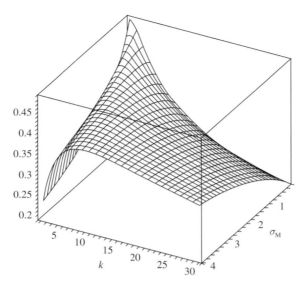

Figure 3.6. Kyle's λ as function of model parameters. This figure plots Kyle's λ_k as a function of σ_u and k, with $\sigma_z = 1$.

Solving for λ_k and β_k from equations (3.32) and (3.33), it is straightforward to derive the equilibrium values of λ_k^* and β_k^*:

$$\lambda_k^* = \frac{1}{1 + k + 2\,\sigma_u^2}\sqrt{\frac{k\,(1 + \sigma_u^2)}{\sigma_z^2}} \quad \text{and} \quad \beta_k^* = \sqrt{\frac{\sigma_z^2}{k\,(1 + \sigma_u^2)}} \tag{3.34}$$

Now let us compare the results obtained under the assumption of heterogeneous signals with the earlier results. With homogeneous signals an increase in k reduces λ_k because it intensifies competition among informed agents. With heterogeneous signals the pattern depends on the precision of the insiders' information. When insiders are getting very precise signals (σ_u^2 is small), λ_k is still a decreasing function of k, as there is no substantial heterogeneity among the insiders' signals (see Figure 3.6). When instead σ_u^2 is large, the opposite may hold, as an increase in k also increases the amount of private information embodied in the order flow. As Figure 3.6 shows, when the number of insiders (k) is small and the signal is noisy (σ_u^2 is large), an increase in their number reduces rather than increases liquidity.

Exercise

Exercise 1
Prove equation (3.18).

Solution

As $p = \overline{F} + \lambda\widetilde{w}$ and $\widetilde{w} = \beta(\widetilde{\delta} + \widetilde{u}) + \widetilde{z}$ are the only stochastic terms, the conditional variance is:

$$Var(\widetilde{F}|p) = Var(\widetilde{F}|w) = Var(\widetilde{F}) - Cov(\widetilde{F}, \widetilde{w})^2/Var(\widetilde{w})$$

with $Var(\widetilde{F}) = \sigma_F^2$, $Cov(\widetilde{F}, \widetilde{w}) = \beta\sigma_F^2$ and $Var(\widetilde{w}) = \beta^2(\sigma_F^2 + \sigma_u^2) + \sigma_z^2$. Combining these gives:

$$Var(\widetilde{F}|w) = \sigma_F^2 - \frac{\beta^2\sigma_F^4}{\beta^2(\sigma_F^2 + \sigma_u^2) + \sigma_z^2} = \sigma_F^2 - \sigma_F^2\beta\lambda = \sigma_F^2\left(1 - \frac{1}{2}\sigma_u^2/\sigma_F^2\right)$$

References

Admati, A. and P. Pfleiderer, 1988, 'A theory of intraday patterns: volume and price variability', *Review of Financial Studies,* 1, 3–40.

Glosten, L. and P. Milgrom, 1985, 'Bid, ask and transaction prices in a specialist market with heterogeneously informed traders', *Journal of Financial Economics,* 14, 71–100.

Grossman, S. and J. Stiglitz, 1980, 'On the impossibility of informationally efficient markets', *American Economic Review,* 70, 393–408.

Kyle, A. 1985, 'Continuous auctions and insider trading', *Econometrica,* 53, 1315–35.

Subrahmanyam, A. 1991, 'Risk aversion, market liquidity and price efficiency', *Review of Financial Studies,* 4, 417–41.

4 Dealer markets: information-based models

Here we discuss the model of Glosten and Milgrom (1985), which captures the notion of asymmetric information, explicitly characterizing the bid–ask spread. The model assumes risk neutrality, asymmetric information and a quote-driven protocol. Within this market protocol, dealers post bid and ask quotes that are subsequently chosen by their customers. The latter are asymmetrically informed and arrive at the market-place sequentially. The assumption of asymmetric information generates adverse selection costs, which oblige dealers to quote different prices for buying and selling, i.e. to open the bid–ask spread. The spread is the premium that dealers demand for trading with agents with superior information.

In Glosten and Milgrom (1985) it is assumed that customers' trades provide information about the future value of the risky asset. However, the model constrains trades to a size of one unit, so only the direction of orders (buy or sell) provides information to dealers. This hypothesis would subsequently be generalized in the model of Easley and O'Hara (1987), which embodies the signalling role of trade sizes. In this framework, market-makers set prices conditional on all the information they can extract from the order flow. Since, by observing the insiders' orders, liquidity providers can infer information on the future value, both models set out a process of price discovery and provide insights into the process of adjustment of quoted prices.

The chapter ends with exercises that enable these models to be used, with minor adaptations, to discuss diverse strategies for different traders and market regulations, such as splitting of large orders by liquidity traders, price improvement offered to regular clients by market-makers, and the effects of transaction size regulation on market quality.

4.1 A model with adverse selection costs

Glosten and Milgrom (1985) assume a market-place where market-makers quote bid–ask prices and trade one single security with two types of agent, insiders (informed traders) and liquidity traders (uninformed traders). The insiders receive a perfectly informative signal about the security's value prior to trading. All traders are risk-neutral and arrive at the market-place sequentially (one agent at a time) and choose to buy or sell. The size of the order is equal to one unit, and agents may only trade once, so that insiders cannot submit orders of infinite size. In fact, if they were allowed to, insiders, being risk-neutral, would trade an infinite number of shares.

Following O'Hara (1995), we assume that nature chooses the future value of the security, $\widetilde{V}$, which can be $\overline{V}$ (high value) with probability θ and $\underline{V}$ (low value) with probability $(1 - \theta)$:

$$\widetilde{V} \sim \left\{ \begin{array}{cc} \overline{V} & \theta \\ \underline{V} & (1 - \theta) \end{array} \right\}$$

The market-makers face an informed trader with probability α and an uninformed trader with probability $1 - \alpha$. The insider is supposed to choose the trade that maximizes his profit (buying when $\widetilde{V} = \overline{V}$ and selling when $\widetilde{V} = \underline{V}$), while liquidity traders will buy and sell with probability $\frac{1}{2}$. Trading occurs as a sequence of bilateral trading opportunities.

4.1.1   The equilibrium prices

At time t, market-makers compete on the price of the security, realizing an expected profit, Π_t, equal to zero.[1] This is a Bertrand-type competition among dealers who undercut each other, driving expected profits to zero. For example, if two dealers compete they will end up setting a price that is equal to their conditional estimate of the future value of the asset, $E(\widetilde{V}|\Phi_t)$. Here Φ_t denotes the information on the direction of trade (given unitary trade size); if the incoming trade is a buy order (B_t), then dealers will offer an ask price, a_t; conversely, if it is a sell order (S_t), then they will offer a bid price, b_t. This conditional expectation given an incoming buy order can be interpreted as the opportunity costs that dealers face when selling the asset:

$$E(\Pi_t^A|\Phi_t) = E[(a_t - \widetilde{V})|\Phi_t] = 0$$
$$a_t = E(\widetilde{V}|\Phi_t)$$

and similarly for the bid price. In this way, once dealers have observed the direction of the trade – B_t for the ask price and S_t for the bid price – they will consider their price-setting rule as fair and have no regrets. In other words, prices are regret-free and incorporate all the information available at time t. The dealers will use the information to update their estimate of the future value of the asset, the process being completed when all the private information is incorporated into prices. Notice that this learning process affects only *dealers'* beliefs, whereas by definition the uninformed traders do not learn anything from the market prices. In this way the probabilities of informed and uninformed trades are constant over time.

The trading process is depicted in Figure 4.1. S_t and B_t indicate a sell or a buy order transmitted to the market-maker. The price quoted thus equals the expected value of

---

[1] In real financial markets, dealers compete with one another or with the limit orders received by their customers (see, for example, NASDAQ's order handling rules of 1997).

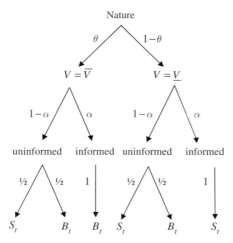

Figure 4.1. The trading process.

the security conditional on the information on the possible direction of the next trade. The bid and ask prices are therefore:

$$a_t = E\left[\widetilde{V} \mid B_t\right] = \underline{V}\Pr\left\{\widetilde{V} = \underline{V} \mid B_t\right\} + \overline{V}\Pr\left\{\widetilde{V} = \overline{V} \mid B_t\right\} \tag{4.1}$$

and:

$$b_t = E\left[\widetilde{V} \mid S_t\right] = \underline{V}\Pr\left\{\widetilde{V} = \underline{V} \mid S_t\right\} + \overline{V}\Pr\left\{\widetilde{V} = \overline{V} \mid S_t\right\} \tag{4.2}$$

respectively.

Let us determine, as an example, the bid price b_t from equation (4.2). This requires computation of the conditional probabilities $\Pr\left\{\widetilde{V} = \underline{V} \mid S_t\right\}$ and $\Pr\left\{\widetilde{V} = \overline{V} \mid S_t\right\}$. Dealers exploit the information on the direction of the incoming orders and update their expectations on the future value using Bayes' rule. Thus we obtain:

$$\Pr\left\{\widetilde{V} = \overline{V} \mid S_t\right\} = \frac{\Pr\left\{\overline{V}, S_t\right\}}{\Pr\left\{S_t\right\}} = \Pr\left\{\widetilde{V} = \overline{V}\right\}\frac{\Pr\left\{S_t \mid \widetilde{V} = \overline{V}\right\}}{\Pr\left\{S_t\right\}}$$

$$= \frac{\Pr\left\{\widetilde{V} = \overline{V}\right\}\Pr\left\{S_t \mid \widetilde{V} = \overline{V}\right\}}{\Pr\left\{\widetilde{V} = \underline{V}\right\}\Pr\left\{S_t \mid \widetilde{V} = \underline{V}\right\} + \Pr\left\{\widetilde{V} = \overline{V}\right\}\Pr\left\{S_t \mid \widetilde{V} = \overline{V}\right\}}$$

$$\tag{4.3}$$

and:

$$\Pr\left\{\widetilde{V} = \underline{V} \mid S_t\right\} = \frac{\Pr\left\{\widetilde{V} = \underline{V}\right\}\Pr\left\{S_t \mid \widetilde{V} = \underline{V}\right\}}{\Pr\left\{\widetilde{V} = \underline{V}\right\}\Pr\left\{S_t \mid \widetilde{V} = \underline{V}\right\} + \Pr\left\{\widetilde{V} = \overline{V}\right\}\Pr\left\{S_t \mid \widetilde{V} = \overline{V}\right\}}$$

$$\tag{4.4}$$

Before observing the order flow, dealers assign a probability equal to $\Pr\left\{\widetilde{V} = \overline{V}\right\}$ to the future value of the asset. It follows that the factor $\Pr\left\{S_t \mid \widetilde{V} = \overline{V}\right\}/\Pr\left\{S_t\right\}$ on the right-hand side of equation (4.3) corresponds to the adverse selection component. By setting $\theta = \frac{1}{2}$, we see that $\Pr \{ S_t \mid \widetilde{V} = \overline{V} \}/\Pr \{ S_t \} = 1 + \alpha$, which shows that the dealers' revision after observing the order flow is larger, the greater the proportion of informed traders in the market, α.

Using the tree diagram shown in Figure 4.1 we get the ask price:

$$a_t = E\left[\widetilde{V} \mid B_t\right] = \frac{1}{2}\underline{V}(1-\alpha) + \frac{1}{2}\overline{V}(1+\alpha) \tag{4.5}$$

and the bid price:

$$b_t = E\left[\widetilde{V} \mid S_t\right] = \frac{1}{2}\underline{V}(1+\alpha) + \frac{1}{2}\overline{V}(1-\alpha) \tag{4.6}$$

so that the spread is equal to:

$$S_t = a_t - b_t = \alpha(\overline{V} - \underline{V}) \tag{4.7}$$

Notice that the spread stems from the probability of informed trading, α, and it is due to adverse selection costs. Furthermore, the variance of the risky asset is equal to:

$$Var(\widetilde{V}) = \theta(\overline{V} - E(\widetilde{V}))^2 + (1-\theta)(\underline{V} - E(\widetilde{V}))^2 = \theta(1-\theta)(\overline{V} - \underline{V})^2 \tag{4.8}$$

where $E(\widetilde{V}) = \theta\overline{V} + (1-\theta)\underline{V}$ equals the expected value of $\widetilde{V}$. It follows that the spread is an increasing function of the variance. This is because the greater the difference between the extreme values of the risky asset, the greater the insiders' information advantage, and thus the greater the market-makers' potential losses.

In terms of price dynamics, from the previous example it follows that when a buy order arrives at time t, the ask and the bid prices at $t+1$ will be equal to:

$$a_{t+1} = E\left[\widetilde{V} \mid B_t, B_{t+1}\right] = \underline{V}\Pr\left\{\widetilde{V} = \underline{V} \mid B_t, B_{t+1}\right\} + \overline{V}\Pr\left\{\widetilde{V} = \overline{V} \mid B_t, B_{t+1}\right\}$$

$$b_{t+1} = E\left[\widetilde{V} \mid B_t, S_{t+1}\right] = \underline{V}\Pr\left\{\widetilde{V} = \underline{V} \mid B_t, S_{t+1}\right\} + \overline{V}\Pr\left\{\widetilde{V} = \overline{V} \mid B_t, S_{t+1}\right\}$$

respectively, where:

$$\Pr\left\{\widetilde{V} = \overline{V} \mid B_t, B_{t+1}\right\} = \Pr\left\{\widetilde{V} = \overline{V} \mid B_t\right\} \frac{\Pr\left\{B_{t+1} \mid \widetilde{V} = \overline{V}\right\}}{\Pr\left\{B_{t+1}\right\}}$$

$$= \frac{\Pr\left\{\widetilde{V} = \overline{V} \mid B_t\right\}\Pr\left\{\widetilde{V} = \overline{V} \mid B_t\right\}\Pr\left\{B_{t+1} \mid \widetilde{V} = \overline{V}\right\}}{\Pr\left\{B_{t+1} \mid \widetilde{V} = \overline{V}\right\} + \Pr\left\{\widetilde{V} = \underline{V} \mid B_t\right\}\Pr\left\{B_{t+1} \mid \widetilde{V} = \underline{V}\right\}}$$

In the case of a sell order at t, the ask and the bid prices will be equal to:

$$a_{t+1} = E\left[\widetilde{V} \mid S_t, B_{t+1}\right] = \underline{V}\Pr\left\{\widetilde{V} = \underline{V} \mid S_t, B_{t+1}\right\} + \overline{V}\Pr\left\{\widetilde{V} = \overline{V} \mid S_t, B_{t+1}\right\}$$

$$b_{t+1} = E\left[\widetilde{V} \mid S_t, S_{t+1}\right] = \underline{V}\Pr\left\{\widetilde{V} = \underline{V} \mid S_t, S_{t+1}\right\} + \overline{V}\Pr\left\{\widetilde{V} = \overline{V} \mid S_t, S_{t+1}\right\}$$

It is easy to show how subsequent orders affect the dealers' quoted prices. For example, a sequence of prices formed by a buy and a sell order leaves the price quoted unchanged (e.g. $a_{t+1} = E\left[\widetilde{V} \mid S_t, B_{t+1}\right] = a_t$). The model permits other empirical implications to be derived as well. In accordance with the information available to the market-maker at time t, the prices quoted in $t + 1$ follow a martingale,[2] i.e. $E\left[p_{t+1} \mid \Phi_t\right] = p_t$, which means that prices are semi-strong efficient. As Chapter 6 shows, if prices are not serially correlated, the estimate of the spread according to Roll (1984) will be zero. Furthermore, it can be shown that the sequence of prices quoted by dealers gradually incorporates the insiders' information and hence generates a sequence of decreasing spreads. Finally, as insiders always trade in the same direction, customers' orders will be serially correlated.

Commenting on this model, O'Hara (1995) stresses that the assumptions concerning the trading protocol are absolutely crucial. Traders may trade only one unit of the asset, and only once, and so are obliged to go back to the pool and wait if they desire to trade further. This makes it impossible for informed traders to trade as much as possible and as often as possible in order to exploit their private information. Furthermore, the model assumes that the population of traders that dealers face is always the same, despite possible learning on the part of uninformed traders who may become more informed over time. The resulting simplification of the analysis comes at the expense of realism.

4.2 Extension: different order sizes

In Glosten and Milgrom (1985) all transactions are of the same size. Instead, we now allow for variation, i.e. large and small trades. Easley and O'Hara (1987) observe that large transactions are usually made at less favourable prices than small transactions. There are at least two possible explanations for this. One is that because larger transactions require the market-maker to leave its optimal position in inventory, the prices for large orders also include this inventory management cost. This concept, which is discussed in Chapter 5, is analysed by Stoll (1978) and by Ho and Stoll (1981). An alternative explanation is given by Easley and O'Hara (1987), who argue that the size of the trade affects the bid and ask prices by revealing the type of agent who submits the order. The authors presume that large trades are driven by better information and that the relation between price and quantity derives from adverse selection costs.

For simplicity, we maintain the assumptions of Glosten and Milgrom (1985) but now allow agents to make trades of two different sizes. As in Glosten and Milgrom, we assume that in addition to market-makers there are insiders and liquidity traders. Orders can be of two sizes, where B_1 and B_2 $(0 < B_1 < B_2)$ indicate the quantity the agents want to buy, and S_1 and S_2 $(0 < S_1 < S_2)$, the quantity they want to sell. We define $\beta/2$ and $(1 - \beta)/2$ as the respective probabilities that the uninformed traders will make large (B_2 and S_2) and small (B_1 and S_1) trades.

---

[2] We know that $p_t = E(V \mid \Phi_t)$, where Φ_t represents the information available to the market-makers at t. Thus $E(p_{t+1} \mid \Phi_t) = E(E(V \mid \Phi_{t,t+1}) \mid \Phi_t)$. Given the law of iterated expectations according to which $E_t = E_t E_{t+1} E_{t+2}...$ (where $E_t(.) = E(. \mid \Phi_t)$), we have $E(E(V \mid \Phi_{t,t+1}) \mid \Phi_t) = E(V \mid \Phi_t) = p_t$. In this way, we demonstrate that the prices follow a martingale, $E(p_{t+1} \mid \Phi_t) = p_t$, and that the best predictor for the prices quoted at $t + 1$, given the information available after the trade t, Φ_t, is the quote at t.

The market-makers compete on the price of the security and realize expected profits equal to zero. Unlike Glosten and Milgrom (1985), however, this model has dealers who set prices taking into account that informed traders maximize their expected profits, given their private information, and that in doing so they can choose whether to trade large or small quantities. But, of course, the insiders' strategies will also depend upon the dealers' pricing rule. It follows that the equilibrium will require both the competitive outcome and the realization of market-makers' conjectures about the informed traders' strategies.

4.2.1 *Equilibrium*

Easley and O'Hara's model can result in two different possible equilibria, depending on the parameters α and β. If the informed traders have an incentive to make small as well as large trades, they will not be separated from the uninformed traders and we will have a *pooling equilibrium* (Figure 4.2). If, however, the informed traders have an incentive to trade only large quantities, they will separate themselves from the uninformed traders, so that a *semi-separating equilibrium* prevails[3] (Figure 4.3).

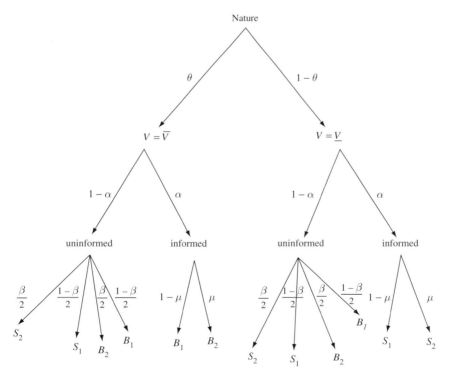

Figure 4.2. The trading game in the case of pooling equilibrium.

---

[3] We describe this equilibrium as 'semi-separating' rather than 'separating', since the insiders' orders are not completely separated from those of the uninformed traders, in that the latter can make both large and small orders.

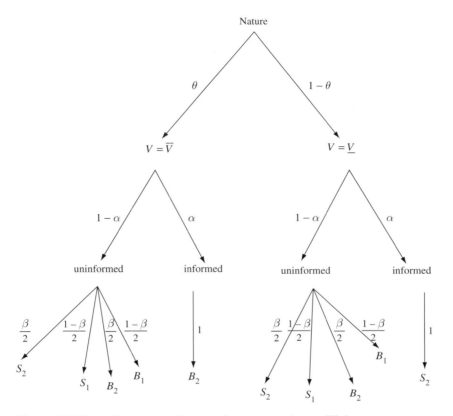

Figure 4.3. The trading game in the case of semi-separating equilibrium.

Pooling equilibrium For simplicity, we suppose that $B_1 = S_1 = 1$ and $B_2 = S_2 = 2$. We obtain a pooling equilibrium when the insiders have the incentive to make small as well as large trades with probability $(1 - \mu)$ and μ, respectively.

The necessary condition for the insiders to trade one unit as well as two units is that the expected profit from trading two units at price a_2 is equal to the expected profit from trading one unit at price a_1:

$$2(1 - a_2) = 1 - a_1 \tag{4.9}$$

where, for simplicity, we let $\overline{V} = 1$ and $\underline{V} = 0$. We can now derive the equilibrium ask price at $t = 1$:

$$
\begin{aligned}
a_1 &= E\left[\tilde{V} \mid B_1\right] = \underline{V} \Pr\left\{\tilde{V} = \underline{V} \mid B_1\right\} + \overline{V} \Pr\left\{\tilde{V} = \overline{V} \mid B_1\right\} \\
&= \frac{1/2(1 - \alpha)(1 - \beta) + \alpha(1 - \mu)}{(1 - \alpha)(1 - \beta) + \alpha(1 - \mu)}
\end{aligned} \tag{4.10}
$$

Following the same procedure we obtain:

$$a_2 = \frac{1/2(1-\alpha)\beta + \alpha\mu}{(1-\alpha)\beta + \alpha\mu} \tag{4.11}$$

Substituting the ask prices (4.10) and (4.11) into (4.9), we derive the probability, μ, that the insider will submit a large order:

$$\mu = \beta + \frac{\beta(1-\beta)}{\alpha(1+\beta)} \tag{4.12}$$

and substituting μ again into (4.10) and (4.11) we obtain:

$$a_1 = \frac{1}{2}[(1-\beta) + \alpha(1+\beta)] \tag{4.13}$$

$$a_2 = \frac{1}{4}[(3-\beta) + \alpha(1+\beta)]$$

As the model is symmetrical, the bid prices can be derived by the same procedure.

Semi-separating equilibrium For certain values of α and β, a semi-separating equilibrium can exist; an equilibrium, that is, in which the insiders always trade the largest quantity. In order for the insiders to submit large orders, the following condition must hold:

$$2\,[1 - a_2(\alpha, \beta, \mu = 1)] \geqslant [1 - a_1(\alpha, \beta, \mu = 1)] \tag{4.14}$$

When the insiders trade only large quantities, then μ equals 1 and the ask prices are:

$$a_1(\alpha, \beta, \mu = 1) = \frac{1/2(1-\alpha)(1-\beta)}{(1-\alpha)(1-\beta)} = \frac{1}{2} \tag{4.15}$$

$$a_2(\alpha, \beta, \mu = 1) = \frac{1/2(1-\alpha)\beta + \alpha}{(1-\alpha)\beta + \alpha} \tag{4.16}$$

Substituting (4.15) and (4.16) into (4.14) we have the necessary condition for the semi-separating equilibrium, i.e. $\beta \geqslant \alpha/(1-\alpha)$. This equilibrium warrants the following comments:

(1) Whenever the semi-separating equilibrium prevails, we have $a_1 = 1/2$; in fact, if the insiders decide not to trade the small quantity, there is no adverse selection problem for that quantity and the ask price for small orders is equal to the unconditional expected value of $\widetilde{V}$, $a_1 = E(\widetilde{V})$;
(2) If the insiders trade only large quantities, we expect the ask price to be greater than in the pooling equilibrium: $a_2(\alpha, \beta, \mu = 1) > a_2$;
(3) The higher the proportion of large orders from uninformed traders, β, relative to the proportion of insiders, α, in the market-place, the greater the probability that a semi-separating equilibrium will prevail, i.e. that we are in the condition where $2(1 - a_2) \geqslant 1 - a_1$ and $\beta \geqslant \alpha/(1-\alpha)$. In this case the insiders exploit their

information to the hilt by submitting only large orders. Intuitively, the greater the number of uninformed traders making large trades, the smaller the adverse selection costs incorporated in the price of large orders, hence the greater the advantage for insiders to make large trades.

Exercises

Exercise 1

An alternative way of calculating the bid and ask prices can be developed using the tree diagram presented in Figure 4.4. Here g is the probability that an uninformed trader will come to the market, q the probability that an informed trader will come; both these probabilities were denoted earlier by $(1 - \alpha)$ and α.

Firstly, find the probability that an uninformed trader submitted an order, given that this is a buy order. Similarly, calculate the probability that an informed trader submitted the same order. Secondly, calculate the ask price as the conditional expectation of the asset value given the buy order. Finally, compute the bid–ask spread.

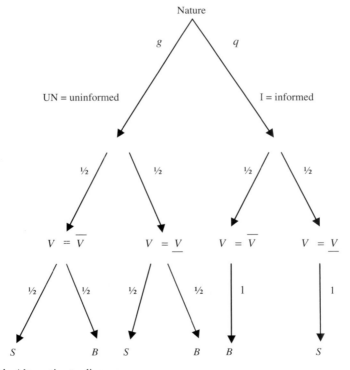

Figure 4.4. Alternative trading game.

Solution

The bid and ask prices quoted by the market-maker are equal to the expected value of the risky asset, conditional on the information available (the order is either buy or sell). In this case, to find the equilibrium ask price we use the equation:

$$a = E\left[\widetilde{V} \mid B\right] = \Pr\{UN \mid B\} E\left[\widetilde{V} \mid UN, B\right] + \Pr\{I \mid B\} E\left[\widetilde{V} \mid I, B\right]$$

where the conditional probabilities of an uninformed and informed trader are:

$$\Pr\{UN \mid B\} = \frac{\Pr\{UN\}\Pr\{B \mid UN\}}{\Pr\{UN\}\Pr\{B \mid UN\} + \Pr\{I\}\Pr\{B \mid I\}}$$

$$= \frac{g(1/2)}{g(1/2) + q(1/2)} = \frac{g}{g + q}$$

$$\Pr\{I \mid B\} = \frac{q(1/2)}{g(1/2) + q(1/2)} = \frac{q}{g + q}$$

From this, we obtain the ask price:

$$a = \frac{g}{g + q} E(\widetilde{V}) + \frac{q}{g + q} \overline{V} = E(\widetilde{V}) + \frac{q}{g + q}(\overline{V} - E(\widetilde{V}))$$

With an analogous procedure we get the bid price, which equals:

$$b = E\left[\widetilde{V} \mid S\right] = \frac{g}{g + q} E(\widetilde{V}) + \frac{q}{g + q} \underline{V} = E(\widetilde{V}) + \frac{q}{g + q}(\underline{V} - E(\widetilde{V}))$$

We can now calculate the equilibrium spread:

$$S = a - b = \frac{q}{g + q}(\overline{V} - \underline{V})$$

It is easy to verify that both methods yield the same result. Substituting $g = 1 - \alpha$ and $q = \alpha$ into the last equation we get equation (4.7). This indicates that, if we exclude the case of no agents coming to the market (i.e. we assume that $g + q = 1$), the spread is only a function of α.

Exercise 2

Assume that the probability of informed trading, α, is equal to 0.5 and that $\underline{V} = 0$ and $\overline{V} = 1$. Using equations (4.5) and (4.6), compute the ask and bid quoted prices at both time t and time $t + 1$. Provide some intuitions for these results.

Solution

$a_t = E\left[\widetilde{V} \mid B_t\right] = \frac{3}{4}$; $b_t = E\left[\widetilde{V} \mid S_t\right] = \frac{1}{4}$. Assume that $p_t = a_t = \frac{3}{4}$, then $a_{t+1} = E\left[\widetilde{V} \mid B_t, B_{t+1}\right] = \frac{9}{10}$ and $b_{t+1} = E\left[\widetilde{V} \mid B_t, S_{t+1}\right] = \frac{1}{2}$. Alternatively, if $p_t = E\left[\widetilde{V} \mid S_t\right] = \frac{1}{4}$, then $a_{t+1} = E\left[\widetilde{V} \mid S_t, B_{t+1}\right] = \frac{1}{2}$ and $b_{t+1} = E\left[\widetilde{V} \mid S_t, S_{t+1}\right] = \frac{1}{10}$. Notice that the first transaction represents a signal on the future value of the asset: after a buy order, dealers revise their expectations upwards and set $a_t = \frac{3}{4} > \frac{1}{2}$; conversely, after a sell order they revise them downwards and set $b_t = \frac{1}{4} < \frac{1}{2}$.

Exercise 3

Under the same assumptions as in Exercise 2, show that prices follow a martingale.

Solution

Assume once more that $p_t = a_t = E[\widetilde{V} \mid B_t] = \frac{3}{4}$; then $a_{t+1} = E[\widetilde{V} \mid B_t, B_{t+1}] = \frac{9}{10}$ and $b_{t+1} = E[\widetilde{V} \mid B_t, S_{t+1}] = \frac{1}{2}$. Now $E[p_{t+1} \mid \Phi_t] = a_{t+1} \Pr(B_{t+1} \mid B_t) + b_{t+1} \Pr(S_{t+1} \mid B_t) = \frac{3}{4} = p_t$, where $\Pr(B_{t+1} \mid B_t) = \frac{5}{8}$ and therefore $\Pr(S_{t+1} \mid B_t) = \frac{3}{8}$.

Exercise 4

Regulators often impose a minimum quote size (MQS) on the prices quoted by liquidity providers. Use the Easley and O'Hara model to compare MQS with a regime without constraint. To this end, measure liquidity by the bid–ask spread and compare the trading volumes and number of trades under the two regimes.

Solution

With minimum quote size, the equilibrium ask price that drives dealers' expected profits to zero must satisfy the following condition $E[\pi_{Ask}] = \Pr(\overline{V})E[\pi_{Ask} \mid \overline{V}] + \Pr(\underline{V})E[\pi_{Ask} \mid \underline{V}] = 0$, i.e. $\Pr(\overline{V})[1(A_Q - 1)\Pr(1 \mid \overline{V}) + 2(A_Q - 1)\Pr(2 \mid \overline{V})] + \Pr(\underline{V})[1(A_Q - 0)\Pr(1 \mid \underline{V}) + 2(A_Q - 0)\Pr(2 \mid \underline{V})] = 0$. Substituting for the conditional probabilities and solving for A_Q, we get the equilibrium ask price under the regime with MQS: $A_Q = (1/2)[\beta(\alpha - 1) - 3\alpha - 1]/[\beta(\alpha - 1) - \alpha - 1]$.

References

Easley D. and M. O'Hara, 1987, 'Price, trade and information in securities markets', *Journal of Financial Economics*, 19, 69–90.

Glosten L. and J. Milgrom, 1985, 'Bid, ask and transaction prices in a specialist market with heterogeneously informed traders', *Journal of Financial Economics*, 14, 71–100.

Ho, T. and H. Stoll, 1981, 'Optimal dealer pricing under transactions and return uncertainty', *Journal of Financial Economics*, 9, 47–73.

O'Hara, M. 1995, *Market Microstructure Theory*, Oxford: Blackwell.

Roll, R. 1984, 'A simple implicit measure of the bid–ask spread in an efficient market', *Journal of Finance*, 39, 1127–39.

Stoll H. 1978, 'The supply of dealer services in securities markets', *Journal of Finance*, 33, 1133–51.

5 Inventory models

Chapter 4 discussed a model where dealers quote bid and ask prices that deviate from the fundamental value of the asset in order to offset the adverse selection costs that arise in the case of asymmetric information. We therefore assumed risk neutrality, so that dealers would be concerned only with adverse selection costs. In real markets, however, dealers also act as mandatory liquidity suppliers and are obliged to quote prices continuously. This means they will frequently hold undesired portfolio positions that do not lie on their efficient frontier. The costs that dealers must sustain for holding undesired positions – called 'inventory costs' – are another determinant of the bid–ask spread. In fact, through opposite changes in the bid–ask quotations, dealers can encourage transactions by their customers that will rebalance their portfolio. Clearly, in this context, it is crucial to assume that dealers are risk-averse, since only the risk-averse are concerned about the possible losses due to future adverse price changes.

Inventory models assign an important role to market-makers who offer the opportunity to trade at all times and therefore act as immediacy providers. The initial modelling approach (Garman, 1976) to the market-makers' control problem assumes that their objective is to avoid bankruptcy (the 'ruin problem'), which could be caused by the uncertainty induced by the arrival of non-synchronous buy and sell orders. As O'Hara (1995) suggests, this approach is not realistic since it assumes that a dealer quotes his prices only at the beginning of the trading game, so his inventory plays no role in the decision.

More realistically, Stoll (1978) and Ho and Stoll (1981, 1983) assume that the dealer is a risk-averse liquidity provider who absorbs temporary imbalances in the order flow. The dealer therefore often holds an inventory of assets that deviates from the desired portfolio position. Since he bears the risk of price fluctuations, the dealer requires compensation in terms of a bid–ask spread. Stoll (1978), Amihud and Mendelson (1980) and Ho and Stoll (1980, 1981, 1983) are the first models that formalize this idea. Biais (1993) also introduces incomplete information about the other dealers' inventory positions.

In the following section we introduce Stoll's modelling approach to inventory costs, which considers a one-dealer market, and then extend the model both on the supply side (by introducing a number of competitive dealers) and on the demand side (by allowing for a rational customer who trades both for risk-sharing and to speculate on his private information). The model is then further extended by assuming that liquidity suppliers and liquidity demanders both behave non-competitively and hence take the price impact of their net demand into account.

5.1   The Stoll model

As in Stoll (1978), we consider a two-period model in which a dealer quotes bid and ask prices. The dealer is risk-averse and demands compensation whenever he acts as liquidity supplier; for this reason he moves away from his efficient portfolio frontier, setting prices such that the expected utility of his terminal wealth when the portfolio is on the efficient frontier, W^{EF}, is equal to the expected utility of his terminal wealth, W^{dealer}, as computed when he takes the other side of a customer order x_i. This allows the dealer to be compensated for the liquidity he supplies to the market. We assume a CARA utility function with a coefficient of risk aversion equal to A.

The other relevant assumptions are the following: the dealer chooses an initial portfolio of risky assets equal to:

$$\Sigma_{h=1}^{N} p_h q_h^* = W_0 \tag{5.1}$$

where p_h is the price of the asset h and q_h^* is the optimal choice of the asset h's holding at time $t = 0$; the terminal wealth of the initial portfolio when no trade occurs between time $t = 0$ and $t = 1$ is thus equal to:

$$\widetilde{W}^{EF} = \Sigma_{h=1}^{N}(\widetilde{F}_h - p_h)q_h^* = \frac{\Sigma_{h=1}^{N}(\widetilde{F}_h - p_h)q_h^*}{\Sigma_{h=1}^{N} p_h q_h^*} \Sigma_{h=1}^{N} p_h q_h^* = R^* W_0 \tag{5.2}$$

where $\widetilde{F}_h \sim N(\overline{F}, \sigma_h^2)$ is the price of the asset h at $t = 1$, and R^* is the return on the risky asset portfolio that lies on the dealer's efficient frontier. The terminal wealth of the new portfolio when a trade equal to $q_i - q_i^* = -x_i$ occurs at time $t = 0$ is instead:

$$\widetilde{W}^{dealer} = \Sigma_{h=1}^{N}(\widetilde{F}_h - p_h)q_h^* + (\widetilde{F}_i - p_i)(-x_i) \tag{5.3}$$

where p_i is equal to the ask price p_i^A, when the incoming customer submits a buy order of size $x_i > 0$ and the dealer sells $-x_i = q_i - q_i^* < 0$; conversely, p_i is equal to the bid price p_i^B, when the customer sells $x_i < 0$ and the dealer buys $-x_i = q_i - q_i^* > 0$ from this customer.

Following Stoll, we further assume that the dealer quotes competitive prices. To achieve this, he sets the price so that the expected utility from the end-of-period wealth of the initial portfolio ($E[U(\widetilde{W}^{EF})]$) is equal to the expected utility from the end-of-period wealth from the new portfolio, which also includes x_i ($E[U(\widetilde{W}^{dealer})]$):

$$E[U(\widetilde{W}^{EF})] = E[U(\widetilde{W}^{dealer})] \tag{5.4}$$

Given normality of the asset returns and an exponential utility function, this is equivalent to setting:

$$E[\widetilde{W}^{EF}] - \frac{A}{2} Var[\widetilde{W}^{EF}] = E[\widetilde{W}^{dealer}] - \frac{A}{2} Var[\widetilde{W}^{dealer}] \tag{5.5}$$

where $E[\widetilde{W}^{EF}] = \Sigma_{h=1}^{N}(\overline{F}_h - p_h)q_h^*$ and $Var[\widetilde{W}^{EF}] = \sigma_*^2 W_0^2$ with $\sigma_*^2 = Var(R^*)$. The expectation and variance of the dealer's wealth are then:

$$E[\widetilde{W}^{dealer}] = E[\widetilde{W}^{EF}] + (\overline{F}_i - p_i)(-x_i),$$

$$Var[\widetilde{W}^{dealer}] = Var[\widetilde{W}^{EF}] + Var[(\widetilde{F}_i - p_i)(-x_i)] + 2Cov[\widetilde{W}^{EF}, (\widetilde{F}_i - p_i)(-x_i)]$$

The expression for the variance can be written as:

$$Var[\widetilde{W}^{dealer}] = \sigma_*^2 W_0^2 + x_i^2 \sigma_i^2 - 2W_0 x_i \sigma_{*,i}$$

where $\sigma_{*,i}$ is the covariance of the asset i with the portfolio of risky assets lying on the efficient frontier and σ_i^2 is the variance of the ith asset. Substituting these variances and expected values into equation (5.5) we derive:

$$\begin{aligned}(\overline{F}_i - p_i)(-x_i) &= E[\widetilde{W}^{dealer}] - E[\widetilde{W}^{EF}] \\ &= \frac{A}{2}[Var(\widetilde{W}^{dealer}) - Var(\widetilde{W}^{EF})] = \frac{A}{2}[x_i^2\sigma_i^2 - 2W_0 x_i \sigma_{*,i}]\end{aligned}$$

from which the price can be solved as

$$p_i = \overline{F}_i - AW_0\sigma_{*,i} + \frac{A}{2}x_i\sigma_i^2 \tag{5.6}$$

The first two parts of this expression represent the equilibrium price, which is equal to the expected payoff minus a discount for covariance with the efficient frontier portfolio (systematic risk). The third part reflects the additional risk added by the transaction. Notice that the customer's order, x_i, is positive when the dealer buys and negative when he sells; hence equation (5.6) can be used to derive the bid (p_i^B) and ask (p_i^A) prices for the asset i as follows:

$$p_i^A = \overline{F}_i - AW_0\sigma_{*,i} + \frac{A}{2}\sigma_i^2|x_i| \qquad \text{with } x_i > 0 \text{ (dealer sells)}$$

$$p_i^B = \overline{F}_i - AW_0\sigma_{*,i} - \frac{A}{2}\sigma_i^2|x_i| \qquad \text{with } x_i < 0 \text{ (dealer buys)}$$

with bid–ask spread $S_i = p_i^A - p_i^B = A\sigma_i^2|x_i|$. Some observations on these results are in order.

The slope of the price function, $(A/2)\sigma_i^2$, depends on the dealer's risk aversion and the riskiness of the asset. Therefore, an empirical prediction of this model is that assets with high return variance will have high transaction costs. Notice that it is the total variance that matters here, not the covariance with the market return.

The bid–ask spread of the asset S_i is an increasing function of the dealer's risk aversion, A, of the asset volatility, σ_i^2, and of the trade size, $|x_i|$. This is because in this model the spread reflects the costs that dealers face when they accommodate their customers' orders. Since inventory costs increase with the size of the transaction, the equilibrium price is increasing in the trade size. Finally, expression (5.6) shows that the spread does not depend upon the dealer's initial asset holdings.

5.1.1 Pricing with initial inventory

Now we introduce the assumption that there is competition in the form of threat of entry into the market and that the dealer is still a monopolist, and we suppose his position in asset i already deviates from the optimal position q_i^* by an initial inventory I_i. This inventory can be either positive or negative, indicating a position either larger or smaller than optimal. Hence, after a trade of size x_i the quantity held by the dealer is $q_i - q_i^* = I_i - x_i$. We can work out the expected payoff and variance to find:

$$E[\widetilde{W}^{dealer}] = E[\widetilde{W}^{EF}] + (\overline{F}_i - p_i)(I_i - x_i)$$

and

$$Var[\widetilde{W}^{dealer}] = Var[\widetilde{W}^{EF}] + (I_i - x_i)^2\sigma_i^2 + 2W_0(I_i - x_i)\sigma_{*,i}$$

Substituting these variances and expected values into equation (5.5), we derive the quoted price for a trade of size x_i in asset i:

$$p_i = \overline{F}_i - AW_0\sigma_{*,i} - \frac{A}{2}(I_i - x_i)\sigma_i^2 \tag{5.7}$$

We can write this compactly as a set of bid and ask quotes:

$$p_i^A = p_i(I_i) + \frac{A}{2}\sigma_i^2|x_i| \qquad \text{with } x_i > 0 \text{ (dealer sells)}$$

$$p_i^B = p_i(I_i) - \frac{A}{2}\sigma_i^2|x_i| \qquad \text{with } x_i < 0 \text{ (dealer buys)}$$

with the midpoint of the quote equal to:

$$p_i(I_i) = \overline{F}_i - AW_0\sigma_{*,i} - \frac{A}{2}\sigma_i^2 I_i$$

The location of this midpoint depends on the level of the inventory: with high initial inventory, the dealer quotes lower prices; with low initial inventory he quotes prices higher than the equilibrium price. The bid–ask spread for a round-trip trade of size $|x_i|$ is again independent of the initial asset holdings and also independent of the inventory level:

$$S_i = p_i^A - p_i^B = A\sigma_i^2|x_i| \tag{5.8}$$

5.2 Order-driven markets

Let us now introduce competition among liquidity suppliers and hence consider a market with multiple dealers. With a multiplicity of dealers, we also need an assumption regarding the market structure within which the dealers operate. From Chapter 1 we know that market structures can be classified according to two criteria: the trading session and the execution system. Trading sessions organized as call markets work with uniform pricing rules, whereas continuous auctions are governed by discriminatory pricing rules.

5.2.1 Competitive dealers

Let us start by considering the simplest batch market with M risk-averse dealers submitting limit orders for a single risky asset, and Z liquidity traders submitting market orders. Let the aggregate market orders be equal to $\widetilde{x} \sim (\overline{x}, \sigma_x^2)$, and each dealer's endowment equal to I_j, with $\overline{I} = \left(\sum_{j=1}^{M} I_j\right)/M$. Furthermore, we maintain the previous chapters' assumptions of a CARA utility function and a coefficient of risk aversion A; we also retain the assumption of normality of the future value of the risky asset $\widetilde{F} \sim N(\overline{F}, \sigma^2)$. It follows that each dealer will submit a limit order that is shaped as a demand function specifying for each price, p, the number of shares he wishes to trade. This demand function is the solution to each dealer j's expected utility maximization of terminal wealth, $\widetilde{W}_j$:

$$\underset{q_j}{\text{Max }} E[\widetilde{W}_j] - \frac{A}{2} Var[\widetilde{W}_j] \tag{5.9}$$

with $E[\widetilde{W}_j] = (\overline{F} - p)q_j + I_j\overline{F}$ and $Var[\widetilde{W}_j] = \sigma^2[q_j^2 + I_j^2 + 2I_jq_j]$.

From the first-order conditions we obtain:

$$q_j = \frac{\overline{F} - p}{A\sigma^2} - I_j = \frac{\overline{F} - I_jA\sigma^2 - p}{A\sigma^2} = \frac{\varphi_j - p}{A\sigma^2} \tag{5.10}$$

where $\varphi_j = \overline{F} - I_jA\sigma^2$ is the dealer's marginal evaluation for the asset.[1] Notice that the higher the dealer's expected value of the risky asset, $\overline{F}$, the larger the order, whereas the greater the dealer's inventory, the lower his marginal evaluation for the asset and the smaller his net demand. Clearly, the dealer will buy provided that his marginal evaluation of the asset is higher than the price, p.

Given the agents' orders, the uniform pricing rule can be obtained from the market-clearing condition:

$$\sum_{j=1}^{M} q_j + \widetilde{x} = 0 \tag{5.11}$$

Substituting q_j from equation (5.10) and solving for p, we obtain:

$$\widetilde{p} = \overline{F} - \overline{I}A\sigma^2 + \frac{A\sigma^2}{M}\widetilde{x} \tag{5.12}$$

---

[1] We should notice that this interpretation of the dealer's marginal evaluation of the risky asset is consistent with Biais, Martimort and Rochet (2000); here dealers only face risk-bearing costs, whereas there they also face adverse selection costs.

Notice that $(A\sigma^2/M)\widetilde{x}$ is the price impact of a trade of size $\widetilde{x}$; clearly, the greater the dealers' risk aversion and the volatility of the asset, the heavier the burden of the inventory costs perceived by the dealers and the greater the price impact; increasing the number of dealers, M, however, will reduce the average dealer's exposure and hence the price impact of a liquidity trader's order. Note also that the market price is a random variable with variance equal to: $Var(\widetilde{p}) = [A\sigma^2/M]^2\sigma_x^2$; this is a measure of the price risk that liquidity traders face when submitting their market orders. Hence an increase in volatility will be associated with a decrease in market liquidity.

To obtain the post-trade quantity allocation of dealers, we can substitute the equilibrium price (5.12) into the dealers' demand function (5.10) and obtain:

$$q_j^* = (\overline{I} - I_j) - \frac{\widetilde{x}}{M} \tag{5.13}$$

which shows that the quantity traded reflects the distance between each dealer's inventory and the average inventory; it also shows that inventory hedging is not complete in this market, since trading does not eliminate the difference between I_j and $\overline{I}$, and the post-trading dealer's demand still depends on I_j.

From equation (5.12) it is easy to derive the bid and ask prices, as well as the spread S:

$$p^A = \varphi + \frac{A\sigma^2}{M}|x| \quad \text{for } x > 0 \tag{5.14}$$

$$p^B = \varphi - \frac{A\sigma^2}{M}|x| \quad \text{for } x < 0$$

with $\varphi = \overline{F} - \overline{I}A\sigma^2$

$$S = \frac{2A\sigma^2}{M}|x| \tag{5.15}$$

Notice that φ is the bid–ask midquote and is a negative function of the average endowment shock $\overline{I}$. It follows that dealers should adjust their bid and ask prices according to the size of their endowment; when it is large, they will lower their bid and ask prices to induce their customers to buy the asset, but when their holding of the risky asset decreases they will do the opposite. It follows that dealers' spread should be mean-reverting. Finally, equation (5.15) shows that the spread should be increasing in the volatility of the asset and decreasing in the number of dealers.

So far it has been assumed that customers submit random demands; as shown in Exercise 1, the model is easily extended to include rational agents who trade to hedge their initial endowment shock.

5.2.2 Imperfect competition
We will now extend the model to posit that dealers behave strategically; this is a reasonable assumption when the number of dealers is not very large. When agents behave

strategically they recognize that their net demand will affect the market price and scale back their trade accordingly. Therefore, under this new assumption of imperfect competition traders behave less aggressively and, consequently, will supply less liquidity. Including imperfect competition produces a model reminiscent of Kyle (1989) where the Cournot–Nash equilibrium price is the result of competition in quantities.

Within this Cournot game we assume that each dealer holds the following conjecture on the other $M - 1$ dealers' demand:

$$q_{h \neq j} = \xi - \beta p - \gamma I_h \quad \forall h = 1, \ldots, M \tag{5.16}$$

where ξ, β and γ are positive parameters, and, computing the residual demand in the market, a dealer can infer the market equilibrium from the market-clearing condition:

$$\sum_{h \neq j}^{M} (\xi - \gamma I_h - \beta p) + q_j + \widetilde{x} = 0 \tag{5.17}$$

and the residual supply curve:

$$\widetilde{p} = \lambda[(M - 1)\xi - \sum_{h \neq j}^{M} \gamma I_h + q_j + \widetilde{x}] \tag{5.18}$$

where $\lambda \equiv 1/[(M - 1)\beta]$.

It follows that the dealer's optimization problem can be solved by substituting this expression for the market price into his objective function (5.9), and computing the following first-order condition and optimal demand curve:

$$q_j = \frac{1}{\lambda + A\sigma^2}\overline{F} - \frac{1}{\lambda + A\sigma^2}p - \frac{A\sigma^2}{\lambda + A\sigma^2}I_j \tag{5.19}$$

Assuming symmetry among dealers,[2] an equilibrium can be obtained by equating expression (5.19) to the dealer's conjectured equilibrium demand function to obtain:

$$\beta = \frac{M - 2}{(M - 1)A\sigma^2}$$
$$\gamma = A\sigma^2\beta$$
$$\xi = \overline{F}\beta$$

and hence:

$$q_j = \frac{M - 2}{(M - 1)A\sigma^2}\left(\overline{F} - p\right) - \frac{M - 2}{M - 1}I_j \tag{5.20}$$

---

[2] See Viswanathan and Wang (2002).

Substituting the equilibrium strategy into the market-clearing condition (5.11), we can derive the equilibrium price,[3] $\widetilde{p}_{ic}$, and spread, $\widetilde{S}_{ic}$:

$$\widetilde{p}_{ic} = \overline{F} - A\sigma^2 \overline{I} + \frac{A\sigma^2(M-1)}{M-2} \frac{\widetilde{x}}{M} = \varphi + \frac{A\sigma^2(M-1)}{M-2} \frac{\widetilde{x}}{M} \qquad (5.21)$$

$$\widetilde{S}_{ic} = 2\frac{A\sigma^2(M-1)}{M-2} \frac{|\widetilde{x}|}{M} \qquad (5.22)$$

Comparing expression (5.21) with the equilibrium price (5.12) for the model with competitive dealers, we observe that with imperfect competition liquidity decreases; this can be inferred by considering both the price impact of an order of size $\widetilde{x}$, which is greater under imperfect competition, and the bid–ask spread, $\widetilde{S}_{ic}$, which is wider. As mentioned earlier, the increase in the cost of trading for noise traders that results from imperfect competition is due to the fact that dealers take the price impact of their own trades into account and consequently offer less liquidity to the market.

5.3 Dealers and informed traders

Consider a market with M competitive dealers facing a rational investor who trades both to hedge his endowment shock, I^L, and to speculate on the signal, $\widetilde{\delta}$, that he received at the outset. This introduces asymmetric information and hence adverse selection costs. Other things being equal to the model discussed in section 5.2.1, it is convenient to assume that the future value of the risky asset is equal to $\widetilde{F} = \overline{F} + \widetilde{\delta} + \widetilde{\varepsilon}$ with $E[\widetilde{F}] = \overline{F}$, $Var[\widetilde{F}] = \sigma^2$ and $Var[\widetilde{F}|\overline{F} + \delta] = \sigma_\varepsilon^2$, and $\widetilde{\delta}, \widetilde{\varepsilon} \sim (0, \sigma_\varepsilon^2)$ and I^L jointly normal and independent.

The informed investor observes $\overline{F} + \widetilde{\delta}$ and solves the maximization problem:

$$\underset{x}{\text{Max}} \quad E[\widetilde{W}_x] - \frac{\rho}{2} Var[\widetilde{W}_x] = (\overline{F} + \widetilde{\delta})(x + I^L) - xp - \frac{\rho}{2}\sigma_\varepsilon^2(I^L + x)^2 \qquad (5.23)$$

From the first-order condition, we obtain the demand function:

$$\widetilde{x} = \frac{\overline{F} + \widetilde{\delta} - \rho\sigma_\varepsilon^2 I^L - p}{\rho\sigma_\varepsilon^2} = \frac{\widetilde{\Omega} - p}{\rho\sigma_\varepsilon^2} \qquad (5.24)$$

where $\widetilde{\Omega} = \overline{F} + \widetilde{\delta} - \rho\sigma_\varepsilon^2 I^L = p + \rho\sigma_\varepsilon^2 x$ is the investor's marginal evaluation of the risky asset. Notice that, if the price p is observable, and the product $\rho\sigma_\varepsilon^2$ a constant, it follows that x is a sufficient statistic for $\widetilde{\Omega}$.

Each dealer's objective function is:

$$\underset{q_j}{\text{Max}} \; E[\widetilde{W}_j|\Omega] - \frac{A}{2} Var[\widetilde{W}_j|\Omega] = E(\widetilde{F}|\Omega)(q_j + I_j) - q_j p - \frac{A}{2} Var(\widetilde{F}|\Omega)(q_j + I_j)^2$$

and from the first-order condition, we can derive the demand function:

$$q_j = \frac{E(\widetilde{F}|\Omega) - p}{A\,Var(\widetilde{F}|\Omega)} - I_j = \frac{E(\widetilde{F}|\Omega) - I_j A\,Var(\widetilde{F}|\Omega) - p}{A\,Var(\widetilde{F}|\Omega)} = \frac{\varphi_j - p}{A\,Var(\widetilde{F}|\Omega)} \qquad (5.25)$$

---

[3] It can be shown that this equilibrium in linear strategies is not unique (Klemperer and Meyer, 1989).

Using the Theorem of Projection for Normal Distributions (see Chapter 2), we can compute the conditional expectation $E(\widetilde{F}|\Omega) = \alpha\widetilde{\Omega} + (1 - \alpha)\overline{F} = \alpha(\widetilde{p} + \rho\sigma_\varepsilon^2 x) + (1 - \alpha)\overline{F}$, with $\alpha = Cov(\widetilde{F}, \widetilde{\Omega})/Var(\widetilde{\Omega}) = Var(\widetilde{\delta})/Var(\widetilde{\Omega})$, which is related to the informativeness of the informed traders' signal. Notice that the more precise this signal, the higher the dealer's adverse selection costs and the greater the presumable price reaction to an order submission should be.[4]

Substituting expression (5.25) into the market-clearing condition:

$$\sum_{j=1}^{M} q_j + \widetilde{x} = 0$$

the equilibrium price can be computed as:

$$\widetilde{p} = \frac{[(\alpha - 1)\overline{F} + A \, Var(\widetilde{F}|\Omega)\overline{I}][M\rho\sigma_\varepsilon^2 + A \, Var(\widetilde{F}|\Omega)]}{M\rho\sigma_\varepsilon^2 + A \, Var(\widetilde{F}|\Omega)(\alpha - 1)} + \frac{\alpha M\rho\sigma_\varepsilon^2 + A \, Var(\widetilde{F}|\Omega)}{M(1 - \alpha)}\widetilde{x}$$

or

$$\widetilde{p} = \Gamma + \lambda\widetilde{x} \tag{5.26}$$

As expected, the equilibrium price is a function of the informativeness of the signal: the higher α, the less liquid the market.

Exercises

Exercise 1
Extend the model considered in Section 5.2.1 to include risk-averse customers who trade to hedge their endowment shock, and comment on the empirical implications of this version of the model.

Solution
Again assuming a CARA utility function with the parameter of risk aversion equal to ρ, the liquidity trader (i.e. the dealer's customer), holding an endowment equal to I^L, will choose to trade the quantity that maximizes his end-of-period expected utility:

$$\underset{x}{\text{Max }} E[\widetilde{W}_x] - \frac{\rho}{2}Var[\widetilde{W}_x] \tag{5.27}$$

with $E[\widetilde{W}_x] = (\overline{F} - p)x + I^L\overline{F}$ and $Var[\widetilde{W}_x] = \sigma^2[x^2 + I^{L\,2} + 2I^Lx]$.
From the first-order condition we obtain:

$$x = \frac{\overline{F} - p}{\rho\sigma^2} - I^L = \frac{\overline{F} - \rho I^L\sigma^2 - p}{\rho\sigma^2} \tag{5.28}$$

---

[4] See Seppi (1992) on this issue.

where $\overline{F} - I^L \rho \sigma^2$ is the liquidity trader's marginal valuation of the asset. Hence, the liquidity trader's optimal demand can be derived by substituting the price equation (5.12) into the liquidity demand (5.28) to obtain:

$$x = \frac{A\overline{I} - \rho I^L}{\rho + A/M} \tag{5.29}$$

Notice from expression (5.29) that the liquidity trader's demand is a positive function of the average inventory of the liquidity suppliers. In fact, as their inventory increases, liquidity suppliers' evaluation of the asset decreases and so therefore does the price they offer, which in turn enhances liquidity traders' demand. Various empirical findings are consistent with the results obtained. Madhavan and Sofianos (1998) and Manaster and Mann (1996) show that market-makers holding short and long positions are, respectively, more likely to buy and to sell; with similar arguments, Reiss and Werner (1998) explain interdealer trading at the London Stock Exchange.

Exercise 2

This exercise is an extension of the model presented in section 5.3. Assume that the informed trader behaves strategically by taking the price impact of his trade into account. Show how the equilibrium price function changes under this assumption.

Solution

Consider equation (5.26) as the informed trader's conjecture on the equilibrium price and substitute it into his objective function (5.23) to obtain, from the first-order condition, the new demand function:

$$x = \frac{\overline{F} + \widetilde{\delta} - \rho \sigma_\varepsilon^2 I^L - \Gamma}{\rho \sigma_\varepsilon^2 + 2\lambda} = \frac{\widetilde{\Omega} - \Gamma}{\rho \sigma_\varepsilon^2 + 2\lambda} \tag{5.30}$$

As we have already seen in Chapter 2, when traders behave strategically, they take the price impact of their own orders into account and trade less aggressively; this is evident from a comparison of expressions (5.30) and (5.24) which shows that when the informed trader behaves strategically, his demand sensitivity to the signal $\widetilde{\Omega}$ diminishes. The equilibrium price function can now be obtained by the same procedure used for the model presented in section 5.3.

References

Amihud, Y. and H. Mendelson, 1980, 'Dealership market. Market making with inventory', *Journal of Financial Economics,* 8, 31–53.

Biais, B. 1993, 'Price formation and equilibrium liquidity in fragmented and centralized markets', *Journal of Finance,* 48, 157–85.

Biais, B., D. Martimort and J. C. Rochet, 2000, 'Competing mechanisms in a common value environment', *Econometrica,* 68, 799–837.

Garman, M. 1976, 'Market microstructure', *Journal of Financial Economics,* 3, 257–75.

Ho, T. and H. Stoll, 1980, 'On dealer markets under competition', *Journal of Finance,* 35, 259–67.

1981, 'Optimal dealer pricing under transactions and return uncertainty', *Journal of Financial Economics*, 9, 47–73.

1983, 'The dynamics of dealer markets under competition', *Journal of Finance*, 38, 218–31.

Klemperer, P. D. and M. A. Meyer, 1989, 'Supply function equilibria in oligopoly under uncertainty', *Econometrica,* 57, 1243–77.

Kyle, A. 1989, 'Informed speculation with imperfect competition', *Review of Economic Studies*, 56, 317–56.

Madhavan, A. and G. Sofianos, 1998, 'An empirical analysis of NYSE specialist trading', *Journal of Financial Economics,* 48, 189–210.

Manaster, S. and C. S. Mann, 1996, 'Life in the pit: competitive market making and inventory control', *Review of Financial Studies,* 9, 953–75.

O'Hara, M. 1995, *Market Microstructure Theory*, Oxford: Blackwell.

Reiss, P. and I. Werner, 1998, 'Does risk sharing motivate inter-dealer trading?', *Journal of Finance,* 53, 1657–704.

Seppi, D. 1992, 'Block trading and information revelation around quarterly earning announcements', *Review of Financial Studies,* 5, 281–305.

Stoll H. R. 1978, 'The supply of dealer services in securities markets', *Journal of Finance*, 33, 1133–51.

Viswanathan, S. and J. Wang, 2002, 'Market architecture: limit-order books versus dealership markets', *Journal of Financial Markets,* 5, 127–67.

6 Empirical models of market microstructure

The bid–ask spread is the difference between the price at which liquidity suppliers are willing to sell (ask) and the price at which they are willing to buy (bid). In the theoretical models discussed so far, the existence of the spread is due to the adverse selection costs arising with asymmetric information and to inventory costs. This chapter concerns the basic empirical models of market microstructure, which take another component of the bid–ask spread into account, namely order processing costs. Order processing costs are the costs associated with the handling of a transaction and are typically modelled as fixed costs per share.

We emphasize that each trade has a buyer and a seller, so the costs for one party are the trading profits for another party. It is natural to look at costs from the perspective of an impatient trader, who consumes liquidity by placing market orders and pays the bid–ask spread. Adverse selection and inventory costs depend on traders' behaviour, type and preferences, and on the characteristics of the trading process. By nature, inventory costs exist only in quote-driven markets, where intermediaries have the institutional obligation to supply liquidity continuously; adverse selection and order-processing costs, on the other hand, may exist in any financial market.

In Section 6.1 we start by defining several measures of transaction costs. In Section 6.2 we define *Roll's estimator*, which is a particularly easy way to estimate the spread from transaction prices. In Section 6.3 we examine models with asymmetric information where the trading process affects the equilibrium price. Finally, in Section 6.4 we discuss the type of intraday data available for market microstructure studies and consider a measure of the probability of informed trading.

6.1 Definitions of transaction costs

In this section, we adopt the following hypotheses when considering empirical models of the bid–ask spread:

(1) Let P_t^* be the equilibrium price of the asset at time t. We assume that $P_t^* = E\left(P_T^*|\Phi_t\right)$, i.e. the markets are informationally efficient and P_t^* is a martingale with respect to the information set Φ_t. Following the definition of Fama (1970),

we refer to semi-strong efficiency when Φ_t incorporates all the public information available at time t.

(2) There is no rationing either on the demand side or on the supply side.

However, on account of market microstructure frictions, transaction prices may deviate from the equilibrium price, generating transaction costs. As we have noted, the bid–ask spread is a frequently used indicator of market liquidity. This differential is an important component of trading costs, often referred to as implicit transaction costs to distinguish them from explicit costs such as brokerage fees and taxes. We will offer different measures of the spread, each one focusing on a different interpretation. The *quoted spread*, or the difference between the best ask and best bid prices offered by liquidity suppliers, is an estimate of the costs that a generic investor incurs for a round-trip transaction, i.e. a purchase followed by a sale. On the other hand, the *realized spread* is an estimate of the gain a market-maker can expect to make from two consecutive transactions. We show that the two definitions coincide when transaction costs consist solely in order-processing costs. We will also show that the difference between the quoted and the realized spread, which is always positive or at least zero, is a positive function of adverse selection and inventory costs. This difference can also be affected by the number of transactions at prices within the spread, as well as by order fragmentation. Furthermore, we will provide a definition of the effective spread, which is twice the difference between the transaction price and the midpoint of the quoted bid–ask spread and is therefore a better proxy of transaction costs when quoted prices are not binding.

We start with the most common estimator of trading costs, the quoted spread.

- **Definition 1:** The *quoted spread, S^Q*, is the average difference between the best ask and the best bid prices:

$$S^Q = \frac{1}{T} \sum_{t=1}^{T} (A_t - B_t) \tag{6.1}$$

The quoted spread can be estimated using a sample of $t = 1, ..., T$ bid and ask quotes, for example from intraday data. By dividing the bid–ask difference in equation (6.1) by the quote midpoint (i.e. the average of the bid and the ask quote), we obtain an estimator of the relative spread:

$$s^Q = \frac{1}{T} \sum_{t=1}^{T} \frac{A_t - B_t}{(A_t + B_t)/2} \tag{6.2}$$

The relative spread can also be obtained by using the logarithm of the bid and ask price in equation (6.1); this gives very similar numerical results to those of equation (6.2).

The quoted spread has several drawbacks. It may vary over the day (typically U-shaped) and therefore may not be a good measure of actual trading costs. For example, if trading is busiest when the spread is small, the average trading cost incurred will be smaller than a simple calendar-time weighted average of quoted spreads. One solution is to weight the bid–ask quote observations by the duration between quotes or between trades. Another problem is that the quotes may not be binding, or may be valid for small volumes only. To measure the actual trading costs, measures based on the prices of actual transactions are therefore often preferred.

We now turn to some alternative definitions of transaction costs.

- **Definition 2:** The *transaction costs* at time t are equal to:

$$Q_t \left(P_t - P_t^* \right) \tag{6.3}$$

where P_t^* is equal to the equilibrium price, or fundamental value, and P_t denotes the transaction price at t. The variable Q_t indicates whether the transaction was buyer-initiated ('buy', $Q_t = 1$) or seller-initiated ('sell', $Q_t = -1$).

In general, 'transaction cost' is the cost of a single transaction (buy or sell), whereas spread is defined as the costs associated with a round-trip transaction, i.e. a purchase followed by a sale of the same amount (assuming the equilibrium price does not change). From this, a natural estimator for the spread is:

$$S = \frac{1}{T} \sum_{t=1}^{T} 2 Q_t (P_t - P_t^*) \tag{6.4}$$

where T is the number of observations over a given period. Notice that taking the price P_t denominated in a particular currency yields the quoted spread in currency units, whereas taking the logarithm ($\ln P_t$) gives the relative spread, which is preferable when several stocks are compared.

The fundamental value of the security P_t^* is typically not observable, but the transaction prices P_t are. We must introduce a definition of spread as a function of observable variables. An operational measure of spread is the absolute difference between the transaction price and the midpoint of bid and ask quotes. This is usually called the effective spread.

- **Definition 3:** The *effective spread* is defined as

$$S^E = \frac{1}{T} \sum_{t=1}^{T} 2 Q_t (P_t - M_t), \quad M_t = \frac{A_t + B_t}{2} \tag{6.5}$$

Again, taking the price and bid and ask quotes denominated in a particular currency yields the quoted spread in currency units, whereas taking their logarithm gives the relative spread. Data on the buy/sell indicator Q_t are not always available. In that case, a feasible measure is the absolute difference between the transaction price P_t and the midpoint of bid and ask quotes.

- **Definition 3A:** The *effective spread* can be estimated by

$$S^E = \frac{1}{T} \sum_{t=1}^{T} 2|P_t - M_t| \tag{6.6}$$

The effective spread proxies the equilibrium price by the midpoint of bid and ask quotes prevailing at the time of the trade. However, if there is asymmetric information in the market, the trade itself may affect the equilibrium price. An alternative proxy for the equilibrium price is therefore the midpoint of bid and ask quotes *after* the transaction. This leads to the following spread measure.

- **Definition 4:** The *realized spread* is defined as

$$S^R = \frac{1}{T} \sum_{t=1}^{T} 2Q_t (P_t - M_{t+1}) \tag{6.7}$$

The rationale for this measure is given by Biais, Foucault and Hillion (1997), who point out that the realized spread is equal to:

$$S^R = E (\Delta P_t | P_{t-1} = B_{t-1}) - E (\Delta P_t | P_{t-1} = A_{t-1}) \tag{6.8}$$

where $\Delta P_t = P_t - P_{t-1}$, A_{t-1} is the ask price, meaning that the transaction at time $t-1$ was initiated by a buyer, and B_{t-1} the bid price quoted at time $t - 1$, being therefore a transaction initiated by a seller. Equation (6.8) indicates the market-maker's expected gain between time $t - 1$ and t. Figure 6.1 illustrates the different components of the realized spread between $t - 1$ and t. As the example shows, the minus sign in equation (6.8) indicates that a negative variation in the price after a sale ($\Delta P_t | P_{t-1} = A_{t-1} < 0$) represents a profit (or, better, an opportunity gain) for the market-maker. Looking at Figure 6.1, in fact, one can see that starting from a spread equal to $A_{t-1} - B_{t-1}$, after a sale by the market-maker at $t - 1$ ($P_{t-1} = A_{t-1}$), if the midquote decreases as is assumed in Figure 6.1, the market-maker can either sell again at t, and $\Delta P_t | P_{t-1} = A_{t-1}$ becomes $A_t - A_{t-1}$, or he can buy with $\Delta P_t | A_{t-1} = B_t - A_{t-1}$. Now, if A_t and B_t are lower than A_{t-1}, the two consecutive transactions (sell–sell and sell–buy) must be accounted for as profits in the realized spread, and hence premultiplied by a minus as in equation (6.8).

In general the realized spread (S^R) is smaller than the quoted spread (S^Q); however, as we show with Roll's model later in this chapter, if transaction costs consist only of order-processing costs, the two coincide.

To estimate the quoted spread, data on the bid and ask prices quoted by the market-maker are sufficient, whereas to estimate the realized and the effective spread, data on both transaction prices and best bid and ask prices are necessary. It follows that the possibility of estimating the spread depends crucially on the availability and quality of the data. The recent availability of data sets at high frequency, i.e. time series where

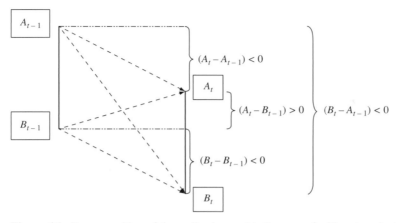

Figure 6.1. Decomposition of the realized spread in the case of midquote reduction.

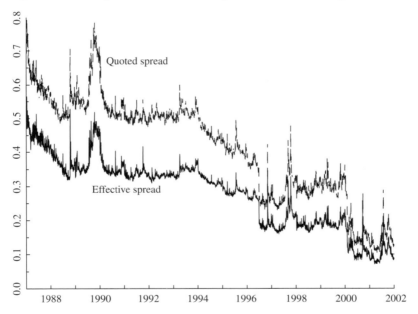

Figure 6.2. Percentage quoted and effective spread for NYSE stocks.

all the prices quoted during the day are registered, allows more accurate estimates to be made.

Chordia, Roll and Subrahmanyam (2001) used detailed data from the New York Stock Exchange (NYSE) Trade and Quote (TAQ) database to construct daily estimates of the quoted and effective spreads for virtually all stocks listed on the NYSE. Figure 6.2 shows the quoted and effective spreads, averaged over all NYSE stocks for the period 1988–2002.[1] A few conclusions can be drawn from this graph.

---

[1] These data were kindly provided by Avanidhar Subrahmanyam on his website.

- The effective spread is always lower than the quoted spread. This confirms our intuition that most actual trades are made at times when quoted spreads are relatively low, or involve stocks with low spreads.
- The level of transaction costs has come down greatly over time. The average effective spread narrowed from 0.5% at the beginning of 1988 to 0.1% at the end of 2002. Note that these numbers are an average over all NYSE stocks, and the trading costs of large-capitalization firms is typically even smaller, whereas for small caps they can be much higher.
- The figures show that, apart from the general downward trend, there is considerable variation in trading costs. On several occasions, such as during the 1998 financial crisis, there is a sudden, large jump in the spread and a general deterioration in financial market liquidity. This so-called 'liquidity risk' and its implication for asset prices will be studied further in Chapter 7.

6.2   Estimating the bid–ask spread from transaction prices

The measures of the spread discussed above require observations on transaction prices and bid–ask quotes. Very often, however, quoted prices are either unavailable, unreliable or difficult to handle. As noted, quotes may not be binding or the spread may vary in the course of the trading day, so estimation of the spread based on transaction prices is usually preferred. Roll (1984) offers a very parsimonious model for estimating spread, using the time series of the prices at which trades were made. This model shows that when transaction costs consist of order processing costs only, i.e. in the absence of both adverse selection and inventory costs, the quoted spread coincides with the realized spread.

6.2.1   Roll's model
The assumptions underlying Roll's (1984) model are:

(1) information is homogeneous;
(2) orders are executed either at the best ask or at the best bid price;
(3) there is no rounding of transaction prices; this assumes that prices can be quoted on an infinitely fine grid and there is no rounding to the nearest 'tick';
(4) the trading process has no impact on the equilibrium price M_t;
(5) the probabilities of buying and selling are equal, specifically:

$$\Pr(Q_t = 1|\Phi_{t-1}) = \Pr(Q_t = -1|\Phi_{t-1}) = \frac{1}{2} \quad \forall t \tag{6.9}$$

(6) the probability of continuation is equal to that of reversal:

$$\Pr(Q_t = Q_{t-1}|\Phi_{t-1}) = \frac{1}{2} \quad \forall t$$

where Q_t is again a variable that take the values $+1$ (-1) in case of a purchase (sale) on behalf of the market-maker's counterpart. This assumption may be valid, for example, when inventory costs are zero and agents do not fragment their orders.

In later models these assumptions are progressively relaxed.

Roll demonstrates that it is possible to estimate spread by computing the auto-covariance of transaction prices. Below we show how in the absence of transaction costs this auto-covariance is equal to zero, whereas with transaction costs, it is negative and a function of the spread. This allows us to estimate the spread by using transaction prices alone. This method proves useful when quoted bid and ask prices are not available.

Suppose that the transaction price is equal to the equilibrium price:

$$P_t = P_t^* \tag{6.10}$$

This means that the spread is zero. Further, suppose that the variation of the underlying asset price is a random walk:

$$\Delta P_t^* = P_t^* - P_{t-1}^* = \Gamma + U_t \tag{6.11}$$

where Γ is a constant equal to the unconditional expected value of ΔM_t in the time interval Δt, corresponding to the expected variation in the equilibrium price, and U_t is a random variable with zero mean and variance σ_U^2, representing the revision of the equilibrium price generated in the period Δt by the unexpected arrival of public information. This variable can be interpreted as fundamental, publicly available news about the firm's value. Technically, we assume that $E(U_t|\Phi_{t-1}) = 0$ where Φ_{t-1} contains all public information, i.e. all past observations on transaction prices and quotes. With the price drift $\Gamma = 0$, which is a reasonable approximation for intraday data, we obtain from (6.10) and (6.11):

$$\Delta P_t = \Delta P_t^* = U_t \tag{6.12}$$

In this case the auto-covariance of the price variations is equal to:

$$Cov\,(\Delta P_t, \Delta P_{t-1}) = Cov\,(U_t, U_{t-1}) = 0 \tag{6.13}$$

If we now introduce transaction costs that justify the existence of a constant spread S, whose midpoint is assumed to be equal to the equilibrium price P_t^*, the transaction price becomes:

$$P_t = P_t^* + \frac{S}{2}Q_t \tag{6.14}$$

where Q_t is a dummy variable taking the value $+1$ for a buy and -1 for a sell order with equal probability. Now it can be demonstrated that the auto-covariance of the

Table 6.1. *Joint probabilities of subsequent price changes*

		ΔQ_{t-1}			
		-2	0	$+2$	
	-2	0	$\frac{1}{8}$	$\frac{1}{8}$	$\frac{1}{4}$
ΔQ_t	0	$\frac{1}{8}$	$\frac{1}{4}$	$\frac{1}{8}$	$\frac{1}{2}$
	$+2$	$\frac{1}{8}$	$\frac{1}{8}$	0	$\frac{1}{4}$
		$\frac{1}{4}$	$\frac{1}{2}$	$\frac{1}{4}$	1

price variations is no longer zero but, given the initial assumptions, negative. In fact, the price change becomes:

$$\Delta P_t = P_t^* - P_{t-1}^* + \frac{S}{2}(Q_t - Q_{t-1})$$

$$= U_t + \frac{S}{2}\Delta Q_t \qquad (6.15)$$

The negative serial correlation in returns may seem somewhat surprising at first sight, but this result emerges from Table 6.1 on the joint probabilities of subsequent price changes.

Notice first that the off-diagonal values show that it is more likely that an upturn will be followed by a downturn, and vice versa, which explains:

$$E(\Delta Q_t \Delta Q_{t-1}) = -1 \qquad (6.16)$$

Since:

$$E(\Delta Q_t) = E(\Delta Q_{t-1}) = 0 \qquad (6.17)$$

and, by assumption, $Cov(U_t, U_{t-1}) = 0$, the auto-covariance of the price change is equal to:

$$Cov(\Delta P_t, \Delta P_{t-1}) = Cov\left[\left(U_t + \frac{S}{2}\Delta Q_t\right), \left(U_{t-1} + \frac{S}{2}\Delta Q_{t-1}\right)\right]$$

$$= -\frac{S^2}{4} < 0 \qquad (6.18)$$

Equation (6.18) shows that the existence of a bid–ask spread induces negative autocorrelation in the transaction price changes. By inverting (6.18), Roll illustrates how the quoted spread can be estimated using only transaction prices:

$$S(Roll) = 2\sqrt{-Cov(\Delta P_t, \Delta P_{t-1})} \qquad (6.19)$$

Notice that for Rolls estimator to exist, the covariance of price changes must be negative; a disadvantage of this procedure is that when prices show positive serial correlation, Roll's spread cannot be computed. Notice also that the implicit assumption in Roll's model is that trading does not affect the midpoint of bid–ask quotes.

Roll's estimator is very parsimonious; in fact, to estimate the spread from equation (6.15), one could run the following regression of ΔP_t on ΔQ_t, where Q_t is again the 'sign' of the trade:

$$\Delta P_t = \beta_0 + \beta_1 \Delta Q_t + e_t \tag{6.20}$$

The slope coefficient estimates the half-spread $S/2$. To do this, however, both prices and 'direction' data (Q_t) on a sequence of trades $t = 1, \ldots, T$ are needed. If trade direction Q_t is not observed, one can only use Roll's estimator of the spread.

6.2.2 Extensions of Roll's model

To consider the intraday dynamics of the bid–ask spread, or the conditions that might prevail when markets are under stress, it can be interesting to relax Roll's fairly restrictive assumptions on the process of arrival of buy and sell orders. We accordingly now remove assumption (5) of Roll's model.

Roll's model assumes that the probabilities of a purchase and of a sale are both equal to $\frac{1}{2}$. However, when transaction prices at any particular time of the day are analysed, it is not certain that the probability of a buy order, α, is equal to that of a sell order, i.e. $1 - \alpha$. As a consequence, calculating the transaction price covariance as in (6.18), we obtain:

$$Cov\,(\Delta P_t, \Delta P_{t-1}) = \frac{(S)^2}{4} E\,(\Delta Q_t \Delta Q_{t-1}) = -(S)^2\,[\alpha\,(1 - \alpha)] \tag{6.21}$$

Hence, the estimate of the quoted spread is equal to:

$$S = \sqrt{-\frac{Cov\,(\Delta P_t, \Delta P_{t-1})}{[\alpha\,(1 - \alpha)]}} \tag{6.22}$$

Since the denominator, $[\alpha\,(1 - \alpha)]$, has a maximum at $\frac{1}{4}$ for $\alpha = \frac{1}{2}$, as in Roll's model, it follows that for $\alpha \neq 1/2$, Roll underestimates the spread.

Choi, Salandro and Shastri (1988) consider the possibility of serial correlation of buy and sell orders. An implicit hypothesis in Roll is that investors' orders are not serially correlated, meaning that the probability of a buy order is equal to that of a sell order and, further, is independent of the preceding transaction. However, in some cases (for example when traders fragment their orders), serial dependence between sell and buy orders can be verified. In these cases the probability of continuation is equal to:

$$\Pr\,(Q_{t+1} = Q_t) = (1 - q) \neq \frac{1}{2} \tag{6.23}$$

and the covariance between the transaction price variations results in:

$$Cov\,(\Delta P_t, \Delta P_{t-1}) = \frac{(S^Q)^2}{4}\left[-4q^2\right] = -S^2 q^2 \tag{6.24}$$

whereas the spread estimator proves to be:

$$S\,(css) = \frac{1}{q}\sqrt{-Cov\,(\Delta P_t, \Delta P_{t-1})} \tag{6.25}$$

For $q < \frac{1}{2}$ Roll's model underestimates the spread, and for $q > \frac{1}{2}$ it overestimates it. Typically, intraday data exhibit positive serial correlation in the order flow, hence $q < \frac{1}{2}$, and Roll's model will underestimate the spread.

6.3   Price effects of trading

This section extends the model presented so far to incorporate price effects of trading due to adverse selection costs. Inventory costs will be discussed in the next section. In such a situation, the trading process affects the equilibrium price. More specifically, a buyer-initiated order will drive the equilibrium price upwards, as it sends a signal that the asset is currently undervalued. Conversely, a seller-initiated trade pushes the equilibrium price downwards.

6.3.1   The Glosten and Harris model

When no agent has privileged information, the midpoint of the bid–ask quote, or 'true' price, is a random walk, independent of the trading process:

$$P_t^* = P_{t-1}^* + U_t \tag{6.26}$$

Market microstructure models with asymmetric information effects, based on the Glosten and Milgrom (1985) approach, imply that the trading process has an impact on the equilibrium price, as follows:

$$P_t^* = P_{t-1}^* + (1 - \pi) \frac{S}{2} Q_t + U_t \tag{6.27}$$

where π is the parameter indicating order processing costs as a fraction of total costs, and $(1 - \pi)$ the fraction of adverse selection costs. Notice the timing convention: P_t^* indicates the equilibrium price including the information revealed by the transaction at time t; it incorporates the public information U_t, as well as the private information revealed by the order flow Q_t. It follows that there are two innovations in the true price, one due to the arrival of public information, U_t, and the other due to adverse selection, which equals the revision in the expectations conditional on the order arrival. Clearly, buy orders cause an upward revision of these expectations, sell orders a downward revision.

If the equilibrium price reflects adverse selection costs, $(1 - \pi)(S/2)Q_t$, then the transaction price P_t reflects order processing costs:

$$P_t = P_t^* + \pi \frac{S}{2} Q_t \tag{6.28}$$

The quote midpoint (before the trade) will not reflect the new information yet, but will include the public information. This leads to $M_t = P_{t-1}^* + U_t$ and the equations of the model will look like:

$$P_t = M_t + \frac{S}{2} Q_t \tag{6.29}$$

$$M_t = M_{t-1} + (1 - \pi) \frac{S}{2} Q_{t-1} + U_t \tag{6.30}$$

Clearly, if we assume that $\pi = 1$, the model reduces to Roll's model.

Taking the first difference of P_t from (6.28) we obtain the reduced form for the transaction price changes:

$$\Delta P_t = \Delta P_t^* + \pi \frac{S}{2} \Delta Q_t \tag{6.31}$$

$$= (1 - \pi) \frac{S}{2} Q_t + \pi \frac{S}{2} \Delta Q_t + U_t$$

$$= \frac{S}{2} Q_t - \pi \frac{S}{2} Q_{t-1} + U_t \tag{6.32}$$

The parameters S and π can be estimated from the regression coefficients in a regression of ΔP_t on Q_t and ΔQ_t, where the level variable Q_t estimates the adverse selection component that embodies the permanent price effect, and the difference variable ΔQ_t estimates the fixed cost component, i.e. the temporary price effect. Alternatively, the parameters S and π can be estimated from the regression coefficients in a regression of ΔP_t on Q_t and Q_{t-1}, where the contemporaneous variable Q_t estimates the total cost, and the lagged variable Q_{t-1} estimates (minus) the order processing cost component.

Glosten and Harris (1988) generalize this model by allowing the order processing cost and adverse selection cost to be functions of trade size. Assume as before that the spread incorporates two components, permanent and transitory:

$$P_t = M_t + (C_t + Z_t) Q_t \tag{6.33}$$

$$M_t = M_{t-1} + Z_{t-1} Q_{t-1} + U_t \tag{6.34}$$

where Z_t is the price impact of a trade due to adverse selection, and the spread now consists of an order processing cost component, C_t, and a price impact component, Z_t:

$$\frac{S_t}{2} = C_t + Z_t \tag{6.35}$$

Notice that in the previous notation $C_t = \pi S/2$ and $Z_t = (1 - \pi) S/2$. According to the new notation, the transaction price variation is equal to:

$$\Delta P_t = \Delta(C_t Q_t) + Z_t Q_t + U_t \tag{6.36}$$

Assuming that both spread components are linear in trade size q_t, we obtain:

$$C_t = C_0 + C_1 q_t \tag{6.37}$$

$$Z_t = Z_0 + Z_1 q_t \qquad (6.38)$$

The reduced-form model for price changes is:

$$\Delta P_t = C_0 \Delta Q_t + C_1 \Delta x_t + Z_0 Q_t + Z_1 x_t + U_t \qquad (6.39)$$

where $x_t = q_t Q_t$ is the 'signed' trade size. The coefficient Z_1 has a nice interpretation as Kyle's lambda, i.e. the slope of the price impact curve due to asymmetric information effects.

To estimate the Glosten–Harris model of price impact, intraday data are needed. However, sometimes such data are unavailable, or are only available for a limited time span, or costly to collect. Consequently, a popular alternative for estimating the price impact of trading is to use daily data on prices and trading volume (or net order flow).

Roll's estimator can be applied to daily data for the estimation of the bid–ask spread; nevertheless, it does not always provide a sensible estimate, as $Cov(\Delta P_{t+1}, \Delta P_t)$ is not always negative for daily data. For regressions of price changes on order flow, Evans and Lyons (2002), among others, use daily data in the foreign exchange market. They run regressions of the type:

$$\Delta P_t = \lambda X_t + U_t \qquad (6.40)$$

where X_t is the net order flow (buy volume minus sell volume) on a particular day and ΔP_t is the open-to-close price change. This method can be seen as a time aggregation of the Glosten–Harris price impact regressions (see the adjoining box entitled 'Transaction cost estimates').

Transaction cost estimates

Glosten and Harris (1988) estimate their model using NYSE common stock transaction prices, excluding opening trades, which are determined by a call auction. For twenty stocks they examine the first 800 successive transactions starting in December 1981. They estimate equation (6.39) with restrictions $C_1 = Z_0 = 0$ (i.e. the order processing costs per share are fixed and the adverse selection costs per share increase with trade size) which they find the most useful and parsimonious specification for their analysis. Their results show that the fixed spread component is equal to 4.44 cents, whereas the adverse selection cost measures 1.13 for a 1,000-share trade and and 11.30 for 10,000 shares. It follows that according to equations (6.37) and (6.38) the estimated spread is:

- for a 1,000-share trade (from 6.35): 2(4.44+1.13)=11.14 cents per share; consequently, the adverse selection amounts to about 20% of the total spread, the remaining 80% being due to fixed costs;
- for a 10,000-share trade, adverse selection costs amount to 70% (11.30/15.50) of the spread, the latter being equal to 2(4.44+11.30)=31 cents per share.

Notice that the bid–ask spreads here are measured in cents. To translate this to the relative spread, one needs the share price. In the sample period used by Glosten and Harris (1988), the average share price is close to $20. Hence, the bid–ask spread is around 0.5% for a 1,000-share trade and 1.5% for a 10,000-share trade. The data are from the 1980s, and in recent years transaction costs have declined significantly.

6.3.2   Estimation of illiquidity using daily data

The most popular method for measuring implicit transaction costs using daily data is the ILLIQ measure of Amihud (2002). The idea is to measure Kyle's lambda (i.e. the price impact of trading) as the absolute price change on a particular day divided by the absolute order flow that same day. This ratio is then averaged over a number of days D (say, all the days in a month) to obtain a measure of illiquidity for that period. In practice, for many exchanges the net order flow (buy minus sell) is not available and is proxied by gross order flow (buy plus sell orders), denoted here by V_t:

$$ILLIQ_t = \frac{1}{D} \sum_{d=1}^{D} \frac{|\Delta P_d|}{V_d} \tag{6.41}$$

Proxying the net order flow with gross trading volume may overstate liquidity, as the latter may be much larger than the former. Nevertheless, the ILLIQ measure is useful when only daily data on prices and volume are available. The ILLIQ measure has been used commonly in recent years in the literature on the relation between liquidity and asset pricing. We return to that literature in Chapter 7.

Hasbrouck (2006) compares several measures of trading costs based on daily data with the (more accurate) effective spread measure estimated from intraday data. The measures based on daily data are (i) Roll's estimator (ii) an improved version of Roll's estimator using Gibbs sampling, and (iii) ILLIQ. Table 6.2 shows that the ILLIQ has the highest rank correlation with the effective spread.

Table 6.2. *Spearman rank correlations between liquidity proxies*

	Effective spread	Roll's estimator	Gibbs' estimator	ILLIQ
Effective spread	1.000			
Roll's estimator	0.636	1.000		
Gibbs' estimator	0.872	0.791	1.000	
ILLIQ	0.937	0.592	0.778	1.000

Source: Hasbrouck (2006), Table 2.

6.4   The probability of informed trading

The purpose of this section is to describe the types of data typically used in empirical microstructure work. We also discuss how to classify trades as buy or sell, and how the probability of information can be estimated using intraday buy and sell order-flow data.

6.4.1   Intraday data

Empirical research on the microstructure of exchanges ordinarily uses intraday price and trade data. However, the format and quality of the data differ greatly by exchange and data source. For measuring quoted spreads, a record of simultaneous bid and ask quotes is needed. In dealership or hybrid markets (with a designated specialist or market-makers with quote obligations), such data are sometimes available. However, one needs to be careful because the quotes may only be indicative (as they are, for example, in the foreign exchange markets) or there may be better prices available from a competing order book.

For the other measures discussed, prices of actual transactions are needed, and typically one also needs to know whether the transaction was initiated by the buyer ('buy') or by the seller ('sell'). For some markets, this classification into buys and sells is easy to establish, since trading is at best quotes or the best prices available in the limit order book (LOB). An important exception is the NYSE, where trading can be within the specialist's quotes, because either the specialist improves on his quoted price, or trading is with the LOB. Moreover, the NYSE data sources (notably the TAQ database) have two separate files for trades and quotes and the timing is not exactly simultaneous. This sometimes makes it difficult to classify a trade as buy or sell. Lee and Ready (1991) developed a classification method that has become the standard measure for the TAQ data. In recent years, many high-quality data sets have become available from electronic limit order book markets, where all trades are cleared against the limit order book. This permits unambiguous classification of trades as buys or sells.

6.4.2   Inferring trade direction

Some intraday data series do not contain a buy/sell identifier for trades. As most estimators of transaction costs require this information, an algorithm is necessary to classify trades as buy or sell. When bid/ask quotes (or best buy/sell limit order prices) are available, a natural method is to compare the trade price with the quotes prevailing at the time of the trade. Trades at or above the ask (or best sell limit price) will be classified as buys, trades at or below the bid (or best buy limit price) will be classified as sells.[2] This algorithm will leave trades within the quotes unclassified. Trades

---

[2] Because of possible reporting lags, care has to be taken that the time matching of trades and quotes is correct. Lee and Ready (1991) suggest that taking quotes available at least five seconds before the reported trade time gives reliable classifications.

within the quotes may be either 'crosses' (trades negotiated outside the central market place) or trades where a floor broker or the order book improved on the price of the specialist's quote, as often happens on hybrid markets like the NYSE.

In the absence of quote data, or for trades that fall within the quotes, Lee and Ready (1991) advocate the so-called 'tick test'. In the tick test, the price of a trade is compared to the price of the previous trade. The algorithm is as follows:

- if the price of the current trade is above the price of the previous trade (an 'uptick'), the trade is classified as a buy;
- if the price is below that of the previous trade (a 'downtick'), the trade is classified as a sell;
- if the price is equal to the price of the previous trade and the previous trade was a buy (a 'zero-uptick'), the trade is classified as a buy;
- if the price is equal to the price of the previous trade and the previous trade was a sell (a 'zero-downtick'), the trade is classified as a sell.

Lee and Ready (1991) show that this algorithm is very reliable and classifies most trades in the same way as the classification based on a comparison with bid and ask quotes.[3]

6.4.3 The PIN model

Easley, Kiefer, O'Hara and Paperman (1996) develop a method to estimate the probability that there was informed trading in the market on a particular day. The method builds on an extension of the Glosten and Milgrom (1985) model, which was explained in Section 4.1. The extension is that there is a probability $1 - \alpha$ every day that there is no news, and a probability α of news, which can be either good news (with conditional probability δ) or bad news (with conditional probability $1 - \delta$). This gives the following information structure

$$\text{Pr} \ (news) = \alpha \ \begin{cases} \text{Pr} \ (good \ news|news) = \delta \\ \text{Pr} \ (bad \ news|news) = 1 - \delta \end{cases} \tag{6.42}$$

$$\text{Pr} \ (no \ news) = 1 - \alpha \tag{6.43}$$

During the course of the day, trades arrive according to Poisson processes. The arrival rate of uninformed buy orders is ϵ_B and that of uninformed sell orders ϵ_S. On days with information, informed trades arrive at rate μ. The informed trades are buys when information is good, sells when it is bad; there are no informed trades when there is no news. As in the Glosten and Milgrom (1985) model, the bid–ask spread at the opening of the trading day can be derived from a zero profit condition for the dealer, and is equal to:

$$S = \frac{\alpha \mu}{\alpha \mu + \epsilon_B + \epsilon_S} [V_H - V_L] \tag{6.44}$$

---

[3] See also Boehmer, Grammig and Theissen (2007).

where V_H and V_L are the high and low value of the asset, respectively. The probability that the first trade of the day is informed can be derived from this model as well. This is:

$$PIN = \frac{\alpha\mu}{\alpha\mu + \epsilon_B + \epsilon_S} \tag{6.45}$$

This quantity is called the 'probability of informed trading' (PIN) and is closely related to the covariance between the number of buy trades (N_B) and the number of sell trades (N_S). Duarte and Young (2007) show that this covariance equals:

$$Cov(N_B, N_S) = -\alpha^2\mu^2\delta(1-\delta) \tag{6.46}$$

The intuition for this negative covariance is quite simple. On days with good news, there are more buys than average, on days with bad news there are more sells than average. Plotting N_B versus N_S for many days then gives a negative relation between these variables. The strength of the relation is determined by the expected informed trading intensity ($\alpha\mu$).

Easley, Hvidkjaer and O'Hara (2002) show that PIN is a useful measure of liquidity and is a determinant of the cross-section of stock returns; we return to this point in Chapter 7. We now discuss the estimation of PIN from daily data on the number of buy and sell transactions.

6.4.4   *Maximum likelihood estimation of PIN*

Easley, Kiefer, O'Hara and Paperman (1996) suggest estimating PIN by maximum likelihood. Given the information structure, the probabilities of the number of buy and sell trades on a given day can be determined from the Poisson arrival process, which implies a Poisson distribution for the number of trades on a given day. The Poisson distribution has the following properties: suppose the arrival rate per day for the number of trades N is λ. Then the expected number of buy trades per day is $E(N) = \lambda$, and the variance of the number of trades is $Var(N) = \lambda$, and the uncentred second moment is $E(N^2) = \lambda + \lambda^2$. The probability density function, used to construct the likelihood function, is:

$$P(N = n) = e^{-\lambda}\frac{\lambda^n}{n!} \tag{6.47}$$

In the Easley *et al.* model, the arrival rates depend on the information available on each day, which can be good news, bad news or no news. Given the information structure outlined above, the arrival rates of the number of buy (N_B) and sell (N_S) trades are:

$$E(N_B|good\ news) = \epsilon_B + \mu, \quad E(N_S|good\ news) = \epsilon_S$$
$$E(N_B|bad\ news) = \epsilon_B, \quad\quad E(N_S|bad\ news) = \epsilon_S + \mu$$
$$E(N_B|no\ news) = \epsilon_B, \quad\quad E(N_S|no\ news) = \epsilon_S$$

Of course, the econometrician does not know whether there is good, bad or no news. However, he observes the number of buy trades (B) and the number of sell trades (S).

Given the probabilities of good, bad or no information, and the conditional probabilities of the number of buys and sells given the information, the following likelihood function can be constructed:

$$L(B, S; \psi) = \alpha \delta e^{-(\epsilon_B + \mu)} \frac{(\epsilon_B + \mu)^B}{B!} e^{-\epsilon_S} \frac{(\epsilon_S)^S}{S!}$$
$$+ \alpha(1 - \delta) e^{-\epsilon_B} \frac{(\epsilon_B)^B}{B!} e^{-(\epsilon_S + \mu)} \frac{(\epsilon_S + \mu)^S}{S!}$$
$$+ (1 - \alpha) e^{-\epsilon_B} \frac{(\epsilon_B)^B}{B!} e^{-\epsilon_S} \frac{(\epsilon_S)^S}{S!} \tag{6.48}$$

This likelihood can be multiplied over several days (typically, all the days of a month) with observations (B_t, S_t) to obtain the likelihood function:

$$L(\psi) = \prod_{t=1}^{T} L(B_t, S_t; \psi) \tag{6.49}$$

Maximizing this function with respect to the parameters $\psi = (\alpha, \delta, \mu, \epsilon_B, \epsilon_S)$ gives maximum likelihood estimates of the parameters. Often, in the estimation the arrival rate of uninformed buy and sell orders is assumed equal, i.e. $\epsilon_B = \epsilon_S = \epsilon$; this reduces the number of parameters to be estimated by one.

6.5   Empirical inventory models

Here we specify empirical versions of the theoretical inventory models presented in Chapter 5 and provide a brief overview of the main empirical findings in this literature.

6.5.1   The Ho and Stoll model

Ho and Stoll (1981) extend Stoll's (1978) model, discussed in section 5.1, to a dynamic setting with random arrival of buy and sell orders (Poisson processes with arrival rates λ_a and λ_b). They assume that one monopolistic, passive specialist sets bid and ask prices as a markup, a_t and b_t, on the midpoint M_t:

$$ask_t = M_t + a_t, \quad bid_t = M_t - b_t \tag{6.50}$$

and that the number of orders is declining in markup (elastic demand/supply). Ho and Stoll specify complicated dynamics for prices, inventory and wealth and find conclusions consistent with Stoll (1978) and equations (5.6) and (5.7):

$$ask_t = M_t + a_t = P_t^* - \beta I_t \ + (K + \xi |x_t|) \tag{6.51}$$
$$bid_t = M_t - b_t = P_t^* - \beta I_t \ - (K + \xi |x_t|) \tag{6.52}$$

with $\xi = \frac{1}{2} \sigma^2 AT$ and $M_t = P_t^* - \beta I_t$. Notice that the location of the midpoint of bid and ask quotes (M_t) depends on inventory level:

$$M_t = P_t^* - \beta I_t \tag{6.53}$$

The markups a_t and b_t depend on a fixed component (K), reflecting the specialists' monopoly power, and on a component ξx_t, proportional to trade size depending on the volatility of the stock price (σ^2), risk aversion (A) and time horizon (T). As before, the bid–ask spread is independent of the inventory level:

$$S = a_t + b_t = 2(K + \xi |x_t|). \tag{6.54}$$

The main difference from the spread in Stoll's model, equation (5.8), is that now the spread also depends on T, which is the difference between the time when a trade takes place and the end of the trading game. The longer this period, the higher the risk-bearing costs the dealer faces when he holds a non-optimal portfolio of risky assets.

It follows that in the Ho and Stoll model, trading affects future bid and ask prices. In fact, change in inventory is negative in signed trade size ($\Delta I_t = -|x_{t-1}| Q_{t-1} = x_{t-1}$); this moves the quote midpoint in the direction of trade, meaning that a buyer- (seller-) initiated transaction ($x_t > 0$ ($x_t < 0$)) pushes the price up (down), and its effect is proportional to trade size. Algebraically:

$$\Delta M_t = \Delta P_t^* - \beta \Delta I_t = \beta x_{t-1} \tag{6.55}$$

However, trading does not affect the 'true' price P_t^*.

6.5.2 Transaction cost estimation with inventory costs

Ho and Macris (1984) propose the following framework to test the empirical implications of Ho and Stoll (1981):

$$P_t = M_t + \frac{S}{2} Q_t \tag{6.56}$$

$$M_t = P_t^* - \beta I_t \tag{6.57}$$

$$P_t^* = P_{t-1}^* + U_t \tag{6.58}$$

where I_t is the prevailing inventory level of the dealer. The reduced-form model is:

$$\Delta P_t = \beta x_{t-1} + \frac{S}{2} \Delta Q_t + U_t \tag{6.59}$$

because change in inventory $-\Delta I_t$ equals the signed trade size x_{t-1}. Notice that the price effect of trading goes in the same direction as the Glosten and Harris (1988) model: buyer-initiated trades raise the quote midpoint, seller-initiated trades lower it. The true price, however, is unaffected by the trade, and quote midpoints will revert to their original level when the market-maker has replenished his inventory.

6.5.3 Transaction cost estimation with adverse selection and inventory costs

Madhavan and Smidt (1991) combine inventory- and information-based models. They assume that each market-maker uses Bayes' rule to update his beliefs on the liquidation value of the asset and set prices conditional on the arrival of both public information and the information embodied in the order flows they observe. It follows that market-makers' quotes will be influenced both by the signed size of the customers' orders,

x_t, and by the information that they can extract from traders' demands, which in turn depend upon the price quoted one period in advance. The parameter λ captures the responsiveness of price to order quantity, hence it embeds the information effect of trade size.

A combination of the inventory- and information-based models gives:

$$P_t = M_t + \frac{S}{2}Q_t + \lambda x_t \tag{6.60}$$

$$M_t = P_{t-1}^* + U_t - \beta I_t \tag{6.61}$$

$$P_t^* = P_{t-1}^* + (1 - \pi)\left[\frac{S}{2}Q_t - \beta I_t\right] + \lambda x_t + U_t \tag{6.62}$$

As before, M_t is the midpoint of bid and ask quotes prevailing at the time of the trade. This midpoint depends on the expected value of the asset just before the trade, $P_{t-1}^* + U_t$, and on the inventory level I_t. The variable P_t^* denotes the expected value of the asset including the information conveyed by the trade and the public information U_t. Notice that this empirical model differs from that of Glosten and Harris (1988) in that it includes the inventory level, which interacts with both the quote midpoint and market-makers' updates. When $\beta = 0$, i.e. when there is no inventory effect, the result is the Glosten–Harris model. The Madhavan–Smidt model also differs from Ho and Macris (1984), since it includes asymmetric information. Letting $\lambda = 0$ and $\pi = 1$, we obtain the Ho–Macris model.

The reduced form of the Madhavan–Smidt model is:

$$\Delta P_t = \lambda x_t + \frac{S}{2}Q_t - \pi\frac{S}{2}Q_{t-1} - \beta I_t + \pi\beta I_{t-1} + U_t \tag{6.63}$$

Madhavan and Smidt estimate this reduced form for all transactions in sixteen stocks of a NYSE specialist for February–December 1987. The inventory is constructed by aggregating the orders recorded by the specialist for operational purposes over a period of one month, and the following results are obtained. First and foremost, the inventory effect is weak. The estimates of the coefficient of inventory β are approximately zero. That is, the data do not indicate that the level of inventory significantly affects prices. The fixed spread component is significant and of similar magnitude for all stocks: $\pi(S/2) = 0.10$; the adverse selection component of this fixed component, $(1 - \pi)$, is around 0.24. The size-dependent price impact parameter λ is between 0.004 and 0.03 for a unit trade size of 1,000 shares; the market is least liquid for small firms, which is reflected by a high value of λ.

6.5.4 Other empirical evidence on inventory control

A clear-cut empirical implication of the inventory model is that in setting their prices dealers take their inventory levels into account. More precisely, when their holding of a risky asset increases, they offer liquidity at better prices so as to induce their customers to buy. The opposite applies when their inventory decreases. There is a vast empirical literature on this issue.[4] Hasbrouck and Sofianos (1993) and Madhavan and Smidt (1993) show that inventory changes have an effect on prices, so that quote revisions are negatively related to the specialists' trades. They also show that quoted prices induce mean reversion in inventory towards the target portfolio. What is ambiguous, however, is the time horizon of inventory mean reversion. Both Hasbrouck and Sofianos (1993) and Subrahmanyam (2008) find evidence that specialists react slowly to inventory shocks, so that inventories can be persistent for up to two months. This slow adjustment is not due to hedging with positions in other stocks since, as Naik and Yadav (2003) more recently showed using data from the London Stock Exchange, dealer firms' quote changes are significantly related to changes in their ordinary inventories, not to changes in equivalent inventories in other stocks. Thus it remains a puzzle why it takes so long for inventory effects to be manifested in financial market data.

Exercises

Exercise 1. Roll's estimator
Demonstrate that when the trading process does not affect the equilibrium price, the quoted spread coincides with the realized spread and it is possible to estimate both using Roll's estimator, defined in equation (6.19).

Solution
Thanks to Definition 4 (section 6.1), we know that the realized spread is equal to:

$$S^R = E\left(\Delta P_t | P_{t-1} = B_{t-1}\right) - E\left(\Delta P_t | P_{t-1} = A_{t-1}\right)$$

Moreover, by (6.13), $P_t = M_t + (S/2)Q_t$, we obtain:

$$A_t = M_t + \frac{S}{2} \quad \text{and} \quad B_t = M_t - \frac{S}{2}$$

for the best ask and the best bid prices respectively.

To calculate the realized spread, we must also find the distribution of ΔP_t, conditional on a purchase (B_{t-1}) and a sale (A_{t-1}) in $t-1$. If we consider the price change in t conditional on a purchase in $t-1$, given the definitions A_t, B_t and ΔM_t, we obtain:

$$(\Delta P_t | P_{t-1} = B_{t-1}) = \begin{cases} A_t - B_{t-1} = U_t + S & \text{with probability} = \frac{1}{2} \\ B_t - B_{t-1} = U_t & \text{with probability} = \frac{1}{2} \end{cases}$$

It follows that the conditional expected value of the price change is equal to:

$$E\left(\Delta P_t | P_{t-1} = B_{t-1}\right) = \frac{1}{2}E(U_t + S) + \frac{1}{2}E(U_t) = \frac{S}{2}$$

---

[4] Hasbrouck and Sofianos (1993) and Madhavan and Sofianos (1998) use data from the NYSE specialists; Lyons (1995) analyses the foreign exchange dealer market; Snell and Tonks (1998), Reiss and Werner (1998) and Hansch, Naik and Viswanathan (1998) examine data from the London equity dealer market.

Accordingly, if we consider the price change at time t conditional on a sale in the period $t - 1$, given the definitions of A_t, B_t and ΔM_t, we obtain:

$$(\Delta P_t | P_{t-1} = A_{t-1}) = \begin{cases} A_t - A_{t-1} = U_t & \text{with probability} = \frac{1}{2} \\ B_t - A_{t-1} = U_t - S & \text{with probability} = \frac{1}{2} \end{cases}$$

and the conditional expected value result as:

$$E(\Delta P_t | P_{t-1} = A_{t-1}) = \frac{1}{2} E(U_t) + \frac{1}{2} E(U_t - S^Q) = -\frac{S}{2}$$

It follows that the realized spread S^R is equal to the quoted spread S:

$$S^R \text{ (Roll)} = E(\Delta P_t | P_{t-1} = B_{t-1}) - E(\Delta P_t | P_{t-1} = A_{t-1})$$
$$= \frac{S}{2} + \frac{S}{2} = S \text{ (Roll)} \tag{6.64}$$

Exercise 2. Asymmetric information and Roll's estimator
In the model with both order processing costs and asymmetric information, as given in equations (6.29) and (6.30), calculate the quoted spread, the realized spread and Roll's estimator as functions of the model parameters π and S. Compare the estimators and discuss the result.

Solution
In order to find an expression for the quoted spread, we must calculate the serial covariance of prices.

By considering equation (6.31) we obtain:

$$\Delta P_t = U_t + \frac{S}{2}(Q_t - \pi Q_{t-1})$$

The covariance of subsequent price changes will be equal to:

$$Cov(\Delta P_t, \Delta P_{t-1}) = Cov\left[\left(U_t + \frac{S}{2}(Q_t - \pi Q_{t-1})\right), \left(U_{t-1} + \frac{S}{2}(Q_{t-1} - \pi Q_{t-2})\right)\right]$$
$$= Cov\left[\left(\pi \frac{S}{2}\Delta Q_t + (1-\pi)\frac{S}{2}Q_t\right), \left(\pi \frac{S}{2}\Delta Q_{t-1} + (1-\pi)\frac{S}{2}Q_{t-1}\right)\right] = -\pi \frac{S^2}{4}$$

$$\tag{6.65}$$

where:

$$E(\Delta Q_t) = E(Q_t) = 0, \quad E\left(Q_{t-1}^2\right) = 1$$

and where:

$$E(\Delta Q_t \Delta Q_{t-1}) = -1$$

From equation (6.65) we see that when order processing costs are zero ($\pi = 0$), the covariance of prices is also zero. If, however, adverse selection costs are zero ($\pi = 1$) as in Roll, the price covariance is equal to $-S^2/4$.

Furthermore, from equation (6.65) we can derive the quoted spread on the basis of the model with asymmetric information $S\,(AI)$:

$$S\,(AI) = \frac{2}{\sqrt{\pi}}\sqrt{-Cov\,(\Delta P_t, \Delta P_{t-1})}$$

whereas in Roll we had:

$$S\,(Roll) = 2\sqrt{-Cov\,(\Delta P_t, \Delta P_{t-1})}.$$

Hence, with adverse selection costs, Roll underestimates the quoted spread.

The results for the *realized spread* are the reverse. As we have seen, the realized spread is given by:

$$s = E\,(\Delta P_t | B_{t-1}) - E\,(\Delta P_t | A_{t-1})$$

where, given that $P_t = M_t + \pi\,(S/2)\,Q_t$, we obtain:

$$A_t = M_t + \pi\frac{S}{2}, \quad B_t = M_t - \pi\frac{S}{2}.$$

In the case of a purchase on behalf of the dealer, the conditional variation of transaction prices is equal to:

$$(\Delta P_t | B_{t-1}) = \begin{cases} A_t - B_{t-1} = U_t + (1 + \pi)\,S/2 & \text{with probability} = \frac{1}{2} \\ B_t - B_{t-1} = U_t - (1 - \pi)\,S/2 & \text{with probability} = \frac{1}{2} \end{cases}$$

It follows that the expected transaction price is:

$$E\,(\Delta P_t | B_{t-1}) = \pi\frac{S}{2}$$

Conversely, in the case of a sale, the conditional variation of transaction prices is equal to:

$$(\Delta P_t | A_{t-1}) = \begin{cases} B_t - A_{t-1} = U_t - (1 + \pi)\,S/2 & \text{with probability} = \frac{1}{2} \\ A_t - A_{t-1} = U_t + (1 - \pi)\,S/2 & \text{with probability} = \frac{1}{2} \end{cases}$$

from which we obtain:

$$E\,(\Delta P_t | A_{t-1}) = -\pi\frac{S}{2}$$

Therefore, the realized spread is equal to:

$$s\,(AI) = E\,(\Delta P_t | B_{t-1}) - E\,(\Delta P_t | A_{t-1})$$
$$= \pi S\,(AI) = 2\sqrt{\pi}\sqrt{-Cov\,(\Delta P_t, \Delta P_{t-1})}$$

In particular, given that $\pi < 1$, the realized spread, s, is smaller than the quoted spread, S.

If order processing costs are the only component of the spread ($\pi = 1$), as in Roll, then the realized spread coincides with the quoted spread. If, however, the transaction cost component consists only of adverse selection costs ($\pi = 0$), the realized spread is equal to zero. Consequently, with adverse selection costs, Roll's estimator overestimates the realized spread.

Exercise 3. Empirical exercise

This exercise applies the transaction cost measures developed in this chapter to data for the stock Accor, a French hotel firm listed on the Paris Bourse. The Bourse operates an electronic limit order market which makes it possible to classify all trades unambiguously as buys or sells.[5] Figure 6.3 plots one day of data. The figure graphs transaction prices and midquotes for Accor on 24 May 1991. Transaction prices are indicated with circles, the midquote is graphed as a solid line.

On the website for this book is a data file, ACCOR.XLS, with all the trades in the period from 24 May 1991 to 25 July 1991. The file has seven columns with:

(1) DATE, in year/month/day format
(2) TIME, in hour/minute/second format
(3) PRICE, the transaction price expressed in French francs (6.55957 francs = 1 euro)
(4) MIDQUOTE, defined as the average of the best buy and sell limit order prices prevailing at the time of the trade
(5) SIZE, in number of shares
(6) SIGN, where +1 indicates a buy and −1 indicates a sell[6]
(7) CROSS, a dummy variable, where 1 indicates the trade is a cross-trade negotiated outside the electronic trading system.

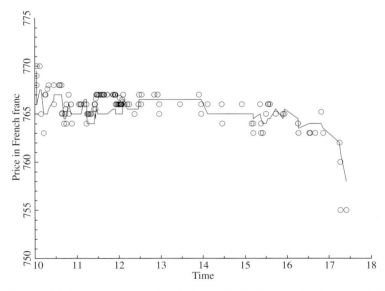

Figure 6.3. Intraday quote and trade data. This depicts data for Accor stock for one day (29 May 1991). The solid line indicates the spread midquotes, whereas circles indicate transaction prices.

---

[5] For a detailed description of the Paris Bourse and the data to which we refer, see De Jong, Nijman and Röell (1995).

[6] Occasionally, the trade sign is a zero. This happens for cross-trades that could not be classified as buy or sell.

Table 6.3. *Solution to Exercise 3*

Measure	S^{eff}	S^{Roll}	C_0	Z_0	C_1	Z_1
Absolute (FF)	1.02	0.84	0.71	0.25	−0.07	0.20
t-statistic			(16.95)	(4.88)	(−0.78)	(1.58)
Relative (b.p.)	13.44	11.21	9.37	3.34	−0.91	2.57
t-statistic			(16.77)	(4.85)	(−0.77)	(1.55)

Using these data, estimate the following measures of transaction costs and compare the results:

- The effective spread
- Roll's estimator
- The Glosten–Harris regression:

$$\Delta P_t = C_0 \Delta Q_t + C_1 \Delta x_t + Z_0 Q_t + Z_1 x_t + U_t$$

If you like, in the estimation you can add an intercept to the last model.

Estimate both absolute spreads (with prices expressed in French francs) and relative spreads.

Solution

Using the first full week of data (27–31 May 1991), we obtain the estimates in Table 6.3. The estimates for the relative spread are expressed in basis points, and have been obtained by redefining the transaction price as $p_t = 10,000 \ln(P_t)$, and likewise for the midquote. The size variable is scaled by 1,000, so that the coefficients C_1 and Z_1 correspond to the marginal impact of a 1,000-share trade (notice that the median trade size for Accor in this sample is 150 shares, so 1,000 shares are a fairly large trade).

References

Amihud, Y. 2002, 'Illiquidity and stock returns: cross-section and time-series effects', *Journal of Financial Markets*, 5, 31–56.

Biais, B., T. Foucault and P. Hillion, 1997, *Microstructure des Marchés Financiers. Institutions, Modèles et Tests Empiriques*, Paris: Presses Universitaires de France.

Boehmer, E., J. Grammig and E. Theissen, 2007, 'Estimating the probability of informed trading – does trade misclassification matter?', *Journal of Financial Markets*, 10, 26–47.

Choi, J.Y., D. Salandro and K. Shastri, 1988, 'On the estimation of bid–ask spreads: theory and evidence', *Journal of Financial and Quantitative Analysis*, 23, 219–30.

Chordia, T., R. Roll and A. Subrahmanyam, 2001, 'Market liquidity and trading activity', *Journal of Finance*, 56, 501–30.

De Jong, F., T. Nijman and A. Röell, 1995, 'A comparison of the cost of trading French shares on the Paris Bourse and on Seaq international', *European Economic Review*, 39, 1277–301.

Duarte, J. and L. Young, 2007, 'Why is PIN priced?' *Journal of Financial Economics*, 70, 223–60.

Easley, D., S. Hvidkjaer and M. O'Hara, 2002, 'Is information risk a determinant of asset returns?', *Journal of Finance*, 57, 2185–221.

Easley, D., N. Kiefer, M. O'Hara and J. Paperman, 1996, 'Liquidity, information and infrequently traded stocks', *Journal of Finance*, 51, 1405–436.

Evans, M. D. D. and R. K. Lyons, 2002, 'Order flow and exchange rate dynamics', *Journal of Political Economy*, 110, 170–80.

Fama, E. 1970, 'Efficient capital markets: a review of theory and empirical work', *Journal of Finance*, 25, 383–417.

Glosten, L. and E. Harris, 1988, 'Estimating the component of the bid/ask spread', *Journal of Financial Economics*, 21, 123–42.

Glosten, L. and P. Milgrom, 1985, 'Bid, ask and transaction prices in a specialist market with heterogeneously informed traders', *Journal of Financial Economics*, 14, 71–100.

Hansch, O., N. Naik and S. Viswanathan, 1998, 'Do inventories matter in dealership markets? Evidence from the London Stock Exchange', *Journal of Finance,* 53, 1623–55.

Hasbrouck, J. 2006, 'Trading costs and returns for US equities: estimating effective costs from daily data', Working Paper, Stern School of Business, New York University.

Hasbrouck, J. and G. Sofianos, 1993, 'The trades of market-makers: an analysis of NYSE specialists', *Journal of Finance,* 48, 1565–94.

Ho, T. and R. Macris, 1984, 'Dealer bid–ask quotes and transaction prices: an empirical study of some AMEX options', *Journal of Finance*, 39, 23–45.

Ho, T. and H. Stoll, 1981, 'Optimal dealer pricing under transactions and return uncertainty', *Journal of Financial Economics*, 9, 47–73.

Lee, C. and M. Ready, 1991, 'Inferring trade direction from intra-day data', *Journal of Finance*, 46, 733–46.

Lyons, R., 1995, 'Test of microstructure hypotheses in the foreign exchange market', *Journal of Financial Economics,* 39, 1–31.

Madhavan, A. and S. Smidt, 1991, 'A Bayesian model of intraday specialist pricing', *Journal of Financial Economics*, 30, 99–134.

1993, 'An analysis of daily changes in specialist inventories and quotations', *Journal of Finance,* 48, 1595–628.

Madhavan, A. and G. Sofianos, 1998, 'An empirical analysis of NYSE specialist trading', *Journal of Financial Economics,* 48, 189–210.

Naik, N. and P. Yadav, 2003, 'Do dealer firms manage inventory on a stock-by-stock or a portfolio basis?', *Journal of Financial Economics,* 69, 325–53.

Reiss, P., and I. Werner, 1998, 'Does risk sharing motivate inter-dealer trading?' *Journal of Finance,* 53, 1657–704.

Roll, R. 1984, 'A simple implicit measure of the bid–ask spread in an efficient market', *Journal of Finance*, 39, 1127–39.

Snell, A. and I. Tonks, 1998, 'Testing for asymmetric information and inventory control effects in market maker behaviour on the London Stock Exchange', *Journal of Empirical Finance*, 5, 1–25.

Stoll, H. R. 1978, 'The supply of dealer services in securities markets', *Journal of Finance*, 33, 1133–51.

Subrahmanyam, A. 2008, 'Lagged order flows and returns: a longer-term perspective', *Quarterly Review of Economics and Finance*, 48, 623–40.

7 Liquidity and asset pricing

The core of this book consists of models of price formation that emphasize the role of transaction costs in financial markets. This chapter discusses the relationship between transaction costs and asset prices. The crucial question is whether transaction costs affect the price of the financial assets. Clearly, transaction costs are a measure of the degree of liquidity, and accordingly the purpose of this chapter is to show how asset prices and liquidity can be related. In the first section we build on the seminal work of Amihud and Mendelson (1986) and discuss models that relate the price of a stock to the level of liquidity. In the second section, we discuss the relationship between expected returns and liquidity risk.

7.1 Transaction costs and expected returns

From the investor's point of view, transaction costs reduce the return on investments, so rational investors will require a compensation for expected transaction costs. This affects the price an investor is willing to pay for an asset. As a result, in equilibrium, transaction costs lead to lower asset prices and therefore to higher expected returns gross of costs. Let's start with a simple example. Suppose an investor buys a stock for $100 (ask price) and holds it for one year. Suppose that after a year the ask price is $104, and the bid price is $102 (hence, the bid–ask spread is $2). To liquidate his position, the investor sells the asset at the bid price i.e. at $102. The return on the asset (measured as the ask–ask price increase) is 4 per cent, but the investor's realized return is only 2 per cent! This illustrates that there is a difference between the gross return (before transaction costs) and the net return (after these costs).

7.1.1 A formal model

In this section we discuss the model of Amihud and Mendelson (1986), which is a generalization of the Gordon dividend growth model for asset valuation, where the value of a share with perpetual dividends d (and no growth of dividends) is $P = d/r$, where r is the risk-adjusted discount rate. The Amihud–Mendelson model has the following parameters: a perpetual per-period dividend d; the required risk-adjusted return r; the relative bid–ask spread S; and the expected trading frequency μ. The parameter μ is the rate at which the investor turns over the asset. For example, a value of $\mu = 0.5$ means that the investor trades 50 per cent of his holdings of the asset per period.

Amihud and Mendelson (1986) show that under these assumptions, the value of the asset is:

$$P = \frac{d}{r + \mu S} \tag{7.1}$$

The logic of this equation is simple: apart from the required net return r, the investor requires a compensation for the expected per-period trading cost μS. The sum of the two is the effective discount rate. The spread can actually have a large impact on the asset price (see Exercises 1 and 2 at the end of this chapter). The proof of equation (7.1) is quite simple. Consider the return on buying the asset and selling after one period. The asset is bought for P_0 and must generate an expected return of $r P_0$. The expected payoff at the end of the holding period equals its price P_1 less the expected transaction costs, $\mu S P_1$, plus the dividend payment d. Equating expected payoff and required return, we find the equilibrium pricing condition:

$$P_1(1 - \mu S) + d = (1 + r) P_0 \tag{7.2}$$

Now observe that the stream of cash flows generated by the asset at time 1 is identical to that generated by the asset at time 0, i.e. the perpetual dividend d. Therefore, the end-of-period price P_1 must be equal to the beginning-of-period price P_0. This gives the equality

$$P(1 - \mu S) + d = (1 + r) P \tag{7.3}$$

Solving this gives the pricing equation (7.1).

The foregoing analysis does not allow for uncertainty in the next period's price. This is, however, easily captured. Let r now be the required, risk-adjusted expected return on the stock, P_1 the end-of-period price and P_0 the initial price; we can now generalize equation (7.2) to:

$$E(P_1)(1 - \mu S) + d = (1 + r) P_0 \tag{7.4}$$

Solving this expression for the expected return on the asset we find:[1]

$$E(R) \equiv E\left(\frac{P_1 - P_0 + d}{P_0}\right) = r + \mu S \tag{7.5}$$

The interpretation of this result is highly intuitive: the expected gross return on the asset equals the risk-adjusted required return r plus the expected trading costs. Using the CAPM to determine risk-adjusted required returns, we find:

$$E(R) = r_f + \beta\left(E(R_m) - r_f\right) + \mu S \tag{7.6}$$

---

[1] In this solution, the small cross-products $\mu S \cdot r$ and $\mu S \cdot d$ are omitted.

where r_f is the risk-free rate, $E(R_m) - r_f$ is the market risk premium and β is the asset's beta. Thus, expected returns are the sum of three components: (i) the risk-free rate of return; (ii) a risk premium, determined by the beta of the asset; and (iii) a liquidity premium, determined by the bid–ask spread and the trading frequency.

Amihud and Mendelson (1986) also discuss an extension of their model where the trading frequency μ is endogenous. With higher transaction costs S, the trading frequency μ may decrease. This leads to a countervailing effect on expected transaction costs. The net result is that the latter are increasing but concave in S. An empirical prediction across assets is that expected returns are an increasing but concave function of the relative bid–ask spread.

7.1.2 Empirical evidence

Amihud and Mendelson (1986) conduct empirical tests of the relationship between expected return and bid–ask spreads. Using data from NYSE stocks for the period 1960–79, and controlling for other determinants of expected returns such as risk and firm size, they estimate the effect of liquidity on average returns. The empirical method involves the calculation, for every stock, of the bid–ask spread and the estimation of the beta (exposure to the market return). The authors then sort all assets into portfolios based on beta and spread, and perform a cross-sectional regression of average monthly portfolio return on the spread and portfolio beta. The cross-sectional regression looks like:

$$\bar{R}_p = \gamma_0 + \gamma_1 \beta_p + \gamma_2 S_p + e_p \tag{7.7}$$

where $\bar{R}_p$ is the average return on portfolio p, β_p is the portfolio's beta and S_p is the average bid–ask spread of the assets in portfolio p. The estimates reported in Amihud and Mendelson (1986) are (converted into percentage returns per month):

$$\bar{R}_p = 0.36 + 0.672\beta_p + 0.211 S_p + u_p \tag{7.8}$$

The value 0.211 is an estimate of the trading frequency μ; it implies that each stock is traded approximately once every five months. In an extended regression with $(S_p)^2$ as an additional explanatory variable, they do not find a significant effect of the squared bid–ask spread. Hence, the theoretically predicted concavity in the spread–expected return relationship appears to be weak or non-existent.

Amihud (2002) repeats Amihud and Mendelson's (1986) empirical analysis with data for 1964–97, using ILLIQ, introduced in equation (6.41), as the measure of illiquidity. Amihud's estimates are:

$$\bar{R}_{pt} = -0.364 + 1.183\beta_{pt} + 0.162 ILLIQ_{pt} + u_{pt} \tag{7.9}$$

These results confirm that illiquidity raises the required return on assets. However, it is well known that liquidity is correlated with firm size, and that small firms tend to have higher average returns. Amihud therefore adds an additional control for market capitalization (SIZE). The result of this model is:

$$\bar{R}_{pt} = 1.922 + 0.217\beta_{pt} + 0.112 ILLIQ_{pt} - 0.134 \ln(SIZE)_{pt} + u_{pt} \quad (7.10)$$

The results show that size is indeed an important determinant of expected returns, but that for any given size, illiquidity is also important (although the coefficient is smaller than without the control for firm size).

Brennan and Subrahmanyam (1996) argue that the proper measure of liquidity is the price impact of order flow. They estimate the price impact from a Glosten–Harris-style regression and Hasbrouck's (1991) model (see Chapters 6 and 9 for details on these models). They construct portfolios of assets sorted both by estimated price impact and by size, also adding a dummy for liquidity quintile to the standard Fama and French (1993) three-factor model. In that model, there are three risk factors: the market return, the return on a long–short portfolio of small firms and large firms (the so-called size factor, or SMB), and the return on a long–short portfolio of value firms and growth firms (the value factor, or HML).[2] The idea is that these factors capture risk, whereas the liquidity quintile dummy captures the additional return expected due to transaction costs. Hence, the model looks like this:

$$R_{it} = \alpha + \sum_{i=2}^{5} \gamma_i L_i + \beta_i R_{Mt} + s_i SMB_t + h_i HML_t + e_{it} \quad (7.11)$$

where *SMB* and *HML* are the returns on the size and value factors. The coefficients γ_i measure the incremental return for the low liquidity portfolios. Brennan and Subrahmanyam (1996) report an additional return of 6.6 per cent per year for the lowest as against the highest liquidity portfolio.

The PIN (probability of informed trading) measure introduced in section 6.4 has also been used extensively in applied asset pricing research. Easley, Hvidkjaer and O'Hara (2002) investigate the relation between asset prices and the PIN estimates for a cross-section of US stocks. They study the expected returns on portfolios sorted by size and PIN. Table 7.1a shows the average excess returns and the estimated PIN of these portfolios. For almost all size classes, the high-PIN portfolio has higher average returns than the low-PIN, which is consistent with liquidity as a priced characteristic. Next, Easley, Hvidkjaer and O'Hara (2002) run Fama–MacBeth regressions of the form:

$$R_{it} = \gamma_{0t} + \gamma_{1t}\hat{\beta}_p + \gamma_{2t} PIN_{i,t-1} + \gamma_{3t} SIZE_{i,t-1} + \gamma_{4t} BM_{i,t-1} + \eta_{it} \quad (7.12)$$

where R_{it} is the excess return of the stock i in month t, $\hat{\beta}_p$ is the estimated market beta of the portfolio in which stock i is classified in that month, $SIZE$ is the logarithm of market capitalization, and BM is the logarithm of the book-to-market ratio. This regression is estimated every month, and the coefficients γ_{kt} are averaged over all months. The results are shown in of Table 7.1b. They conclude that PIN is able to explain differences in expected returns on assets: a difference of 10 percentage points in the estimated PIN (roughly the difference between the high- and low-PIN portfolios)

---

[2] 'Long–short' portfolios are long on one class of assets and short on another, and require no upfront investment.

Table 7.1. *Liquidity and expected returns*

(a) Excess returns and PIN[a]

	Excess returns			PIN		
Size/PIN	Low	Medium	High	Low	Medium	High
Small	0.148	0.202	0.474	0.134	0.186	0.257
2	0.462	0.556	0.743	0.138	0.186	0.247
3	0.647	0.695	0.892	0.137	0.183	0.237
4	0.873	0.837	0.928	0.138	0.180	0.231
Large	0.953	1.000	0.643	0.127	0.175	0.233

Note: [a] Estimates of average excess returns and estimated PIN values for portfolios of US stocks, 1984–1998.

Source: Easley, Hvidkjaer and O'Hara (2002), Table III.

(b) Fama–MacBeth estimates

	Beta	*SIZE*	*BM*	*PIN*	*ILLIQ*
EHO[a]	−0.175	0.161	0.051	1.800	
	(−0.48)	(2.81)	(0.48)	(2.50)	
DY[b]	0.175	0.043	0.268	1.004	
	(0.49)	(0.63)	(2.96)	(1.91)	
DY[b]	0.149	0.088	0.254	0.648	0.0003
	(0.42)	(1.38)	(2.82)	(1.17)	(2.99)

Sources: [a] Easley, Hvidkjaer and O'Hara (2002), Table VI.
         [b] Duarte and Young (2007), Table 9.

implies a difference in expected return of 12*0.18%, which equals about 2% per year. Duarte and Young (2007) criticize these findings; they show that when the data are extended to the period 1983–2004, ILLIQ has greater explanatory power than PIN.

7.2   Liquidity risk and asset prices

The Amihud and Mendelson (1986) pricing model discussed in the previous section shows the sensitivity of asset prices to liquidity. In reality, liquidity is not a constant but fluctuates substantially over time. Figure 6.2, which graphed the quoted and effective bid–ask spread over time, illustrates this point. Recent studies on equity market liquidity, such as Chordia, Roll and Subrahmanyam (2000, 2001) and Hasbrouck and Seppi (2001), show that there is commonality in liquidity, i.e. shocks to the liquidity of individual stocks contain a common component. Moreover, returns on stocks tend to be correlated with changes in market-wide liquidity.

These results warrant investigating liquidity as a priced risk factor. In this setup, it is not only the level of transaction costs that determines asset prices, but also the exposure of returns to fluctuations in market-wide liquidity. Indeed, recent literature has shown that the (systematic) risk associated with common liquidity fluctuations is priced in the cross-section of expected equity returns. Pioneering work in this area was done by Amihud (2002). Important recent papers in this growing literature include Acharya and Pedersen (2005), Pastor and Stambaugh (2003) and Sadka (2006), who all document the significance of liquidity risk for the expected returns on equities.

7.2.1 Liquidity risk factor models

We now describe a stylized model for the pricing of liquidity risk. Let L_t be some measure of market-wide liquidity in month t, for example a market-wide average of the bid–ask spread or ILLIQ. Define the unexpected liquidity as the difference between liquidity and expected liquidity:[3]

$$U_t = L_t - E_{t-1}(L_t) \tag{7.13}$$

The first equation of the model is a simple regression of individual stock returns on the market return and the unexpected change in liquidity:

$$r_{it} = \alpha_i + \beta_i r_{mt} + \delta_i U_t + e_{it} \tag{7.14}$$

Here, r_{it} denotes the excess return[4] on asset i, α_i is a constant term, β_i is the loading on the market excess return r_{mt}, and δ_i is the exposure of the returns on asset i to unexpected changes in the liquidity factor, U_t. Finally, e_{it} represents a zero-expectation error term.

The second equation of the model is an expression for the expected return:

$$E(r_i) = \beta_i E(r_m) + \delta_i \lambda_U \tag{7.15}$$

In this equation, λ_U is the liquidity risk premium, i.e. the additional expected return paid for exposure to the common liquidity risk factor. Compared to equation (7.14), this model imposes the restriction $\alpha_i = \delta_i \lambda_U$ for all assets i. In other words, it requires that the extent to which the assets outperform CAPM (α_i) be proportional to the asset's exposure to the liquidity risk factor. The coefficient λ_U is the price of liquidity risk. Notice that in this model the liquidity level is not a separate determinant of expected returns but only a risk factor. The model can be easily extended with expected liquidity:

$$E(r_i) = \beta_i E(r_m) + \delta_i \lambda_U + \mu E(L_i) \tag{7.16}$$

Empirically, there are two ways to estimate the liquidity risk premium. Pastor and Stambaugh (2003) and Sadka (2006) combine equations (7.14) and (7.15) into one and

---

[3] In practice, unexpected liquidity is often estimated as the residual of an AR(1) model, $L_t = c + \phi L_{t-1} + U_t$. A limiting case is where $\phi = 1$, and the unexpected liquidity equals the first difference, $U_t = L_t - L_{t-1}$.

[4] Excess return is defined as the return less the risk-free rate.

use the generalized method of moments (GMM) for estimation:[5]

$$r_{it} = \beta_i r_{mt} + \delta_i (U_t + \lambda_U) + e_{it}. \tag{7.17}$$

The magnitude of the liquidity risk premium estimated in these papers is economically significant. Pastor and Stambaugh's (2003) results show an expected return difference of 7.5% between most and least liquidity-sensitive stock portfolios. Sadka (2006) finds a liquidity risk premium of 5% to 6% per annum; this premium is measured as the difference in expected returns between a high liquidity-exposure portfolio and a low liquidity-exposure portfolio.

An alternative way to estimate the liquidity risk premium is to perform a two-step estimation. Firstly estimate the exposure coefficients β_i and δ_i from a time-series regression (7.14). The expected returns are proxied by the average return over a long sample period. Then use these estimates in a cross-sectional regression of average excess returns on the estimated factor loadings:

$$\bar{r}_i = \lambda_m \widehat{\beta}_i + \lambda_U \widehat{\delta}_i + u_i, \quad i = 1, \dots, N \tag{7.18}$$

where λ_m and λ_U are the market and liquidity risk premium parameters estimated in this regression. The market risk premium λ_m can be estimated from this equation; alternatively, a value can be imposed. The GMM set-up of equation (7.17) automatically imposes $\widehat{\lambda}_m = \bar{r}_m$, i.e. the market risk premium estimate is equal to the sample average of the market excess return.

A major issue in the literature on empirical market microstructure is the appropriate measure of liquidity. Microstructure theory suggests that the transitory cost plus the price impact of a trade is a good measure of an asset's liquidity. Brennan and Subrahmanyam (1996) suggest using microstructure data to estimate these cost components, using the Glosten and Harris (1988) model. Sadka (2006) and Piqueira (2004) follow this approach and estimate the time series of monthly illiquidity for individual assets from quote and transaction data using the TAQ database for the period 1993–2001.[6] These are probably the most accurate measures of time-varying individual asset liquidity available. Based on these estimates, Sadka (2006) shows that the price impact component, rather than the transitory cost component, is the priced liquidity risk factor.

7.2.2   The liquidity CAPM

Acharya and Pedersen (2005) take a different approach to modelling the relation between liquidity and asset prices. They extend the CAPM to include transaction costs. In their model expected returns are determined by expected transaction costs and the

---

[5] GMM is a general econometric method for the estimation of non-linear models. For an introduction, see Greene (2002), chapter 11.

[6] The TAQ data are provided by the New York Stock Exchange (NYSE) and collect all trades and quotes of shares traded on the NYSE. See www.nysedata.com for more information on these data. Sadka's liquidity data can be found on his website.

asset's beta using net (i.e. after transaction costs) returns. The resulting asset pricing equation is:

$$E(r_i) = \alpha + \mu E(c_i) + \lambda \beta_i^{net} \tag{7.19}$$

where $E(r_i)$ is the expected excess return on asset i, $E(c_i)$ is the expected transaction costs. The coefficient μ measures the implicit trading frequency of the asset (as in Amihud and Mendelson's (1986) model). The coefficient λ is the risk premium for covariance with the market return. The intercept α should be zero and β_i^{net} is the net beta, defined as the coefficient in a regression of *net* (i.e. after transaction costs) returns of asset i on the net returns on the market portfolio:

$$\beta_i^{net} = \frac{Cov(r_{it} - c_{it}, r_{mt} - c_{mt})}{Var(r_{mt} - c_{mt})} \tag{7.20}$$

For additional insight, notice that the net beta can be decomposed into four components, as follows:

$$\beta_i^{net} = \beta_{1i} + \beta_{2i} - \beta_{3i} - \beta_{4i} \tag{7.21}$$
$$= \frac{Cov(r_{it}, r_{mt})}{Var(r_{mt} - c_{mt})} + \frac{Cov(c_{it}, c_{mt})}{Var(r_{mt} - c_{mt})} - \frac{Cov(r_{it}, c_{mt})}{Var(r_{mt} - c_{mt})} - \frac{Cov(c_{it}, r_{mt})}{Var(r_{mt} - c_{mt})}$$

The first component, β_{1i} is the traditional CAPM beta, whereas the other betas measure different aspects of liquidity risk.

In order to reduce estimation error in the betas, Acharya and Pedersen perform their analysis not on individual stock returns but on returns on twenty-five liquidity-based portfolios, sorted according to a monthly ILLIQ measure. Table 7.2a gives some descriptive statistics of the highest and lowest liquidity portfolios. Acharya and Pedersen estimate several restricted and unrestricted versions of the asset pricing equation (7.19). The principal results are summarized in Table 7.2b. Acharya and Pedersen's preferred specification is:

$$E(r_i) = -0.333 + 0.034 E(c_i) + 1.153 \beta_{1i} + 4.334 \beta_i^{liq} \tag{7.22}$$

where β_{1i} is proportional to the standard CAPM beta and $\beta_i^{liq} = \beta_{2i} - \beta_{3i} - \beta_{4i}$ collects all the terms of the net beta that involve transaction costs. These results imply a difference between the returns on the highest- and lowest-liquidity portfolios of 4.6% per year, of which 3.5% is compensation for expected liquidity and the remaining 1.1% is compensation for liquidity risk.[7] Compared to the result found by Pastor and Stambaugh, this estimate of the liquidity risk premium is much lower. One likely reason for this is the inclusion of an expected liquidity component in the Acharya–Pedersen model.

---

[7] These numbers are obtained as follows: the highest-liquidity portfolio has expected transaction costs of 0.25%. The lowest-liquidity portfolio has expected transaction costs of 8.83%. Multiplying the difference in expected transaction costs by the estimated turnover μ from Table 7.2 gives $12*(8.83 - 0.25)*0.034 = 3.52\%$ per annum. The liquidity risk premium is found in analogous fashion from β_i^{liq} and its estimated coefficient.

Table 7.2. *Liquidity CAPM*

(a) Estimates of the liquidity and betas of the highest- and lowest-liquidity portfolios. β_i^{net} is defined as $\beta_{1i} + \beta_{2i} - \beta_{3i} - \beta_{4i}$, β_i^{liq} is defined as $\beta_{2i} - \beta_{3i} - \beta_{4i}$.

Portfolio	$E(r_i)$	$E(c_i)$	β_{1i}	β_{2i}	β_{3i}	β_{4i}	β_i^{net}	β_i^{liq}
1	0.48%	0.25%	0.551	0.000	−0.008	−0.000	0.543	0.008
25	1.10%	8.83%	0.845	0.004	−0.017	−0.045	0.911	0.066

Source: Acharya and Pedersen (2005), Table 1.

(b) Estimates of the liquidity-extended CAPM, equation (7.19)

Intercept	$E(c_i)$	β_i^{net}
−0.512	0.042	1.449
(−1.48)	(2.21)	(2.53)

Intercept	$E(c_i)$	β_{1i}	β_{2i}	β_{3i}	β_{4i}
−0.089	0.033	0.992	−151.152	7.087	−17.542
(−0.16)	(0.16)	(0.47)	(−0.28)	(0.09)	(−1.13)

Intercept	$E(c_i)$	β_{1i}	β_i^{net}
−0.333	0.034	−3.181	4.334
(−0.91)	(—)	(−1.00)	(1.10)

Source: Acharya and Pedersen (2005), Table 4.

Exercises

Exercise 1

Let there be an asset whose expected value at the end of the year is $150. The required risk-adjusted return, determined for example by the CAPM, is 6%. The transaction cost (bid–ask spread) for liquidating the position is $3. How much should an investor pay for this asset? What is the (pre-transaction cost) expected return?

Solution

The net proceeds from holding the security for one year and then selling it are $150 - 3$. A present-value calculation gives the value:

$$P = \frac{150 - 3}{1.06} = 138.68$$

In terms of expected return:

$$E(R) = \frac{150 - P}{P} = 8.16\%$$

Note that this expected return is higher than the risk-adjusted required return (6%), since it includes a compensation for the bid–ask spread (the remaining 2.16%, which is reasonably close to the relative bid–ask spread $3/150 = 2\%$).

Exercise 2

Consider the model from section 7.1 with annual parameters $d = 5, r = 5\%, S = 3\%, \mu = 0.5$. Apply the Amihud and Mendelson (1986) model to find both the asset price if there are no transaction costs and the price with transaction costs. Also, calculate the price change when the bid–ask spread narrows from $S = 3\%$ to $S = 2\%$.

Solution

The price without transaction costs would be:

$$P^* = \frac{5}{0.05} = 100$$

The price with 1.5% expected transaction costs ($\mu S = 0.5 \times 3\%$) is:

$$P = \frac{5}{0.05 + 0.015} = 76.92$$

A reduction of the spread from 3% to 2% would lead to a price of:

$$P = \frac{5}{0.05 + 0.01} = 83.33$$

or an increase of more than 8%. So, stock prices can be very sensitive to fluctuations in liquidity.

References

Acharya, V. V. and L. H. Pedersen, 2005, 'Asset pricing with liquidity risk', *Journal of Financial Economics*, 77, 375–410.

Amihud, Y. 2002, 'Illiquidity and stock returns: cross-section and time-series effects', *Journal of Financial Markets*, 5, 31–56.

Amihud, Y. and H. Mendelson, 1986, 'Asset pricing and the bid–ask spread', *Journal of Financial Economics*, 17, 223–49.

Brennan, M. J. and A. Subrahmanyam, 1996, 'Market microstructure and asset pricing: on the compensation for illiquidity in stock returns', *Journal of Financial Economics*, 41, 441–64.

Chordia, T., R. Roll and A. Subrahmanyam, 2000, 'Commonality in liquidity', *Journal of Financial Economics*, 56, 3–28.

   2001, 'Market liquidity and trading activity', *Journal of Finance*, 52, 501–30.

Duarte, J. and L. Young, 2007, 'Why is PIN priced?', *Journal of Financial Economics*, 70, 223–60.

Easley, D., S. Hvidkjaer and M. O'Hara, 2002, 'Is information risk a determinant of asset returns?', *Journal of Finance*, 57, 2185–221.

Fama, E. F. and K. R. French, 1993, 'Common risk factors in the returns on stocks and bonds', *Journal of Financial Economics*, 33, 3–56.

Glosten, L. and L. Harris, 1988, 'Estimating the components of the bid/ask spread', *Journal of Financial Economics*, 21, 123–42.

Greene, W. H. 2002, *Econometric Analysis*, 5th edn, New York: Prentice Hall.

Hasbrouck, J. 1991, 'Measuring the information content of stock trades', *Journal of Finance*, 46, 179–207.

Hasbrouck, J. and D. Seppi, 2001, 'Common factors in prices, order flows, and liquidity', *Journal of Financial Economics*, 59, 383–411.

Pastor, L. and R. F. Stambaugh, 2003, 'Liquidity risk and expected stock returns', *Journal of Political Economy*, 111, 642–85.

Piqueira, N. S. 2004, 'Stock returns, illiquidity cost and excessive trading activity', unpublished manuscript, Princeton University.

Sadka, R. 2006, 'Momentum and post-earnings-announcement drift anomalies: the role of liquidity risk', *Journal of Financial Economics*, 80, 309–49.

8 Models of the limit order book

The models presented in the previous chapters describe the price formation process in markets with different structures. As we saw in Figure 1.2, among the markets with trade pricing rules, those governed by an order-driven execution system can be organized either as a continuous or as a call auction, while markets with a quote-driven system can be either a bilateral dealer market or a continuous auction that works as a limit order book. Within this outline, the Glosten and Milgrom (1985) model describes a bilateral quote-driven market in which dealers' competition guarantees semi-strong efficiency; Kyle's (1985) model proxies an order-driven call auction market where a specialist, or a number of market-makers, sets the market-clearing price after observing his, or their, customers' aggregated order flow. Finally, the Grossman and Stiglitz (1980) model proxies an order-driven market where all participants can submit their demand schedules simultaneously.[1] Since each demand function is a fairly accurate representation of a large number of small limit orders (Brown and Zhang, 1997), this market can be interpreted as a limit order book. As the next section shows, this interpretation has the advantage of considering all market participants as potential liquidity suppliers, i.e. of embodying the order-driven feature of a limit order book (LOB); it fails, however, to incorporate either the discriminatory pricing rule that characterizes an LOB or the agents' strategic choices between limit orders and market orders. Section 8.1 will introduce the reader to the discriminatory pricing rule and will sketch a basic model that embodies this rule; in this model, however, agents cannot choose the type of order to submit to the LOB, so section 8.2 presents models in which the choice between market and limit orders is endogenous.

8.1 Glosten (1994) and the discriminatory pricing rule

In the models of both Kyle (1985) and Grossman and Stiglitz (1980), the equilibrium auction pricing rule is uniform in the sense that it generates a single price at

---

[1] It is worth noticing that when prices reveal quantities, the two market structures can be strategically equivalent, since submitting a demand schedule conditional on prices is equivalent to observing the quantities.

which all orders are executed; in Glosten and Milgrom (1985) each order is executed at a different price, which is determined by the conditional expectation rule (see Chapter 4); however, the customer pays the same marginal price for each unit in the same order. One of the peculiarities of the LOB, by contrast, is that an order can be satisfied at different prices, as limit sell (buy) orders can be executed at or above (below) their limit price. It follows that within an LOB each market order or marketable limit order larger than the quantity available at the inside spread can be filled at different prices, by absorbing the liquidity available at the best bid offer and then walking up (or down) the book. Because buy (sell) orders can be executed at increasing (decreasing) limit prices, when a liquidity supplier posts his price and quantity he will take into account that his price can be picked up not only by traders willing to trade the quantity he offers, as in Glosten and Milgrom, but also by agents willing to submit larger orders. Hence, if the order size is a proxy for the private information held by the customer submitting the order, the liquidity supplier will quote a price that is higher than the one he would post in a bilateral transaction as in Glosten and Milgrom.

The simple model presented in this section shows how liquidity suppliers choose their limit orders in an LOB. To stress the relevance of the discriminatory pricing rule that governs limit order books, we consider the liquidity supplier's decision problem as a screening game where first a large number of risk-neutral market-makers post prices and quantities and subsequently one strategic informed trader optimally chooses the amount he desires to trade.

Following Biais, Martimort and Rochet (2000), the final value of the risky asset is set equal to $\widetilde{v} = \widetilde{s} + \widetilde{\varepsilon}$ where $\widetilde{s}$ is privately observed by informed traders so that $\widetilde{\varepsilon}$ is a source of noise in the informed traders' signal. $\widetilde{\varepsilon}$ has zero mean and variance σ^2. For simplicity, it is assumed that $\widetilde{s}$ takes discrete values, s^L and s^H (and $-s^L$ and $-s^H$) with equal probability. At the beginning of the trading game, the informed trader also observes, with probability $\frac{1}{3}$, his endowment shock, which can be positive $(+I)$, in which case the agent holds a long position in the asset; negative $(-I)$, when the agent holds a short position; or zero. The extensive form of the screening game is the following:

- firstly, nature chooses s and I, and this information is learned by the informed agent;
- secondly, competitive market-makers post their limit orders;
- thirdly, the strategic risk-averse informed agent optimally chooses the quantity that maximizes his expected utility, and trading takes place;
- finally, $\widetilde{\varepsilon}$ and hence $\widetilde{v}$ are realized.

It is assumed that, if the informed agent trades at time t, his final wealth is equal to:

$$W_t = (q_t + I_t)v_t - p(q_t)q_t \tag{8.1}$$

where q_t is the total quantity that the informed agent trades and $p(q_t)$ is the average price paid for q_t.

In equilibrium the informed trader will submit a market order that can hit one or more of the posted prices; hence the total quantity traded by the agent can be split into various parts, each one executed at a different price. This is again the intuition behind the discriminatory pricing rule of the LOB. As orders can walk up (or down) the book, orders larger than the quantity associated with the best price on the opposite side of the market will be executed at different prices.

As before, the risk-averse informed agent with absolute risk-aversion parameter ρ solves the following maximization problem:

$$\text{Max}_{x} \quad E[\widetilde{W}_t | s_t, I_t] - \frac{\rho}{2} Var[\widetilde{W}_t | s_t, I_t] \tag{8.2}$$

$$= (q_t + I_t)s_t - p(q_t)q_t - \frac{\rho}{2}\sigma^2(q_t + I_t)^2$$

$$= \left(I_t s_t - \frac{\rho}{2}\rho\sigma^2 I_t^2\right) + s_t q_t - \rho\sigma^2 I_t q_t - \frac{\rho}{2}\sigma^2 q_t^2 - p(q_t)q_t \tag{8.3}$$

$$= \left(I_t s_t - \frac{\rho}{2}\rho\sigma^2 I_t^2\right) + \left(\theta_t q_t - \frac{\rho}{2}\sigma^2 q_t^2 - p(q_t)q_t\right) \tag{8.4}$$

where, as in Biais, Martimort and Rochet (2000), $\theta_t = s_t - \rho\sigma^2 I_t$ is a mix of the agent's informational and risk-sharing motivations to trade. θ_t can be interpreted as the agent's marginal valuation for the asset, which is increasing in the signal and, because of risk aversion, decreasing in the size of his initial position, I_t. Notice that the first term of equation (8.4) measures the reservation utility of the agent, that he would get if he did not participate in the market, while the second term measures the agent's gains from trades or, intuitively, his informational rent. θ_t characterizes the informed agent's willingness to trade and because it is a linear combination of his private signal and endowment shock, it represents an ambiguous message from the customer to the liquidity supplier that does not reveal whether the agent is speculating on his private signal or is hedging his endowment shock. Given the distribution of $\widetilde{s}$ and $\widetilde{I}$, and assuming as in Buti (2007) that $s^L = s^H - \rho\sigma^2 I = \rho\sigma^2 I$, with $s^H = 2\rho\sigma^2 I$, then $\widetilde{\theta}$ has the distribution shown in Table 8.1.

Liquidity suppliers know that in the market there are three types of agents, each willing to trade a different quantity signalled by θ_1, θ_2 and θ_3, and they will submit their limit orders conditional on each type. As in Glosten and Milgrom (1985), it is assumed that the risk-neutral liquidity suppliers behave competitively and drive liquidity suppliers' expected profits to zero so that the marginal price they set is equal to their expected future value of the asset $(\widetilde{s})$, conditional on the information they hold on the incoming agent's type $\widetilde{\theta}$ which could hit that price:[2]

$$\pi^{LS} = E\left[(p(\widetilde{\theta}) - \widetilde{s})\, q(\widetilde{\theta}) | \vartheta \geq \widetilde{\theta}\right] = 0$$

where $\widetilde{\theta} \in (\theta_1, \theta_2, \theta_3)$, and $p(\widetilde{\theta})$ and $q(\widetilde{\theta})$ are the marginal quantities and the associated prices offered by the liquidity supplier on the grid of the LOB. Notice that, by assumption, $\widetilde{\theta}$ is increasing in the agents' willingness to trade $(\theta_1 < \theta_2 < \theta_3)$

---

[2] The subscript t is removed from here onward as the model is solved for one period only.

Table 8.1. *Distribution of $\tilde{\theta}$*

			$\tilde{I}$ prob.		
			$\frac{1}{3}$	$\frac{1}{3}$	$\frac{1}{3}$
			$+I$	0	$-I$
$\tilde{s}$ prob.	$\frac{1}{4}$	s^H	$s^H - \rho\sigma^2 I =$ $\rho\sigma^2 I = \theta_1$	$s^H =$ $2\rho\sigma^2 I = \theta_2$	$s^H + \rho\sigma^2 I =$ $3\rho\sigma^2 I = \theta_3$
	$\frac{1}{4}$	s^L	$s^L - \rho\sigma^2 I = 0$	$s^L =$ $\rho\sigma^2 I = \theta_1$	$s^L + \rho\sigma^2 I =$ $2\rho\sigma^2 I = \theta_2$
	$\frac{1}{4}$	$-s^L$	$-s^L - \rho\sigma^2 I =$ $-2\rho\sigma^2 I = -\theta_2$	$-s^L =$ $-\rho\sigma^2 I = -\theta_1$	$-s^L + \rho\sigma^2 I = 0$
	$\frac{1}{4}$	$-s^H$	$-s^H - \rho\sigma^2 I =$ $-3\rho\sigma^2 I = -\theta_3$	$-s^H =$ $-2\rho\sigma^2 I = -\theta_2$	$-s^H + \rho\sigma^2 I =$ $-\rho\sigma^2 I = -\theta_1$

and liquidity suppliers cannot discriminate among types of agent; hence, when posting their limit prices, say for agent θ_1, they anticipate that this price can be hit by any agent with a $\tilde{\theta}$ which is equal to or higher than θ_1. This is due to the fact that any order can walk up or down the LOB. Consequently, the equilibrium ask prices will not be conditioned on the trader's type as in Glosten and Milgrom (1985), but will be *upper-tail expectations*:

$$p(\theta_i) = E[\tilde{v}|\theta \geq \theta_i] = \frac{\sum_{j\geq i}^{3} \Pr(\theta_j)E(\tilde{v}|\theta_j)}{\sum_{j\geq i}^{3} \Pr(\theta_j)} \quad \text{with } i = 1, \ldots, 3 \quad (8.5)$$

(and, symmetrically, the bid prices will be *lower-tail expectations*), where $\Pr(\theta_j)$ is the probability that the incoming agent is of θ_j type.

Given the signal distribution and the (8.5) pricing rule, the three ask prices posted by the liquidity suppliers are:[3]

$$\left.\begin{aligned} p(\theta_3) &= E[\tilde{V}|\theta \geq \theta_3] = 2\rho\sigma^2 I \\ p(\theta_2) &= E[\tilde{V}|\theta \geq \theta_2] = \frac{5}{3}\rho\sigma^2 I \\ p(\theta_1) &= E[\tilde{V}|\theta \geq \theta_1] = \frac{8}{5}\rho\sigma^2 I \end{aligned}\right\} \quad (8.6)$$

As mentioned, liquidity suppliers offer limit prices, so they quote prices and the associated quantities. Liquidity suppliers will offer those quantities that maximize each agent's gains from trade as defined in equation (8.4), by taking into account the fact that at each price $p(\theta_i)$ the agent cannot submit an order larger than $\sum_{j\leq i} q^*(\theta_j)$.

---

[3] Given the symmetric distribution of the signals, the bid prices can be obtained analogously.

It follows that the quantities offered by the liquidity suppliers at each price $p(\theta_i)$ are those that maximize the following traders' gains from trade:

$$\theta_i \sum_{j \leq i} q^*(\theta_j) - \frac{\rho}{2}\sigma^2 \left(\sum_{j \leq i} q^*(\theta_j)\right)^2 - \left(\sum_{j \leq i} p(\theta_j)q^*(\theta_j)\right) \quad \text{with } i = 1, \ldots, 3$$

(8.7)

which are equal to:

$$q^*(\theta_1) = 0$$
$$q^*(\theta_2) = \frac{1}{3}I$$
$$q^*(\theta_3) = \frac{2}{3}I$$

Notice that, given the signal distribution, $p(\theta_1)$ is higher than the signal θ_1 and liquidity suppliers will offer a quantity equal to zero to agents of type θ_1, as they anticipate that nobody will be willing to trade at that price. Notice also that both equilibrium prices and quantities are increasing functions of the signal $\tilde{\theta}$.

Finally, the equilibrium prices can be compared to those prevailing in a dealership market à la Glosten and Milgrom, $p^{GM}(\theta_j)$, where:

$$p^{GM}(\theta_3) = E[\tilde{V}|\theta = \theta_3] = E[\tilde{V}|\theta \geq \theta_3] = 2\rho\sigma^2 I$$
$$p^{GM}(\theta_2) = E[\tilde{V}|\theta = \theta_2] = \frac{3}{2}\rho\sigma^2 I$$
$$p^{GM}(\theta_1) = E[\tilde{V}|\theta = \theta_1] = \frac{3}{2}\rho\sigma^2 I$$

As expected, under the upper-tail expectation rule the prices quoted by the liquidity suppliers are higher than those obtained with the conditional expectation rule, $p(\theta_i) \geq p^{GM}(\theta_i)$.

8.1.1   The model for an LOB with risk-averse imperfectly competitive dealers

As mentioned above, the model in Glosten (1994) shows the working of an LOB under the assumption that liquidity suppliers behave competitively.[4] Viswanathan and Wang (2002) remove the assumption of perfect competition and asymmetric information, and assume that a finite number of risk-averse dealers compete strategically to supply liquidity in an LOB. The model setup draws on section 5.2.2, where a dealership market with imperfectly competitive liquidity provision was presented. As before, M risk-averse dealers face a group of liquidity traders, x; to derive the discriminatory pricing

---

[4] Glosten (1994) also shows that the competitive LOB is competition-proof against any anonymous rival market. By removing the assumption that all liquidity suppliers submit their limit orders simultaneously, Seppi (1997) shows that a monopolistic specialist who competes against an LOB can provide additional liquidity, because of the different timing of the two liquidity provisions. Liquidity providers on the LOB submit their pricing schedules before observing the realization of the incoming order; the specialist, however, can improve his price after observing it. Furthermore, Parlour and Seppi (1993) analyse the competition between a pure LOB and an LOB with specialists, whereas Buti (2007) shows that, because of relationship trading, a non-anonymous specialist market can improve upon a pure LOB.

equilibrium, however, two new assumptions are introduced. Firstly, it is assumed that x, liquidity trading, is uniformly distributed[5] over the interval $[0, 1]$ and hence has a distribution function $G(x) = x$ and density function $g(x) = 1$. Secondly, it is assumed that dealers have mean variance preferences,[6] and for simplicity $I_j = 0$. It follows that each dealer's objective function is the one given in equation (5.9):

$$\underset{q_j}{\text{Max}} \ E[\widetilde{W}_j] - \frac{A}{2} Var[\widetilde{W}_j] \tag{8.8}$$

However, here, the end-of-period profits of bidder j are:

$$\widetilde{W}_j = q_j(p)\widetilde{F} - \int_0^{q_j} p(y)dy$$

where $\int_0^{q_j} p(y) \, dy$ is his total payment under the discriminatory pricing rule.

As x is the total amount of supply, let $h(p) = x - \sum_{i \neq j} q_i(p)$ be bidder j's (upward-sloping) residual supply curve; then, following Viswanathan and Wang (2002), dealer j chooses his optimal bidding strategy both by taking into account the strategies of the other dealers, and by maximizing the following derived mean-variance utility function:[7]

$$E\left[\widetilde{F} \, h(p) - \frac{A\sigma^2}{2} (h(p))^2 - \int_0^{q_j} p(y) \, dy\right] \tag{8.9}$$

Viswanathan and Wang (2002) show that the jth dealer's optimization decision can be solved as a control problem to obtain:

$$p = \overline{F} - A\sigma^2 q_j(p) + \frac{1 - x}{\sum_{i \neq j}^M \frac{dq_i(p)}{dp}} \tag{8.10}$$

Expression (8.10) shows the marginal price offered by dealer j for quantity q. To obtain the jth dealer's equilibrium demand it is assumed that each dealer conjectures the following demand schedule for the other $M - 1$ dealers:

$$q_i = \xi - \beta p \quad \forall \, i = 1, \ldots, M, \, i \neq j \tag{8.11}$$

Substituting into the market-clearing condition $x + \sum_{i=1}^M q_i = 0$, yields $x = M(\xi - \beta p)$; plugging into (8.10) and rearranging terms, we obtain:

$$q_j = \frac{\overline{F}}{A\sigma^2} - \frac{1 - M\xi}{(M - 1)\beta A\sigma^2} - \frac{(2M - 1)}{(M - 1)A\sigma^2} p \tag{8.12}$$

Equating expression (8.12) to the dealer's conjectured demand function, we derive the equilibrium parameters β and ξ:

---

[5] Uniform distribution is the simplest case, but any bounded distribution for x would be fine in this context.
[6] Notice that with discriminatory auctions, CARA utility and normality are no longer equivalent to a quadratic utility function. For simplicity, the latter is assumed here; Appendix F in Viswanathan and Wang (2002) presents a formulation with a CARA utility function.
[7] Notice that this objective function is reminiscent of equation (8.7).

$$\beta = \frac{2M - 1}{(M - 1)A\sigma^2} \tag{8.13}$$

$$\xi = \beta\overline{F} - \frac{1}{M - 1}$$

together with the optimal dealer's demand function:

$$q_j = \frac{(2M - 1)\overline{F} - A\sigma^2}{(M - 1)A\sigma^2} - \frac{2M - 1}{(M - 1)A\sigma^2}p \tag{8.14}$$

or bid schedule:

$$\widetilde{p}_j = \overline{F} - \frac{A\sigma^2}{2M - 1} - \frac{(M - 1)A\sigma^2}{2M - 1}q \tag{8.15}$$

Substituting the equilibrium strategy (8.14) into the market-clearing condition, the following equilibrium price obtains:

$$\widetilde{p} = \overline{F} - \frac{A\sigma^2}{M - 2} - \frac{A\sigma^2(M - 1)}{(2M - 1)}\frac{\widetilde{x}}{M} \tag{8.16}$$

Now conclusions can be drawn from a comparison of the solution derived for the discriminatory pricing rule, expressions (8.15) and (8.16), with the solution derived for the uniform pricing rule in section 5.2.2. Setting $I_j = 0$ for consistency, equations (5.20) and (5.21) read:

$$\widetilde{p}_j = \overline{F} - \frac{(M - 1)A\sigma^2}{M - 2}q \tag{8.17}$$

$$\widetilde{p} = \overline{F} - \frac{A\sigma^2(M - 1)}{M - 2}\frac{\widetilde{x}}{M} \tag{8.18}$$

Firstly, let us note that the equilibrium bidding schedule is flatter in the limit order market (8.15) than in the uniform price market (8.17); this is because with price discrimination, competition for liquidity provision intensifies. Figure 8.1 plots the bid schedule under the discriminatory (8.16) and the uniform pricing rules (8.18) for different numbers of dealers: competition modifies only the slope of the uniform pricing schedule, but for the discriminatory schedule it also changes the intercept.

As mentioned, the model in Viswanathan and Wang (2002) does not allow for asymmetric information among market participants. Biais, Martimort and Rochet (2000) introduce adverse selection in a model with the discriminatory pricing rule and show how imperfect competition among dealers within an LOB can be modelled as a game with multiple principals, where each dealer (principal) chooses his optimal trading strategy under the participation and incentive constraints of the investor (agent).

8.2 The model for an LOB with endogenous choice between limit and market orders

In Glosten (1994), as well as in Viswanathan and Wang (2002) and Biais, Martimort and Rochet (2000), liquidity suppliers can only submit limit orders and liquidity demanders can only use market orders to hit the existing quotes; it follows that in these

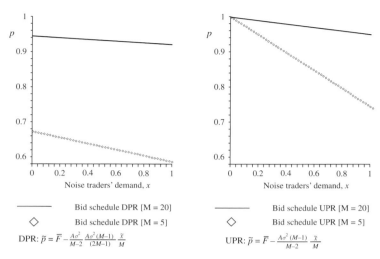

Figure 8.1. Equilibrium bid schedules. Equilibrium bid schedules under both the discriminatory pricing rule (DPR) (equation 8.16) and the uniform pricing rule (UPR) (equation 8.18) for different numbers of dealers ($M = 5, 20$); $A = 2$, $\sigma^2 = 0.5$, $\overline{F} = 1$.

models agents are not allowed to choose between limit and market orders. In real markets, of course, at the very least the agents submitting orders to an LOB can choose between limit and market orders.

The choice between limit and market orders is a strategic element in any trading decision and depends on the relative probability of execution of the two orders, which in turn depends on a variety of factors, such as the asymmetry of the personal evaluations of the risky asset between the agents who submit the orders and those who hit the existing quotes, their degree of patience, their waiting costs and the state of the LOB. In the recent literature there are a few models for an LOB which embody the choice between market and limit orders; with the exception of Goettler, Parlour and Rajan (2008), in these early models there is no asymmetric information on the asset value.[8] It is important, however, to understand the theory on the optimal traders' submission strategies even when transaction costs are not due to informational asymmetries because there is evidence that non-informational frictions can be substantial; for example, Huang and Stoll (1997) show that on average they account for more than 80 per cent of the spread.

---

[8] The microstructure literature has long assumed that informed traders do not submit limit orders but rather exploit their information using market orders. Kumar and Seppi (1998) is one of the few models that have integrated market and limit orders with asymmetric information. Glosten (1989) includes informed traders among limit order submitters and shows how this is consistent with a linear rational expectations equilibrium. Chakravarty and Holden (1995) and Kaniel and Liu (1998) extend the Glosten–Milgrom framework to include limit orders. Within this setting, Chakravarty and Holden show that informed traders optimally chose a combination of limit and market orders whenever the terminal value of the asset is inside the bid–ask spread, whereas Kaniel and Liu show that informed traders decide optimally to submit limit rather than market orders when their private information is long-lived. Finally, in their experimental work, Bloomfield, O'Hara and Saar (2002) show that in an electronic centralized market, liquidity arises endogenously from limit orders placed not only by uninformed traders but also by the informed.

   In the rest of this chapter three models will be outlined in which the choice between limit and market orders is the key element of traders' optimization strategies. The model by Parlour (1998) concentrates on the time priority rule, which governs limit order books, and shows how the choice between market and limit orders depends crucially on the state of both sides of the book at the time the order is submitted. Foucault's (1999) model of price formation focuses instead on the winner's curse problem, which arises when limit order submitters cannot cancel their orders and, due to the arrival of public information, run the risk of being picked off by incoming traders submitting market orders. In the model by Foucault, Kadan and Kandel (2005) the determinants of the price formation process and of the strategic order submission choice are instead the speed of agents' arrival on the market, their waiting costs and the relative number of patient and impatient traders. Although the work is not presented in this chapter, the reader should be aware that Rosu (2004) extends the Foucault, Kadan and Kandel model by allowing both limit order traders to cancel their orders and prices to take continuous values.[9]

8.2.1   The Parlour model

Parlour's (1998) model considers the choice between market and limit orders to show the working of a limit order book. In her simplified world there are only strategic risk-neutral liquidity traders who are endowed with a different evaluation of the risky asset and arrive randomly at the market to submit either a market order (*MO*) or a limit order (*LO*). The novelty of this model is precisely the choice of the type of order to submit. As will be clarified below, this is not a model of price formation, since it assumes an exogenously given bid–ask spread at which traders can submit their orders; however, it introduces the strategic interaction between traders and the state of the limit order book, which is an important element previously disregarded by the literature on the functioning of an LOB. Furthermore, this model does not consider asymmetric information on the fundamental value of the asset; since traders are endowed only with their personal evaluation of the asset, they cannot exploit any information on its future value; it follows that in this model there are no adverse selection costs, nor are there inventory costs, since there are no market-makers offering liquidity. The spread is simply due to order processing costs.

   As mentioned above, the choice each trader faces between market orders and limit orders is influenced by his estimate of the probability of execution, which depends both on the depth of the book at the time of the order submission and on the number of orders that may arrive over the remainder of the day. All traders coming to the marketplace take this updating process into account and in equilibrium the traders' behaviour generates systematic patterns in transaction prices and order placement strategies. The results from this model show that both sides of the book affect agents' order placing

---

[9] Rosu's model also removes two assumptions, namely that buy and sell orders must alternate and that new orders must improve on the current limit orders by at least one tick.

strategies, and enable us to explain some of the well-known price patterns established, for instance, by Biais, Hillion and Spatt (1995).

The model describes traders' interactions during a trading day divided into $T + 1$ periods: $t = 0, \ldots, T$. At time T, trading finishes as during a real trading day. It is assumed that only one risky asset is traded and that it pays v units when the game is over; furthermore, each trader who comes to the market can submit only one order for one unit, and the order is irreversible. The prices at which the trader can buy or sell the asset are given as equal to A (ask price) and B (bid price) respectively, and are symmetric around the final value, v. It is also assumed that the difference between the ask and the bid prices is equal to twice the tick size, k, which is the minimum price increment traders are allowed to quote over the existing price.[10] Hence, at any time t, the book, b_t, is characterized by the number of shares that are available at each of these prices. Notice that, as the ask and bid prices are exogenously fixed, this is not a standard model of price formation. Furthermore, it is assumed that at the ask and bid prices there exists a trading crowd that absorbs any amount of the risky asset offered by the incoming trader. This assumption is necessary to contain the book within the standing ask and bid prices. The existence of the trading crowd does not allow for any competition on prices; however, since the limit orders have time priority over the crowd, it does not prevent the time priority rule from working as it does in real markets. If a trader at time t submits a market buy order ($MOB = -1^A$), it will be transacted at the ask price, A, and executed against the limit order with the highest time priority available on the ask side; if he submits a market sell order ($MOS = -1^B$), it will be transacted at the bid price, B, and hit the limit buy order with the highest precedence on the bid side; if instead he submits a limit buy order ($LOB = +1^B$), or a limit sell order ($LOS = +1^A$), this will be executed only if in the remaining $T - t$ periods the number of market sell or buy orders that reach the market is larger than the number of limit buy or sell orders that are present at the bid or ask price at the time the order is submitted.[11] For instance, if at time $T - 1$ the incoming trader submits a limit buy order at the bid, his order will be executed only if at time T a market sell order is entered; if, however, at time $T - 1$ there is already one limit buy order on the book, the trader's limit buy order will not be executed. This is the reason why, given the model's assumptions, traders submit only market orders at time T.

Traders come to the market sequentially, and at each period only one trader arrives; this trader is characterized by his personal evaluation of the risky asset, β, which can be derived from a continuous distribution with values $[\underline{\beta}, \overline{\beta}]$. Since there is no reason to assume that traders hold asymmetric valuations of the final value of the asset, we need to set β_t so that it is symmetrical around 1:

$$0 \leq \underline{\beta} \leq 1 \leq \overline{\beta}$$

---

[10] The fundamental value of the asset is therefore equal to the spread mid-quote, i.e. $v = (A + B)/2$, with $A = v + k$ and $B = v - k$.

[11] Notice that a market sell order reduces depth on the bid side by one unit (-1^B), whereas a limit sell order increases depth on the ask side by one unit ($+1^A$).

Table 8.2. *Strategies and expected profits*

Strategy	Expected profits
Market sell order (*MOS*)	$B - \beta_t v$
Limit sell order (*LOS*)	$(A - \beta_t v) P_{t+i}^B$
Limit buy order (*LOB*)	$(\beta_t v - B) P_{t+i}^S$
Market buy order (*MOB*)	$\beta_t v - A$

For simplicity, we further assume that traders' valuations of the asset are drawn from a uniform distribution:

$$\beta \sim U[0, 2]$$

Notice that, given his own β, each trader's evaluation of the future value of the asset will be equal to βv. Unlike Parlour (1998), this model does not determine the direction of each agent's trade by an exogenous parameter, but makes it depend only on the value of β. Because of risk-neutrality, each trader arriving at the market at time t maximizes his expected profits by choosing one of the orders listed in Table 8.2.

It follows that he will submit a market buy order if the price he pays for the asset is lower than his valuation ($A < \beta_t v$), and he will submit a market sell order in the contrary case ($\beta_t v < B$). Notice that the profits from a limit buy or sell order depend on the probabilities P_{t+i}^S and P_{t+i}^B, with $i = 1, \ldots, T - t$, of observing a market sell or buy order at time $t + i$. In fact, as mentioned above, the profitability of a limit buy order at time t depends on its probability of execution, i.e. the probability of observing a market sell order at time $t + i$. Notice also that the profits from a sell order are decreasing in β_t, whereas those of a buy order are increasing. It follows that agents whose valuation is very low will sell, whereas those with a high valuation will buy. On account of the recursive structure of this game, there always exists an equilibrium for any parameter formulation. The optimal trading strategy at time t depends on the probability of execution of the limit orders at time $t + 1$, which in turn depends on the future probability of execution at time $t + 2$, and so on up to time T. However, since traders can only submit market orders at time T, the probability of execution of a limit order at time $T - 1$ is known; this allows us to compute, by backward induction, all the probabilities of execution at previous periods back to time t when the order is submitted. Clearly, the higher the number of the remaining periods, the more complicated the model's solution.

We will start by characterizing an agent's optimal order submission strategy at time $T - 1$. Clearly, in order to compute the agent's expected profits at $T - 1$, we need to calculate the probability of observing a market order at time T. This is straightforward: at time T the arriving agent will submit either a market buy or a market sell order depending on whether his valuation of the asset is higher (or lower) than the price he pays (or gets). These conditions are satisfied for these values of β_T:

$$\text{submit } MOB \text{ if } \beta_T v > A \qquad \text{i.e. } \beta_T > \frac{A}{v}$$

$$\text{submit } MOS \text{ if } B > \beta_T v \qquad \text{i.e. } \beta_T < \frac{B}{v}$$

Remembering that β is uniformly distributed between 0 and 2, the probabilities of observing a market buy or a market sell order at T are equal to:

$$P_T^B = \frac{2 - \frac{A}{v}}{2} = \frac{2 - \frac{v+k}{v}}{2} = \frac{v - k}{2v} = \frac{1}{2} - \frac{k}{2v}$$

$$P_T^S = \frac{\frac{B}{v}}{2} = \frac{v - k}{2v} = \frac{1}{2} - \frac{k}{2v}$$

Now we can compute the agent's optimal strategy at time $T-1$, $\phi_{T-1}(\beta_{T-1}, b_{T-1})$, which depends on his personal valuation of the asset, β_{T-1}, and on the state of the book, b_{T-1}. In the following example we will assume that at $T-1$ the book (b_{T-1}) is empty on both sides. Thus we can characterize in terms of $\beta_{T-1}^{(0,0)}$ the solutions obtained. Figure 8.2 shows a graphical representation of the four possible strategies, $\phi_{T-1}(\beta_{T-1}, b_{T-1})$, that each agent may select when coming to the market at time $T-1$. On the horizontal axis the following threshold values for $\beta_{T-1}^{(0,0)}$ are shown:

$$\beta_{T-1}^{(0,0)} \in \begin{cases} [\beta = 0 & \beta^S(P_T^B)] & \phi_{T-1} = -1^B & MOS \\ [\underline{\beta}^S(P_T^B) & \overline{\beta}^S(P_T^B)] & \phi_{T-1} = +1^A & LOS \\ [\underline{\beta}^B(P_T^S) & \overline{\beta}^B(P_T^S)] & \phi_{T-1} = +1^B & LOB \\ [\overline{\beta}^B(P_T^S) & \overline{\beta} = 2] & \phi_{T-1} = -1^A & MOB \end{cases}$$

where:

$$\underline{\beta}^S(P_T^B) = \text{Max} \left[\frac{A}{v} - \frac{2k}{(1 - P_T^B)v}, \underline{\beta} \right] \text{ and}$$

$$\text{for } P_T^B \le \frac{B}{A}, \ \underline{\beta}^S(P_T^B) = \frac{A}{v} - \frac{2k}{(1 - P_T^B)v}$$

$$\overline{\beta}^B(P_T^S) = \text{Min} \left[\frac{B}{v} + \frac{2k}{(1 - P_T^S)v}, \overline{\beta} \right] \text{ and}$$

$$\text{for } P_T^S \le \frac{B}{A}, \ \overline{\beta}^B(P_T^S) = \frac{B}{v} + \frac{2k}{(1 - P_T^S)v}$$

$$\overline{\beta}^S(P_T^B) = \underline{\beta}^B(P_T^S) = 1$$

Agents with very low valuations will choose a market sell order and agents with very high values of β will submit a market buy order. Notice that to simplify the representation it has been assumed that $P_T^{B,S} \le B/A$, i.e. for $\beta = 0$ and $\beta = 2$, the expected

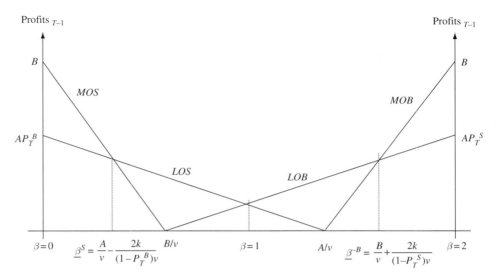

Figure 8.2. Trading profits. Profits from *MOS, LOS, LOB* and *MOB* at $T - 1$ under the hypothesis $P_T^B - P_T^S \leqslant B/A$.

profits from *MOS* and *MOB* are greater than those from *LOS* and *LOB* respectively.[12] This guarantees that *MOS* and *MOB* can be equilibrium strategies.[13] Under these assumptions, $\underline{\beta}^S(P_T^B) = A/v - 2k/[(1 - P_T^B)v]$ and $\overline{\beta}^B(P_T^S) = B/v + 2k/[(1 - P_T^S)v]$.

It is now possible to discuss how the state of the book affects agents' trading strategies. Figure 8.2 shows the intervals of the β values that are consistent with the four strategies; the larger the intervals, the higher the probability of submission. It follows that anything that increases the probability of observing a market order at time T, P_T^B and P_T^S, increases the ranges of β types who submit limit orders and decreases the range of β types who submit market orders at time $T - 1$. For instance, when the probability of observing a market buy order at T, P_T^B, increases, $\underline{\beta}^S(P_T^B)$ moves backwards and the probability of a limit sell order at time $T - 1$ increases.

For this reason, more generally, any trader at time $t - 1$ will take into account both the state of the book at the time of his order and the effect of his own trading strategies on trades in the following period; in fact, by changing the queue, his trade at time $t - 1$ can change the decisions of the traders that arrive during the next period, t. Clearly, a trader's degree of influence on agents' trading strategy in the next period depends on the relative depth of the book at the time of his order. It is therefore relevant to

---

[12] The assumption of equal probability of observing a market buy or a market sell order at the end of the trading game is also realistic, since there is no reason to impose any exogenous asymmetry on traders' behaviour when, at T, they can only submit market orders.

[13] The lowest valuation that is consistent with an *LOS*, $\underline{\beta}^S(P_T^B)$, can be obtained by equating the expected profits from an *MOS* and those from an *LOS*; as Figure 8.2 shows, for $\beta = 0$ the profits from an *MOS* are equal to B and those from an *LOS* are equal to AP_T^B, assuming that $P_T^B \leq B/A$ guarantees that the *MOS* and *LOS* profit functions will cross at $\beta > 0$.

understand more precisely how both the state of the book and the changes in the depth of the book at time $t-1$ affect the transaction probabilities at time t. For the sake of clarity and manageability, we only analyse the trading process up to $T-2$. Firstly, notice that at time $T-1$ only one side of the book matters; an agent willing to sell will only consider the depth of his own side of the book, since at time T no trader will submit limit orders. Conversely, at time $T-2$ the situation may change and, in choosing between a limit and a market order, the seller will also consider the other side of the book. The reason is that the state of the other side of the book may affect the next agent's trading decision. If, for example, the seller at time $T-2$ observes that there are no orders on the book at the bid, he will consider the fact that at time $T-1$ the potential buyer will more likely submit limit than market orders, which reduces the probability of execution of his own limit sell order at time $T-2$. Conversely, if he observes that the bid side is full, he will presume that over the following period the potential buyer will submit a market order, thus increasing the probability of execution of his own limit sell order at $T-2$. It follows that the probability of execution of a LOS at time $T-2$, P_{T-2}^{LOS}, which also depends on the probability of observing a MOB at time $T-1$, P_{T-1}^{B}, will be lower or higher, the emptier or deeper the opposite side of the book, and by contrast it will be higher or lower when its own side, ask, is empty or full:

$$P_{T-2}^{LOS}(0^B, b_{T-2}^A) \leq P_{T-2}^{LOS}(1^B, b_{T-2}^A)$$
$$P_{T-2}^{LOS}(b_{T-2}^B, 0^A) \geq P_{T-2}^{LOS}(b_{T-2}^B, 1^A)$$

As mentioned previously, this line of reasoning allows us to explain the diagonal effect found by Biais, Hillion and Spatt (1995) for the Paris Bourse: small market orders of the same sign are more frequent than small market orders with differing signs. In fact, if a market buy order is submitted at time t, then the depth at the ask is reduced by one unit; this increases (reduces) the probability of execution of LOS (LOB) orders at time $t+1$ and therefore, all else equal, it reduces (increases) the probability of execution of MOS (MOB) orders. It follows that at time $t+1$ there will be a greater probability of observing a market buy than a market sell order.

Finally, it is worth mentioning that this model can also be used to comment on Roll's result. Roll (1984) shows that under the assumption of no adverse selection and no inventory costs (an assumption that is shared by the model discussed so far), the covariance of successive price changes is equal to $-S^2/4$. As was discussed in Chapter 6, this result is obtained by assuming that the probability of reversal is the same as the probability of continuation. Now, if we take into account the effect of the state of the book on agents' decisions, the probability of continuation is greater than that of reversal ($q < \frac{1}{2}$, in Chapter 6 notation) and Roll's model underestimates the effective spread.

8.2.2   The winner's curse problem

As mentioned above, Foucault's (1999) model is based on the assumption that limit order submitters offer valuable options to incoming traders and, if they cannot cancel mispriced orders, they run the risk of being picked off by agents who exploit the new public information. It follows that agents set their bid and ask prices by considering the probability of adverse price changes due to the arrival of public information. Clearly, the greater the variance of the future value of the asset, the higher the risk that limit orders can be mispriced and therefore the wider the bid–ask spread will be.

Foucault (1999) considers a market for a single risky asset whose underlying value follows a random walk:

$$\widetilde{v}_{t+1} = \widetilde{v}_t + \widetilde{\varepsilon}_{t+1} \tag{8.19}$$

where $\widetilde{\varepsilon}_{t+1}$ is the innovation due to the arrival of public information, which can take the values $\pm\sigma$ with equal probabilities.

Traders arrive sequentially and place orders for one unit. Traders differ in their reservation price, i.e. the highest (lowest) price a buyer (seller) is willing to pay (receive) for the asset. For an agent arriving at time t, the reservation price $\widetilde{R}_t$ is given by:

$$\widetilde{R}_t = \widetilde{v}_t + \widetilde{y}_t \tag{8.20}$$

where y_t is the trader's private evaluation of the asset which is time-invariant, independent of the innovation in the asset value and can take two values with equal probabilities:

$$\begin{cases} \widetilde{y}_t = +L > 0 & \text{with } \Pr = \frac{1}{2} \\ \widetilde{y}_t = -L & \text{with } \Pr = \frac{1}{2} \end{cases} \tag{8.21}$$

$\widetilde{y}_t$ has the same interpretation as the parameter β in Parlour's model; however, it differs from that model in that the realization of traders' evaluation is always equal to $|L|$, so that traders' types are only characterized by the sign of $\widetilde{y}_t$. At each interval t there is a probability equal to $(1 - \rho)$ that the trading process will stop. Upon arrival, agents (who are assumed risk-neutral and profit-maximizers) must decide whether to place two limit orders[14] (one on each side of the market) or one market order, and they will take this decision by considering the orders' probability of execution. It is also assumed that in case of indifference between the two strategies, i.e. market and limit order, the trader will always choose the latter.[15] This assumption is introduced to get rid of mixed strategies and hence limit traders to pure strategies only. Once a trader decides to submit limit orders at time t, he cannot revise or cancel his orders, which will expire at the end of the following interval $t + 1$. These assumptions are crucial to understanding the possible states of the book that a trader faces when he comes to the market. In fact, if traders (who arrive sequentially) are only allowed to submit one unit

---

[14] Actually, in equilibrium, traders will obtain profits only from trading on one side of the market. However, to compute the equilibrium spread, it is assumed that each trader will also post a limit price on the other side; this limit order has no effect on his expected profits as it has zero probability of execution.

[15] In the case of perfect competition among liquidity suppliers, opting for market orders would not be viable without mixed strategies. In fact, when profits from limit orders are driven to zero by competition, they would never be posted if mixed strategies are ruled out.

per order (and in the case that they submit limit orders, these orders are cancelled after one period) the incoming trader always observes a book that is either empty or full.[16]

A trader arriving at time t and observing a book with state s_t, must decide on both an order choice strategy (market or limit order), and a quotation strategy, as if he opts for limit orders he has to quote the spread. It follows that to derive the equilibrium spread, one has to derive both the order choice and the quotation strategy. Here only the quotation strategy will be derived as it is sufficient to explain the main intuition offered by the model. Foucault's model is solved under the assumptions of both perfect and imperfect competition among limit order submitters. In what follows we will derive the model with perfect competition. The solution for the bid and ask prices under imperfect competition follows similar arguments. Notice, however, that here the assumption of perfect competition is only a simplifying device, not a realistic representation of the market. In fact, if traders arrive sequentially, there is no room for Bertrand competition as in the Glosten and Milgrom (1985) model. In that model, first dealers compete to quote the best prices, and only subsequently the liquidity takers arrive sequentially, hitting the quotes posted by liquidity suppliers.

With perfect competition the expected profits from limit orders are driven to zero, and hence the equilibrium limit order prices satisfy:

$$B(v_t, y_t) = R_t + E[(\Delta v_{t+1} | I(B) = +1, S_t)] \tag{8.22}$$

$$A(v_t, y_t) = R_t + E[(\Delta v_{t+1} | I(A) = +1), S_t] \tag{8.23}$$

where $\widetilde{S_t} = (\widetilde{v_t}, \widetilde{y_t}, s_t)$ indicates the state of the market at time t and $E[(\Delta \widetilde{v}_{t+1} | ., S_t]$ is the expected change in the asset's value conditional on selling $(I(A) = +1)$ or buying $(I(B) = +1)$ the asset. Notice that the right-hand side of equations (8.23) and (8.22) shows that limit order traders post ask (bid) prices equal to their initial reservation price $(R_t = v_t + y_t)$ adjusted by their conditional expected change in the asset value.

To obtain the equilibrium bid and ask prices, let us assume that a trader of type $+L$ comes into the market at time t and submits his orders.

Firstly we consider his optimal choice of the bid price B_t associated with his limit buy order. According to condition (8.22), the trader has to evaluate the expected price change conditional on the execution of his limit buy order, which is equal to:

$$E[(\Delta v_{t+1} | I(B) = +1, S_t)] = \Pr(\varepsilon_{t+1} = +\sigma | I(B) = +1)(+\sigma) \tag{8.24}$$

$$+ \Pr(\varepsilon_{t+1} = -\sigma | I(B) = +1)(-\sigma) = \pi(B)\sigma - (1 - \pi(B))\sigma = \sigma(2\pi(B) - 1)$$

where $\pi(B)$ is the probability that an increase in the asset value has occurred between time t and $t + 1$, conditional on the execution of the limit buy order with price B at time $t + 1$. Using Bayes' rule, $\pi(B)$ is equal to:

---

[16] Notice that it is assumed that when a trader submits limit orders, the next trader will be able to observe them and decide whether to pick them off; however, immediately after this trader has taken his decision, the limit orders expire.

$$\pi(B) = \frac{\Pr(I(B) = +1|\varepsilon_{t+1} = +\sigma)\Pr(\varepsilon_{t+1} = +\sigma)}{\Pr(I(B) = +1)}$$

$$= \frac{\Pr(I(B) = +1|\varepsilon_{t+1} = +\sigma)\Pr(\varepsilon_{t+1} = +\sigma)}{\Pr(I(B) = +1|\varepsilon_{t+1} = +\sigma)\Pr(\varepsilon_{t+1} = +\sigma) + \Pr(I(B) = +1|\varepsilon_{t+1} = -\sigma)\Pr(\varepsilon_{t+1} = -\sigma)}$$

It follows that to set the optimal bid price, one must calculate the probability of execution of the limit buy order, which in turns depends on the position of the bid price relative to the reservation price of the incoming trader, who will eventually submit a market sell order at time $t+1$ and hit the bid price.

Figure 8.3 shows the possible payoffs for the incoming trader at time $t+1$ when he submits a market sell order (*MOS*) or a market buy order (*MOB*) that will hit either $B(v_t, +L)$ or $A(v_t, +L)$. Notice that by assumption he will choose this option only if his payoff is strictly positive.[17] This is the reason why, when setting his bid price, the previous trader has to calculate all the possible bid prices corresponding to the incoming trader's different cut-off ranges and use them to evaluate and compare his market order payoffs. Table 8.3 reports the bid price ranges as well as the conditional and unconditional probabilities of execution of the limit buy order posted at time t according to the position of its price relative to the incoming trader's cut-off prices, which correspond, under the assumption of perfect competition, to his possible reservation prices. These cut-off prices determine the possible price ranges for the price B_t, and

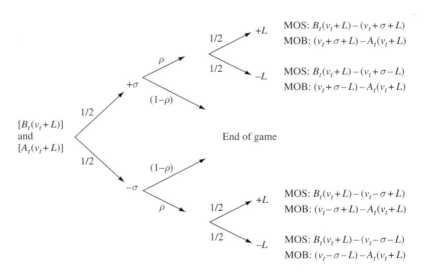

Figure 8.3. Payoff structure. The possible payoffs of an incoming trader who faces the bid price $B_t(V_t + L)$ and the ask price $A_t(V_t + L)$ and submits a market sell order (*MOS*) or a market buy order (*MOB*).

---

[17] Remember that by assumption an incoming trader gets zero expected profits from a limit order, and that in case of indifference between limit and market orders he will choose the latter.

Table 8.3. *Limit buy order unconditional* ($\Pr(I(B) = +1)$) *and conditional* $\Pr(I(B) == +1|\varepsilon_{t+1} = \pm\sigma)$ *execution probabilities, conditional probability of price increase* ($\pi(B)$), *conditional expected price change* ($E[.]$) *and possible bid prices* $B(v_{t+1} + L)$

Bid price ranges	$\Pr(I(B) = +1)$	$\Pr(I(B) = +1\mid \varepsilon_{t+1} = -\sigma)$	$\Pr(I(B) = +1\mid \varepsilon_{t+1} = +\sigma)$	$\pi(B)$	$E[(\Delta v_{t+1}\mid I(B) = +1), S_t]$	$B(v_{t+1}+L)$
$\sigma < L$						
$> v_t+L+\sigma$	ρ	ρ	ρ	$\frac{1}{2}$	0	v_t+L
$\in] v_t+L-\sigma, \; v_t+L+\sigma]$	$\frac{3}{4}\rho$	ρ	$\frac{\rho}{2}$	$\frac{1}{3}$	$-\frac{1}{3}\sigma$	$v_t+L-\frac{1}{3}\sigma$
$\in] v_t-L+\sigma, \; v_t+L-\sigma]$	$\frac{\rho}{2}$	$\frac{\rho}{2}$	$\frac{\rho}{2}$	$\frac{1}{2}$	0	v_t+L
$\in] v_t-L-\sigma, \; v_t-L+\sigma]$	$\frac{\rho}{4}$	$\frac{\rho}{2}$	0	0	$-\sigma$	$v_t+L-\sigma$
$\leq v_t-L-\sigma$	0	0	0	0	$-\sigma$	$v_t+L-\sigma$
$\sigma \geq L$						
$> v_t+L+\sigma$	ρ	ρ	ρ	$\frac{1}{2}$	0	v_t+L
$\in] v_t+\sigma-L, \; v_t+L+\sigma]$	$\frac{3}{4}\rho$	ρ	$\frac{\rho}{2}$	$\frac{1}{3}$	$-\frac{1}{3}\sigma$	$v_t+L-\frac{1}{3}\sigma$
$\in] v_t+\sigma+L, \; v_t+\sigma-L]$	$\frac{\rho}{2}$	$\frac{\rho}{2}$	0	0	$-\sigma$	$v_t+L-\sigma$
$\in] v_t-L-\sigma, \; v_t-\sigma+L]$	$\frac{\rho}{4}$	$\frac{\rho}{2}$	0	0	$-\sigma$	$v_t+L-\sigma$
$\leq v_t-L-\sigma$	0	0	0	0	$-\sigma$	$v_t+L-\sigma$

because they depend on both σ and L, two cases must be considered (first column of Table 8.3): the case with $\sigma < L$ (above), and that with $\sigma \geqslant L$ (below). Columns 2, 3 and 4 of Table 8.3 report the unconditional ($\Pr(I(B) = +1)$) and conditional execution probabilities ($\Pr(I(B) = +1|\varepsilon_{t+1} = \pm\sigma)$) of the limit buy order, column 5 reports the value of the conditional probability of a price increase, $\pi(B)$, column 6 shows the conditional expected price change ($E[(\Delta v_{t+1}|I(B) = +1, S_t)]$) and column 7 the corresponding *possible* equilibrium bid prices ($B_t(v_t + L)$).

Consider the case with $\sigma < L$, and compare the bid prices reported in Table 8.3. First of all, notice from column 7 that the possible equilibrium bid price $B_t(v_t + L) = v_t + L$ cannot be an equilibrium price in the corresponding bid price range ($> v_t + L + \sigma$); if the bidder chooses instead $B_t = v_t + L - \frac{1}{3}\sigma$, he maximizes the probability of execution of his limit order[18] $\left(\frac{3}{4}\rho\right)$. Checking the payoffs for the potential incoming market seller (see *MOS* in Figure 8.3) obtained using $B_t = v_t + L - \frac{1}{3}\sigma$, one can notice that they will be positive if the asset value decreases; conversely, if it increases, that of type $(-L, +\sigma)$, i.e. $v_t + L - \frac{1}{3}\sigma - (v_t - L + \sigma)$, will be positive, provided that $\sigma < \frac{3}{2}L$, whereas the payoff of a trader of type $(+L, +\sigma)$ will be negative. It follows that $B_{t+1} = v_t + L - \frac{1}{3}\sigma$ is the equilibrium bid price for $\sigma < \frac{3}{2}L$. If instead $\sigma \geqslant \frac{3}{2}L$, then $v_t + L - \frac{1}{3}\sigma \leqslant v_t - L + \sigma$, which means that a price of $v_t + L - \frac{1}{3}\sigma$ or lower has zero execution probability if the asset price increases. Consequently, checking all the other possible bid prices, the only solution for $\sigma \geqslant \frac{3}{2}L$ will be $B_{t+1} = v_t + L - \sigma$, with a probability of execution equal to $\rho/4$. Given symmetry, it is straightforward to show that the ask price set by a limit order trader of type $-L$ is equal to $A(v_{t+1}, -L) = v_t - L + \frac{1}{3}\sigma$. Finally, notice that the bid price posted by a trader of type $-L$ must be lower than his reservation price $v_t - L$; if the asset value increases, the reservation price of the incoming trader will be higher than $v_t - L$, hence that bid price will have zero execution probability. Consequently the order will be executed only if the asset value decreases, but in this case the bid price must be set equal to $v_t - L - \sigma$ to break even. Looking at Table 8.3, it can be seen that at this bid price the execution probability of the limit buy order is zero. A similar argument holds for the ask price set by a trader of type $+L$. Summarizing the equilibrium bid and ask prices and spreads, we have:

$$\begin{cases} A(v_t, -L) = v_t - L + \frac{1}{3}\sigma \\ B(v_t, +L) = v_t + L - \frac{1}{3}\sigma \end{cases} \quad \text{if } \sigma < \frac{3}{2}L \quad \text{with execution probability} = \frac{3}{4}\rho$$

$$\begin{cases} A(v_t, -L) = v_t - L + \sigma \\ B(v_t, +L) = v_t + L - \sigma \end{cases} \quad \text{if } \sigma \geqslant \frac{3}{2}L \quad \text{with execution probability} = \frac{1}{4}\rho$$

---

[18] Notice from column 2 that the probability of execution of a limit buy order, $\Pr(I(B) = +1)$, is equal to $\frac{1}{2}\Pr(I(B) = +1|\varepsilon_{t+1} = -\sigma) + \frac{1}{2}\Pr(I(B) = +1|\varepsilon_{t+1} = +\sigma)$, hence, when $\sigma < \frac{3}{2}L$ (and therefore $\sigma \leq L$), for $B_t \in [v_t + L - \sigma, v_t + L + \sigma]$, $\Pr(I(B) = +1) = 0.5\rho/2 + 0.5\rho = \frac{3}{4}\rho$.

$$\begin{cases} A(v_t, +L) = v_t + L + \sigma \\ B(v_t, -L) = v_t - L - \sigma \end{cases} \qquad \text{with execution probability} = 0$$

$$\begin{cases} A(v_t, -L) - B(v_t, -L) = v_t - L + \frac{1}{3}\sigma - v_t + L + \sigma = \frac{4}{3}\sigma \\ A(v_t, +L) - B(v_t, +L) = v_t + L + \sigma - v_t - L + \frac{1}{3}\sigma = \frac{4}{3}\sigma \end{cases} \qquad \text{if } \sigma < \frac{3}{2}L$$

$$\begin{cases} A(v_t, -L) - B(v_t, -L) = v_t - L + \sigma - v_t + L + \sigma = 2\sigma \\ A(v_t, +L) - B(v_t, +L) = v_t + L + \sigma - v_t - L + \sigma = 2\sigma \end{cases} \qquad \text{if } \sigma \geqslant \frac{3}{2}L$$

Notice that when the volatility of the asset price increases, traders shade their offers more markedly relative to their reservation price and the spread is wider. In fact, when volatility is high, the risk of being picked off by an incoming trader is greater, so traders offer to sell (buy) at a higher (lower) price, thus widening the spread. Notice also that the execution probability of a limit order is lower when volatility is high: for example, when volatility is high, traders with type $+L$ quote a lower bid price than when it is low, and their offers will be less attractive; hence the execution probability will be lower.

8.2.3   The LOB as a market for immediacy

Foucault, Kadan and Kandel (2005) develop a model for a limit order market where there are only strategic liquidity traders and the choice between limit and market orders depends only on their degree of impatience. This model focuses on one of the dimensions of liquidity, namely immediacy. Traders who want to trade as soon as possible demand immediacy. This is an important feature of liquidity, insofar as traders value execution speed differently. Hence this model emphasizes the dual role of limit order books as markets where agents can demand and/or supply immediacy. Agents demand immediacy when they submit market orders and they supply immediacy when they post limit orders. Foucault, Kadan and Kandel show that in equilibrium patient traders tend to submit limit orders and impatient traders, market orders. The two key determinants of the limit order dynamics are the ratio of patient to impatient traders and their respective order arrival rates. Further, under several simplifying assumptions, the model derives the expected time to execution for limit orders, the stationary probability distribution of the spread and the expected interval between trades. Hence the model can measure market resiliency by the probability that, after a liquidity shock, the spread will revert to its former level.

The model   Foucault, Kadan and Kandel assume that a risky security is traded in a continuous double auction market organized as a limit order book. There is no asymmetric information and no inventory costs, and market participants, who are strategic and risk-neutral liquidity traders, arrive sequentially and differ in impatience, defined as the cost that liquidity traders suffer for a delay in order execution. Each trader minimizes his total execution costs by choosing a market or a limit order, conditional on the state of the book. There are two categories of traders, type P traders who are relatively patient and incur a waiting cost of δ_P per unit of time, and type I traders who are relatively impatient, as they incur a waiting cost of δ_I, where $\delta_I \geq \delta_P \geq 0$. The proportion of patient traders in the population is θ_P ($1 > \theta_P > 0$), and that of impatient ones is $\theta_I = 1 - \theta_P$. These proportions remain constant over time, and the arrival process is independent of the type distribution.

As in Parlour (1998), Foucault, Kadan and Kandel assume that a *trading crowd* stands ready to sell and buy an unlimited number of shares at prices A and B respectively, which for this reason are constant over time and form the admissible price interval $[B, A]$ that includes all the prices in the limit order book. Prices and spreads are expressed as multiples of the tick size, denoted by $\Delta > 0$. The inside spread is $s \equiv a - b$, where by construction $a \leq A$, $b \geq B$ and $s \leq K \equiv A - B$. In this infinite horizon model, traders come into the market according to a Poisson process with parameter $\lambda > 0$. A *period* is referred to as the time between the arrival of two successive traders, and it is easy to show that $1/\lambda$ is the expected duration of a period. It is also assumed that traders coming into the market can be buyers if their valuation of the security is $V_{buyer} > A\Delta$, and sellers if $V_{seller} < B\Delta$.

Limit orders submitted to the book are executed according to *price priority* and the following assumptions are made to solve for an equilibrium by induction and to keep the model manageable:

(1) Each trader arrives only once, submits a market or a limit order, and leaves the market. Once submitted, orders cannot be cancelled or modified.
(2) Limit orders must be price improving, that is, they must narrow the spread by at least one tick.
(3) Buyers and sellers alternate with certainty; for example, first a buyer arrives, then a seller and so on. The first trader is a buyer with probability 0.5.

Equilibrium   Now we derive the equilibrium spread dynamic starting from traders' maximization function. As equilibrium spreads depend on how willing traders are to improve the price at each possible spread value, it is first necessary to derive the equilibrium price improvement function, which itself is a function of the expected waiting time associated with each j-order's execution, $T(j)$.

Let P_{buyer} and P_{seller} be the execution prices of buyers and sellers. Given the model's structure, a buyer can either submit a market order that will be executed at the best ask price a or submit a limit order with a price higher than the best bid b. Conversely, a seller must choose whether to hit b immediately, or to submit a limit order. Given this choice, the execution prices are:

$$P_{buyer} = a - j \qquad P_{seller} = b + j \qquad j \in \{0, 1, ..., s - 1\} \qquad (8.25)$$

Recalling that each measure is expressed as a multiple of the tick size, it follows that $j = 0$ for a market order, and $j > 0$ for a limit order that creates a spread of size j.

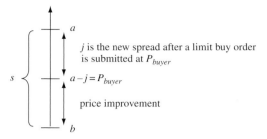

Figure 8.4. Prices within the bid–ask spread.

For example, given a spread $s = a - b$, if a trader submits a limit buy order, he will choose the price P_{buyer} which improves the spread s by $a - b - j$ (see Figure 8.4). Notice also that the greater j, the less aggressive the price posted and the wider the spread (j) after the order placement. Hence a j-limit order is a limit order creating a spread of size j (in ticks), which is ultimately the trader's decision variable.

Let $T(j)$ be the expected time-to-execution of a j-limit order, then the expected waiting cost of a j-limit order is $\delta_i T(j)$, $i \in \{P, I\}$, whereas that of a market order is $T(0) = 0$.

As traders are risk-neutral, the expected profit of trader i can be expressed as:

$$\Pi_i(j) = \begin{cases} V_{buyer} - P_{buyer}\,\Delta - \delta_i T(j) = (V_{buyer} - a\Delta) + j\Delta - \delta_i T(j) & \text{for a buyer} \\ P_{seller}\,\Delta - V_{seller} - \delta_i T(j) = (b\Delta - V_{seller}) + j\Delta - \delta_i T(j) & \text{for a seller} \end{cases} \tag{8.26}$$

where the expressions in parentheses represent the profits associated with a market order. These profits depend on both the trader's valuation and the best quotes at the time of the submission. It follows that the optimal order placement strategy of trader i when the spread is s solves the following optimization problem:

$$\underset{j \in \{0,\dots,s-1\}}{\text{Max}} \pi_i(j) \equiv j\Delta - \delta_i T(j) \tag{8.27}$$

Thus the trader's strategy is a mapping that assigns a j-limit order, $j \in \{0, 1, \dots, s - 1\}$, to each possible spread $s \in \{1, \dots, K\}$. It determines which order to submit given the size of the spread. Let $o_i(.)$ be the order placement strategy of a type i, $i \in \{I, P\}$, trader, whose optimal strategy at time t depends on the response of the subsequent traders, starting from $t + 1$. It follows that a subgame-perfect equilibrium is a group of strategies, $o_P^*(.)$ and $o_I^*(.)$, such that the order chosen by each trader for every possible inside spread maximizes his expected profits when the expected waiting time, $T(j)$, is calculated using the fact that traders follow precisely those strategies. As in equilibrium, $T(j)$ is non-decreasing in j, traders follow a trade-off between execution price and expected waiting time and accordingly submit limit orders only if their price improvement, $j\Delta$, exceeds the waiting cost,[19] $\delta_i T(j)$, i.e. if $j_i\Delta - \delta_i T(j_i) \geq 0$.

[19] Since $T(0) = 0$, from equation (8.27) the payoff from a market order is zero.

It follows that the smallest spread that trader i can establish is the smallest integer j_i^*, such that:

$$\pi_i(j_i^*) = j_i^* \Delta - \delta_i T(j_i^*) \geq 0 \qquad (8.28)$$

where j_i^* is defined as the *reservation spread* for a type i trader:

$$j_i^* = \left\lceil \frac{\delta_i}{\Delta} T(j_i^*) \right\rceil \qquad i \in \{P, I\} \qquad (8.29)$$

and $\lceil x \rceil$ is the ceiling function – the smallest integer larger than or equal to x. Notice that the reservation spread depends both on the expected time to execution, $T(j_i^*)$, and the waiting costs, δ_i. To exclude cases where no traders submit limit orders, it is assumed that $j_P^* < K$, and, as no trader will post a limit order with smaller spreads,[20] patient traders' reservation spread, j_P^*, is called the *competitive spread*. As $\delta_I \geq \delta_P$, and assuming[21] that the expected time function is non-decreasing in j, it follows that patient traders' reservation spread is less than or equal to that of impatient traders ($j_P^* \leq j_I^*$). Analogously the impatient traders' reservation spread, j_I^*, is the maximum spread that can be established in the market.[22] This is because beyond this spread all traders are willing to post limit orders, and, if no one submits market orders, the probability of limit orders' execution is equal to zero. It follows that trading will take place only between j_P^* and j_I^* where patient traders submit limit orders and impatient traders, market orders. Figure 8.5 summarizes agents' reservation spreads, the possible spread between these two, and the maximum ($j^* = K$) and minimum spreads ($j^* = 1$). The spread posted by a limit order trader cannot be smaller than one tick ($j = 1$) as all traders facing such a spread will submit market orders (remember that by assumption two limit orders must improve the price by at least one tick); hence reducing the spread further would not change the order's expected time to execution. Clearly, because $a - b$ cannot be larger than K, the maximum quoted spread is K.

The next step is to show that within the trading interval $[j_P^*, j_I^*]$, patient traders can establish a number of possible spreads n_h. As these n_h spreads will be posted by traders who wish to minimize the expected time to execution, we first have to derive the equilibrium expected waiting time function $T(j)$:

(1) $T(j = 1) = 1/\lambda$: the expected waiting time for a one-tick spread is simply the average time between two arrivals. From assumption 2, it follows that a trader who faces a one-tick spread must submit a market order.
(2) $T(j) = +\infty$ if $\alpha_0(j) = 0$ and $j \in \{2, ..., K - 1\}$, where $\alpha_k(j)$ is the probability that the trader arriving in the next period and observing an inside spread of size j chooses a k-limit order, $k \in \{0, 1, ..., j - 1\}$; if $\alpha_0(j) = 0$, no one will submit a

---

[20] Clearly, for $j < j^*$, $\pi_i(j_i^*) < 0$ and traders will not submit a limit order.
[21] This will however be true in equilibrium.
[22] This derives from the fact that, as Foucault, Kadan and Kandel show, the waiting time function is non-decreasing in J and δ_I represents the highest traders' waiting costs.

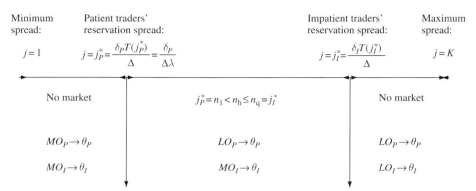

Figure 8.5. Range of possible spreads. The range of possible spreads is partitioned into three regions: (1) $1 \leqslant s \leqslant j_p^*$, where both patient and impatient traders only submit market order MO_P and MO_I with probability θ_P and θ_I respectively; if no traders submit limit orders, there cannot by any trade; (2) $j_P^* < s \leqslant j_I^*$, where patient traders submit limit orders LO_P and impatient traders submit market orders MO_I; (3) $j_I^* < s \leqslant K$, where both patient and impatient traders submit limit orders and, because no traders submit market orders, there cannot be any trade.

market order when the spread is equal to j, and hence the waiting time to execution is $+\infty$.

(3) The generic waiting time function, which is derived in Exercise 3 at the end of this chapter, has the following recursive structure as it depends on the waiting time functions, $T(k)$, of the k-spreads, which are smaller than j:

$$T(j) = \frac{1}{\alpha_o(j)} \left[\frac{1}{\lambda} + \sum_{k=1}^{j-1} \alpha_k(j) T(k) \right] \text{ if } \alpha_o(j) > 0 \text{ and } j \in \{2, \dots, K-1\}$$

(8.30)

Now, to show the existence of a number of spreads $n_h \in \left\{ j_P^*, \dots, j_I^* \right\}$, the model is solved inductively starting from the end-node of the game,[23] which corresponds to the case when the spread is equal to 1; a 1-spread is an end-node here as, by assumption, traders facing this spread must submit a market order. Note that, contrary to the games with a finite time horizon (as in Parlour (1998)), the game-nodes in this model, which is of infinite horizon and stationary (as in Foucault (1999)), are specified in terms of the state variable (the spread) and not in terms of time. This is a standard procedure in any Markov-type game. By considering that traders maximize their expected profits (8.28) and by using the waiting time function (8.30), it is straightforward to show the existence of $n_1 < n_2 < \dots < n_q$ spreads such that, facing a spread in $\langle n_h + 1, n_{h+1} \rangle$ the patient trader submits a n_h–limit order for $h = 1, \dots, q-1$, where $n_1 = j_P^*$ and

---

[23] Let us recall that an 'end-node' is defined as any node of the game tree in which the payoff to the traders is given exogenously.

$n_q = K$. It is easy to understand this result from the example in Exercise 4 at the end of this chapter.

The final requirement is to obtain an equilibrium waiting time function for n_h, $T(n_h)$, and use it to derive a general expression for the equilibrium spread. By exploiting the derived general submission rule (a patient trader facing a spread within the interval $\langle n_{h-1} + 1, n_h \rangle$ will choose n_{h-1}), it is possible to obtain the equilibrium waiting cost function:

$$T(n_h) = \frac{1}{\lambda} \left[1 + 2 \sum_{k=1}^{h-1} \left(\frac{\theta_P}{1 - \theta_P} \right)^k \right] \qquad \forall \ h \in \{2, ..., q - 1\} \tag{8.31}$$

which is related to the proportion of patient to impatient traders. Intuitively, the larger the proportion of impatient traders $(1 - \theta_P)$ who submit market orders, the shorter the expected waiting time for the execution of a n_h-limit order. We derive $T(n_h)$ as part of Exercise 5 below.

Now to find the equilibrium price improvement function, Ψ_h, when the spread is equal to n_h, which determines the aggressiveness of the limit order, Foucault, Kadan and Kandel again exploit the fact that when a trader faces a spread n_{h+1}, he chooses to submit a n_h-limit order. He could decrease the time to execution by submitting a n_{h-1}-limit order, but chooses not to, hence:

$$n_h \Delta - T(n_h)\delta_P \geq n_{h-1}\Delta - T(n_{h-1})\delta_P \qquad \forall \ h \in \{2, ..., q - 1\}$$

or:

$$\Psi_h \equiv n_h - n_{h-1} \geq T(n_h) - T(n_{h-1}) \frac{\delta_P}{\Delta} \qquad \forall \ h \in \{2, ..., q - 1\} \tag{8.32}$$

Similarly, a trader who comes to the market when the spread is n_h, in equilibrium will submit an n_{h-1}-limit order and, hence, must prefer this limit order to the one that creates a spread of $n_h - 1$ ticks. Hence:

$$n_{h-1}\Delta - T(n_{h-1})\delta_P \geq (n_h - 1)\Delta - T(n_h - 1)\delta_P \qquad \forall \ h \in \{2, ..., q - 1\}$$

or:

$$\Psi_h < [T(n_h) - T(n_{h-1})] \frac{\delta_P}{\Delta} + 1 \qquad \forall \ h \in \{2, ..., q - 1\} \tag{8.33}$$

Combining conditions (8.32) and (8.33), Foucault, Kaden and Kandel deduce that:

$$\Psi_h = \left[[T(n_h) - T(n_{h-1})] \frac{\delta_P}{\Delta} \right] = \left[2 \left(\frac{\theta_P}{1 - \theta_P} \right)^{h-1} \frac{\delta_P}{\lambda \Delta} \right] \qquad \forall \ h \in \{2, ..., q - 1\} \tag{8.34}$$

Finally, the equilibrium characterization of Ψ_h, which shows how much traders outbid or undercut posted quotes for each possible spread, allows us to define the equilibrium spreads, which are equal to:

$$n_1 = J_P^*, \quad n_q = K, \quad n_h = n_1 + \sum_{k=2}^{h} \Psi_k \qquad h = 2, ..., q - 1 \tag{8.35}$$

where $\Psi_k = \lceil 2\,(\theta_P/1 - \theta_P)^{k-1}\,(\delta_P/\lambda\Delta)\rceil$ and q is the smallest integer such that

$$J_P^* + \sum_{k=2}^{q} \Psi_k \geq K.$$

Notice that, in equilibrium, traders submit more aggressive orders (the price improvement is larger) when either the proportion of patient traders, θ_P, or their waiting costs, δ_P, increases; they will submit less aggressive orders if instead the order arrival rate, λ, decreases.

Given the model's outcome, Foucault, Kadan and Kandel also define a measure of resiliency, which is the probability, R, that the spread will revert to the competitive level, J_P^*, before the next transaction and when the current spread is K. R is equal to θ_P^{q-1} as it is necessary that $q - 1$ consecutive patient traders submit their orders to narrow the spread from K to the competitive level (equation 8.35).

This model can be extended to discuss issues relating to the degree of liquidity on top of the limit order books. An interesting extension is to include another category of patient traders acting as market-makers to study, for example, the obligations imposed on specialists by the regulators of many of today's order-driven markets.

Exercises

Exercise 1
Considering Parlour's (1998) model, Figure 8.2 shows a graphical representation of the agent's strategies at $T - 1$ under the assumption that the book is empty on both sides. Show how results change when the book is full on one or both sides.

Solution

$$\beta_{T-1}^{(1,0)} \in \begin{cases} [\underline{\beta} = 0 & \underline{\beta}^S(P_T^B) = 0.91) & \phi_{T-1}^S = -1^B & MOS \\ [0.91 & \overline{\beta}^B(P_T^S) = \frac{B}{v} + \frac{k}{(1-P_T^S)v}) & \phi_{T-1}^B = +1^B & LOB \\ [\overline{\beta}^B(P_T^S) & \overline{\beta} = 2] & \phi_{T-1}^B = -1^A & MOB \end{cases}$$

$$\beta_{T-1}^{(0,1)} \in \begin{cases} [\underline{\beta} = 0 & \underline{\beta}^S(P_T^B) = \frac{A}{v} - \frac{k}{(1-P_T^B)v}) & \phi_{T-1}^S = -1^B & MOS \\ [\underline{\beta}^S(P_T^B) & \overline{\beta}^B(P_T^S) = 1.09) & \phi_{T-1}^S = +1^A & LOS \\ [1.09 & \overline{\beta} = 2] & \phi_{T-1}^B = -1^A & MOB \end{cases}$$

$$\beta_{T-1}^{(1,1)} \in \begin{cases} [\underline{\beta} = 0 & \frac{B}{v} = 0.91) & \phi_{T-1}^S = -1^B & MOS \\ [0.91 & 1.09 = \frac{A}{v}) & \phi_{T-1} = 0 & No\ trade \\ [1.09 & \overline{\beta} = 2] & \phi_{T-1}^B = -1^A & MOB \end{cases}$$

Exercise 2
So far, Parlour's model for the LOB has been solved up to period $T - 1$. Under the assumptions specified in the text, compute the equilibrium trading strategies for an agent arriving in the market at time $T - 2$. Assume further that $v = 5.5$ and $k = \frac{1}{2}$.

Solution

The solutions to the model at time $T - 2$ are presented below in terms of intervals for β and hence of probability of execution of different order types. Clearly, the solutions depend on the depth that characterizes both sides of the book.

Time T:

$$\text{submit } MOS \text{ if } B \geqslant \beta_t v \quad \text{i.e.} \quad \beta_T \leqslant \frac{B}{v} = 1 - \frac{k}{v} = 0.91$$

$$\text{submit } MOB \text{ if } \beta_t v \geqslant A \quad \text{i.e.} \quad \beta_T \geqslant \frac{A}{v} = 1 + \frac{k}{v} = 1.09$$

Given $\beta \sim U[0, 2]$, it follows that:

$$P_T^S = \frac{0.90}{2} \simeq 0.46 \quad \text{and} \quad P_T^B = \frac{2 - 1.09}{2} \simeq 0.46$$

Notice that at time T the larger the tick size, k, the larger the 'No trade' region.

Time $T-1$:

$$\beta_{T-1}^{(0,0)} \in \begin{cases} [0 \quad 0.76) & MOS: B - \beta_{T-1} v & P_{T-1}^S = 0.38 \\ [0.76 \quad 1) & LOS: (A - \beta_{T-1} v) P_T^B & P_{T-1}^{LOS} = 0.12 \\ [1 \quad 1.24) & LOB: (\beta_{T-1} v - B) P_T^S & P_{T-1}^{LOB} = 0.12 \\ [1.24 \quad 2] & MOB: \beta_{T-1} v - A & P_{T-1}^B = 0.38 \end{cases}$$

$$\beta_{T-1}^{(0,1)} \in \begin{cases} [0 \quad 0.76) & MOS: B - \beta_{T-1} v & P_{T-1}^S = 0.38 \\ [0.76 \quad 1) & LOS: (A - \beta_{T-1} v) P_T^B & P_{T-1}^{LOS} = 0.12 \\ [1 \quad 1.09) & \text{No trade} & P_{T-1}^{NT} = 0.05 \\ [1.09 \quad 2] & MOB: \beta_{T-1} v - A & P_{T-1}^B = 0.46 \end{cases}$$

$$\beta_{T-1}^{(1,0)} \in \begin{cases} [0 \quad 0.91) & MOS: B - \beta_{T-1} v & P_{T-1}^S = 0.46 \\ [0.91 \quad 1) & \text{No trade} & P_{T-1}^{NT} = 0.05 \\ [1 \quad 1.24) & LOB: (\beta_{T-1} v - B) P_T^S & P_{T-1}^{LOB} = 0.12 \\ [1.24 \quad 2] & MOB: \beta_{T-1} v - A & P_{T-1}^B = 0.38 \end{cases}$$

$$\beta_{T-1}^{(1,1)} \in \begin{cases} [0 \quad 0.91) & MOS: B - \beta_{T-1} v & P_{T-1}^S = 0.46 \\ [0.91 \quad 1.09) & \text{No trade} & P_{T-1}^{NT} = 0.09 \\ [1.09 \quad 2] & MOB: \beta_{T-1} v - A & P_{T-1}^B = 0.46 \end{cases}$$

Time $T-2$:

$$\beta_{T-2}^{(0,0)} \in \begin{cases} [\underline{\beta} = 0 \quad \underline{\beta}^S(P_{T-1}^B, P_T^B) = 0.54) & MOS: B - \beta_{T-2} v & P_{T-2}^S = 0.27 \\ [\underline{\beta}^S(P_{T-1}^B, P_T^B) = 0.54 \quad 1) & \begin{array}{l} LOS: (A - \beta_{T-2} v) P_{T-1}^B + \\ + (A - \beta_{T-2} v)(1 - P_{T-1}^B) P_T^B \end{array} & P_{T-2}^{LOS} = 0.23 \\ [1 \quad \overline{\beta}^B(P_{T-1}^S, P_T^S) = 1.46) & \begin{array}{l} LOB: (\beta_{T-2} v - B) P_{T-1}^S + \\ + (\beta_{T-2} v - B)(1 - P_{T-1}^S) P_T^S \end{array} & P_{T-2}^{LOB} = 0.23 \\ [\overline{\beta}^B(P_{T-1}^S, P_T^S) = 1.46 \quad 2] & MOB: \beta_{T-2} v - A & P_{T-2}^B = 0.27 \end{cases}$$

$$\beta_{T-2}^{(1,1)} \in \begin{cases} [\beta = 0 \quad \beta^S(P_{T-1}^B, P_T^B) = 0.86) \\ [\underline{\beta}^S(P_{T-1}^B, P_T^B) = 0.86 \quad 1) \\ [1 \quad \overline{\beta}^B(P_{T-1}^S, P_T^S) = 1.14) \\ [\overline{\beta}^B(P_{T-1}^S, P_T^S) = 1.14 \quad 2] \end{cases}$$

MOS: $B - \beta_{T-2}\,v$	$P_{T-1}^S = 0.43$
LOS: $(A - \beta_{T-2}\,v)P_{T-1}^B P_T^B$	$P_{T-1}^{LOS} = 0.07$
LOB: $(\beta_{T-2}\,v - B)P_{T-1}^S P_T^S$	$P_{T-1}^{LOB} = 0.07$
MOB: $\beta_{T-2}\,v - A$	$P_{T-1}^B = 0.43$

$$\beta_{T-2}^{(2,2)} \in \begin{cases} [0 \quad 0.91) \\ [0.91 \quad 1.09) \\ [1.09 \quad 2] \end{cases}$$

MOS: $B - \beta_{T-2}\,v$	$P_{T-2}^S = 0.46$
No trade	$P_{T-1}^{NT} = 0.09$
MOB: $\beta_{T-2}\,v - A$	$P_{T-1}^B = 0.46$

Notice also that, as expected, an increase in the book's depth increases the probability of observing a market order and reduces that of observing a limit order.

It is now straightforward to compute the solutions for the cases with asymmetric books, which are left to the reader.

Exercise 3

Consider Foucault, Kadan and Kandel's model and show how the generic waiting time function for a j-limit order, $T(j)$, discussed at point 3 on p. 150 can be derived from the model's assumptions.

Solution

Let us consider a buyer who submits a j-limit order with $j > 1$. With probability $\alpha_0(j)$ the next trader, who is a seller, submits a market order and the expected waiting time of the buyer is $1/\lambda$. With probability $\alpha_k(j)$ the seller instead submits a k-limit order and the initial buyer's waiting time is $1/\lambda + T(k) + T(j)$ as he has to wait $1/\lambda$ for the seller to arrive, $T(k)$ for the seller's order to be cleared and the spread to revert to j, and, finally, $T(j)$ for the j-limit order to be executed. Hence:

$$T(j) = \frac{\alpha_0(j)}{\lambda} + \sum_{k=1}^{j-1} \alpha_k(j)\left[\frac{1}{\lambda} + T(k) + T(j)\right]$$

$$= T(j)[\alpha_1(j) + \cdots + \alpha_{j-1}(j)] + \frac{1}{\lambda}[\alpha_0(j) + \cdots + \alpha_{j-1}(j)] + \sum_{k=1}^{j-1} \alpha_k(j)T(k)$$

and exploiting the fact that $\sum_{k=0}^{j-1} \alpha_k(j) = 1 \ \forall j = 1, ..., K - 1$, we obtain:

$$T(j) = \frac{1}{\alpha_o(j)}\left[\frac{1}{\lambda} + \sum_{k=1}^{j-1} \alpha_k(j)T(k)\right].$$

Exercise 4 [24]

Consider Foucault, Kadan and Kandel's (2005) model and assume that the tick size is $\Delta = \$0.125$ and the arrival rate is $\lambda = 1$. The lower price bound of the book is set to $B\Delta = \$20$, and the upper bound is set to $A\Delta = \$22.50$. Thus, the maximal spread

---

[24] We thank Ohad Kadan for suggesting this exercise.

is $K = 20$ ($K\Delta = \$2.50$). Further, $\delta_P = 0.1$, $\delta_I = 0.25$ and $\theta_P = 0.55$. Derive the equilibrium strategies by backward induction.

Solution
The equilibrium must be derived by backward induction. The game starts with a spread $s = K = 20$. But to solve for the equilibrium we start with the end-nodes of the game, i.e. $s = 1$. By assumption, when facing a spread of 1 both types submit a market order.

Consider now a spread $s = 2$. A trader who arrives and observes a spread of two ticks has to choose between a 1-limit order and a market order. Since $T(0) = 0$, the payoff from a market order is zero (equation 8.28).

Since $T(1) = 1$, the payoff of submitting a 1-limit order is (using equation 8.30):

$$\pi_i(1) = \Delta - \delta_i$$

Thus, if $i = P$ (patient) the payoff is $\pi_i(1) = 0.125 - 0.1 = 0.025$, whereas if $i = I$ (impatient) the payoff is $\pi_i(1) = 0.125 - 0.25 = -0.125$. Hence, facing a spread of two ticks, a patient trader will choose a 1-limit order (the payoff is higher than that of a market order) while the impatient type chooses a market order. Hence, $\alpha_1(2) = \theta_P = 0.55$ and $\alpha_0(2) = 1 - \theta_P = 0.45$, and using (8.30):

$$T(2) = \frac{1}{0.45}[1 + 0.55 \cdot T(1)] = 3.44$$

Consider now a spread $s = 3$. A trader who comes to the market and observes a spread of three ticks has to choose among a market order, a 1-limit order, and a 2-limit order. If he submits a 2-limit order his payoff will be:

$$\pi_i(2) = 2\Delta - \delta_i T(2) = 0.25 - 3.44\delta_i$$

Thus, if $i = P$ we have $\pi_i(2) = -0.094$, while if $i = I$ we have $\pi_i(2) = -0.61$. If the trader submits a 1-limit order or a market order the payoffs are as calculated in the case $s = 1$. We conclude that with a spread of three ticks a patient trader will submit a 1-limit order, and an impatient trader will submit a market order. It follows that $\alpha_0(3) = 0.45$, $\alpha_1(3) = 0.55$ and $\alpha_2(3) = 0$. Consequently, using (8.30), $T(3) = T(2) = 3.44$.

Consider now a spread $s = 4$. The trader has to choose among limit orders with one, two or three ticks, and a market order. If he chooses a 3-limit order his payoff is:

$$\pi_i(3) = 3\Delta - 3.44\delta_i$$

If $i = P$ we have $\pi_i(3) = 0.031$, and if $i = I$ we have $\pi_i(3) = -0.485$. The payoffs for submitting a market order and 1- or 2-limit orders are as calculated above. We conclude that with a spread of four ticks, a patient trader will submit a 3-limit order while an impatient one will submit a market order. Hence, $\alpha_3(4) = 0.55$, $\alpha_2(4) = 0$, $\alpha_1(4) = 0$ and $\alpha_0(4) = 0.45$, and using (8.30):

$$T(4) = \frac{1}{0.45}(1 + 0.55 \cdot 3.44) = 6.43$$

We continue in this way to the case $s = K = 20$. In so doing we derive the equilibrium strategy shown in Table 8.4. It can be seen that the impatient type always

Table 8.4. *Equilibrium strategy*

Current spread	Submitted spread			
s	*Type P*	n_h	*Type I*	n_h
1	0	n_0	0	n_0
2	1	n_1	0	n_0
3	1	n_1	0	n_0
4	3	n_2	0	n_0
5	3	n_2	0	n_0
6	3	n_2	0	n_0
7	6	n_3	0	n_0
8	6	n_3	0	n_0
9	6	n_3	0	n_0
10	9	n_4	0	n_0
11	9	n_4	0	n_0
12	9	n_4	0	n_0
13	9	n_4	0	n_0
14	13	n_5	0	n_0
15	13	n_5	0	n_0
16	13	n_5	0	n_0
17	13	n_5	0	n_0
18	13	n_5	0	n_0
19	18	n_6	0	n_0
20	18	n_6	0	n_0

submits a market order, regardless of the spread. The patient type instead submits six different spreads ($n_1 = 1, n_2 = 3, n_3 = 6, \ldots, n_6 = 18$) when facing spreads between $s = 1$ and $s = 20$. These are the equilibrium spreads. The other spreads are off the equilibrium path, but they are still very important for the specification of the equilibrium. Patient traders' reservation spread, which is the lowest one observed in equilibrium, is 1. Notice also that when a patient trader faces a spread equal to $n_{h-1}+1$ $\in \langle n_{h-1}, n_h \rangle$, he submits n_{h-1}.

Exercise 5
Consider the possible sequence of spreads in Foucault, Kadan and Kandel's (2005) model, $n_1 < n_2 < \ldots < n_q$, such that, facing a spread in $\langle n_{h-1} + 1, n_h \rangle$ the patient trader submits an n_{h-1}-limit order for $h = 1, \cdots, q - 1$ and the impatient trader submits a market order. Now derive the equilibrium waiting costs function by exploiting point 2 on p. 149.

Solution
When the quoted spread is $s \in \langle n_{h-1}+1, n_h \rangle$, we have that $\alpha_0(s) = 1-\theta_P, \alpha_{h-1}(s) = \theta_P$ and $\alpha_k(s) = 0 \; \forall \, h \notin \{0, ..., n_{h-1}\}$, thus equation (8.30) yields:

$$T(s) = \frac{1}{1-\theta_P}\left[\frac{1}{\lambda} + \theta_P T(n_{h-1})\right] \forall s \in \langle n_{h-1}+1, n_h \rangle$$

which means that $T(\cdot)$ is constant for all $s \in \langle n_{h-1}+1, n_h \rangle$. Hence we can recursively derive:

$$\begin{aligned}
T(n_{h+1}) - T(n_h) &= \frac{\theta_P}{1-\theta_P}[T(n_h) - T(n_{h-1})] \\
&= \frac{\theta_P}{1-\theta_P}\left[\frac{\theta_P}{1-\theta_P}(T(n_{h-1}) - T(n_h))\right] \\
&= \cdots = \left(\frac{\theta_P}{1-\theta_P}\right)^{h-1}[T(n_2) - T(n_1)]
\end{aligned}$$

where:

$$T(n_2) - T(n_1) = \frac{1}{1-\theta_P}\left[\frac{1}{\lambda} + \theta_P T(n_1)\right] - T(n_1)$$

and, since $T(n_1) = 1/\lambda$ we have:

$$T(n_2) - T(n_1) = \frac{2\theta_P}{\lambda(1-\theta_P)}.$$

This allows us to obtain:

$$T(n_{h+1}) - T(n_h) = \left(\frac{\theta_P}{1-\theta_P}\right)^{h}\frac{2}{\lambda} \quad \text{or} \quad T(n_h) = T(n_{h-1}) + \left(\frac{\theta_P}{1-\theta_P}\right)^{h-1}\frac{2}{\lambda}$$

so that again substituting recursively for:

$$T(n_{h-1}) = T(n_{h-2}) + \left(\frac{\theta_P}{1-\theta_P}\right)^{h-2}\frac{2}{\lambda}$$

we obtain:

$$T(n_h) = \frac{1}{\lambda}\left[1 + 2\sum_{k=1}^{h-1}\left(\frac{\theta_P}{1-\theta_P}\right)^{k}\right]$$

References

Biais, B., P. Hillion and C. Spatt, 1995, 'An empirical analysis of the limit order book and the order flow in the Paris Bourse', *Journal of Finance*, 50, 1655–89.

Biais, B., D. Martimort and J. C. Rochet, 2000, 'Competing mechanisms in a common value environment', *Econometrica*, 4, 799–837.

Bloomfield, R., M. O'Hara and G. Saar, 2002, 'The "make or take" decision in an electronic market: evidence on the evolution of liquidity', Working Paper, Stern School of Business, New York University.

Brown, P. and M. Zhang, 1997, 'Market orders and market efficiency', *Journal of Finance*, 52, 277–308.

Buti, S. 2007, 'A challenger to the limit order book: the NYSE specialist' *Research Report Series*, SS, Swedish Institute for Financial Research, Stockholm.

Chakravarty, S. and C. W. Holden, 1995, 'An integrated model of market and limit orders', *Journal of Financial Intermediation*, 4, 213–41.

Foucault, T. 1999, 'Order flow composition and trading costs in a dynamic limit order market', *Journal of Financial Markets*, 2, 99–134.

Foucault, T., O. Kadan and E. Kandel, 2005, 'Limit order book as a market for liquidity', *Review of Financial Studies*, 4, 1171–217.

Glosten, L. 1989, 'Insider trading, liquidity and the role of monopolist specialist', *Journal of Business*, 52, 211–35.

    1994, 'Is the electronic open limit order book inevitable?', *Journal of Finance*, 49, 1127–60.

Glosten, L. and P. Milgrom, 1985, 'Bid, ask and transaction prices in a specialist market with heterogeneously informed traders', *Journal of Financial Economics*, 13, 71–100.

Goettler, R., C. Parlour and U. Rajan, 2008, 'Informed traders and limit order markets', *Journal of Financial Economics*, forthcoming.

Grossman, S. and J. Stiglitz, 1980, 'On the impossibility of informationally efficient markets', *American Economic Review*, 70, 393–408.

Huang, R. and H. Stoll, 1997, 'The components of the bid–ask spread: a general approach', *Review of Financial Studies*, 12, 61–94.

Kaniel, R. and H. Liu, 1998, 'So what orders do informed traders use?', *Journal of Business*, 79, 1867–913.

Kumar, P. and D. J. Seppi, 1998, 'Limit and market orders with optimising traders', Working Paper, Bauer College of Business, University of Houston.

Kyle, A. 1985, 'Continuous auctions and insider trading', *Econometrica*, 53, 1315–35.

Parlour, C. 1998, 'Price dynamics in limit order markets', *Review of Financial Studies,* 11, 789–816.

Parlour, C. and D. Seppi, 1993, 'Liquidity based competition for order flow', *Review of Financial Studies*, 16, 301–43.

Roll, R. 1984, 'A simple implicit measure of the effective bid–ask spread in an efficient market', *Journal of Finance*, 39, 1127–39.

Rosu, I. 2004, 'A dynamic model of the limit order book', Working Paper, Massachusetts Institute of Technology.

Seppi, D. 1990, 'Equilibrium block trading and asymmetric information', *Journal of Finance*, 45, 73–94.

    1997, 'Liquidity provision with limit orders and strategic specialist', *Review of Financial Studies,* 10, 103–50.

Viswanathan, S. and J. D. Wang, 2002, 'Market architecture: limit order books versus dealership markets', *Journal of Financial Markets,* 5, 127–67.

9   Price discovery

In the foregoing chapters we have seen that in the short run, the prices of financial instruments may deviate from their fundamental value on account of microstructure frictions such as bid–ask bounce, inventory control and order imbalances. Chapter 6 introduced empirical models for estimating transaction costs and the price impact of a trade. These models were quite simple: they assumed that the price impact of a trade was immediate. In reality, this is not always so, and there may be lagged effects or slow adjustments. We therefore need a richer dynamic structure in order to model prices and trades on financial markets. In this chapter, we introduce dynamic time-series models for prices and trades, and show how they can be used to describe the market's convergence on the new equilibrium price after a shock.

This chapter extends the simple empirical models of Chapter 6 to a full dynamic setting. We show how time-series models for prices and trades can be used to study these questions. Throughout the chapter, we focus more on the structure and interpretation of the models than on the econometric and sampling issues that often arise in estimating dynamic time series using microstructure data. Section 9.1 introduces a dynamic model for prices and order flow, with lagged effects of order flow on prices and order-flow dynamics. Section 9.2 generalizes that model to the vector autoregressive model, which was introduced into microstructure by Hasbrouck (1988, 1991, 1993, 1995) and has since become the standard reference model in the literature. We then turn to a formal decomposition of prices into permanent and transitory components, where the permanent component is interpreted as the equilibrium value of the asset, or the *efficient price*. Section 9.3 examines *price discovery*, i.e. the process of convergence on the efficient price, and the role of order flow in this process. Section 9.4 studies price discovery for securities that are traded in multiple market-places. The appendix gives some tools for dealing with dynamic econometric models and lag polynomials.

9.1   Price effects of trading

In Chapter 6 we discussed methods for estimating the information content of trades and the effect of inventory control on prices. The models that we discussed generally assume that only one of the effects (information or inventory control) is present. However, the empirical predictions of the asymmetric information and inventory control market microstructure models are very similar. Both theories predict that prices will move in the direction of the trade: a buyer-initiated order increases bid and ask prices, whereas a seller-initiated trade decreases bid and ask prices. This makes it difficult to distinguish the two theories empirically, unless good data on inventories are available. However, this is rarely the case.

Fortunately, in the absence of inventory data there is another way to separate information effects from inventory effects. Theoretically, information effects arise because trades reflect new information. This information will be incorporated in the price. If the market is efficient, the impact will be immediate and permanent. In contrast, inventory effects arise due to liquidity providers' inventory imbalances. If the liquidity providers actively manage their inventory, these imbalances will be temporary. As a direct consequence, the price effect of trades will also be temporary and will reverse in the future. This gives a handle to distinguish information from inventory control effects: information has permanent price effects whereas inventory effects are transitory.

9.1.1 Hasbrouck's model

Hasbrouck (1988) suggests an empirical model for estimating the permanent and transitory price effects of trading. Let x_t denote the signed order flow, and r_t the return, which equals the relative change in prices between two transactions.[1] Under the asymmetric information theory, the return responds to the unexpected part of the order flow:

$$r_t = \alpha(x_t - E_{t-1}x_t) + u_t \qquad (9.1)$$

The first term on the right-hand side of this equation is the surprise in the order flow. By construction, this surprise is unpredictable. The variable u_t denotes the return due to publicly available information arriving between the trades. If the market is semi-strong-form efficient, the public information u_t is unpredictable. Denoting the order-flow surprise by $\varepsilon_t = x_t - E_{t-1}x_t$, the returns are simply:

$$r_t = \alpha\varepsilon_t + u_t \qquad (9.2)$$

with the property that both ε_t and u_t are unpredictable:

$$E_t(\varepsilon_{t+i}) = 0, \quad E_t(u_{t+i}) = 0, \quad i > 0$$

It immediately follows that in a pure asymmetric information model, returns are unpredictable and the price follows a random walk. Hence, any shock to the prices is permanent, and consequently so are the price effects of trading.

---

[1] In empirical work, r_t is typically defined as $r_t = m_t - m_{t-1}$, where m_t is the logarithm of the midpoint of bid and ask quotes observed right after trade t. Alternatively, the difference between the transaction prices can be taken, $r_t = p_t - p_{t-1}$. For the purpose of measuring the price impact of trades, the definition based on quote midpoints is the most natural.

In the inventory control models of Chapter 5, returns are related to the trade size by:

$$r_t = \beta x_t + u_t \tag{9.3}$$

where x_t is the signed order flow at time t. Notice that if order flow were unpredictable, the asymmetric information model (9.1) would be empirically identical to the inventory control model (9.3). However, the inventory control theory predicts that order flow is predictable and exhibits reversals. In the long run, if the liquidity provider's inventory is stationary, the order flow will be reversed completely. Again denoting the unexpected order flow by ε_t, we can write the order flow itself as a sum of lagged surprises:

$$x_t = \varepsilon_t + \theta_1 \varepsilon_{t-1} + \theta_2 \varepsilon_{t-2} + \cdots \tag{9.4}$$

In time-series econometrics, equation (9.4) is called the moving average (MA) representation of x_t. If inventory is stationary, order flow in the long run is completely reversed and the coefficients of the MA representation should add up to zero, i.e. $1 + \sum_{i=1}^{\infty} \theta_i = 0$. Substituting (9.4) in (9.3), the equation for the returns in the pure inventory control model becomes:

$$r_t = \beta(\varepsilon_t + \theta_1 \varepsilon_{t-1} + \theta_2 \varepsilon_{t-2} + \cdots) + u_t \tag{9.5}$$

The coefficients of the shocks to order flow again should add up to zero. In the long run, prices are determined only by the public information u_t.

In the more general setting where both information effects and inventory control are present, we can write a general equation for the return:

$$r_t = \beta_0 \varepsilon_t + \beta_1 \varepsilon_{t-1} + \beta_2 \varepsilon_{t-2} + \cdots + u_t \tag{9.6}$$

The coefficient β_0 measures the immediate price impact of a trade, which is the sum of the information and inventory effects. The information effect can now be identified as the permanent impact on prices of a shock to the order flow. This is equal to the sum of the coefficients in equation (9.6):

$$\alpha = \sum_{i=0}^{\infty} \beta_i \tag{9.7}$$

9.1.2 A reduced-form approach

The approach outlined in the previous subsection suggests estimating the surprise in the order flow from the moving average representation (9.4) of x_t. In practice, this approach is not particularly convenient, as there may be many lags and many parameters θ_i to estimate. In addition, the return equation (9.6) cannot be estimated directly from the return and order-flow data. In this section we demonstrate that the information effect can also be estimated by a regression of returns on order flow, and an equation for the dynamics of order flow itself.

One can simply estimate a regression of the returns r_t on current order flow and several lags of the order flow:

$$r_t = b_0 x_t + b_1 x_{t-1} + \cdots + b_K x_{t-K} + u_t \qquad (9.8)$$

This equation generalizes the Glosten and Harris (1988) model, (6.39), which can be obtained by assuming $b_2 = \cdots = b_K = 0$. The leading coefficient, b_0, measures the contemporaneous impact of order flow on price. This is a sum of the information effect and inventory control effect. To isolate the information effect, we need to estimate how much of the price impact is permanent. For this, we also need an equation for the dynamics of order flow itself. An autoregressive model is most convenient:

$$x_t = \varphi_1 x_{t-1} + \cdots + \varphi_p x_{t-p} + \varepsilon_t \qquad (9.9)$$

With this model for return order flow, it is easily shown, using the methods discussed in the appendix to this chapter, that the permanent price effect of a trade is:[2]

$$\alpha(\varepsilon_t) = \frac{b_0 + b_1 + \cdots + b_k}{1 - \varphi_1 - \cdots - \varphi_p} \varepsilon_t \qquad (9.10)$$

This permanent effect can be interpreted as the information component, and the difference between the immediate and permanent effect as the inventory control component of transaction costs.

9.2   A generalized model for prices and trades

Although very useful for separating permanent (information) effects from temporary (inventory control) effects, a limitation of the framework in the previous section is that the order flow is assumed to evolve exogenously. In particular, there are no feedback effects from prices or returns to order flow. In this section we discuss a generalization of the model to take such feedback into account. This model is the vector autoregression, or VAR for short, introduced into market microstructure by Hasbrouck (1991).[3]

The first equation in the VAR model is a regression of returns on current order flow, lagged order flows and lagged returns. This reads as:

$$r_t = b_0 x_t + b_1 x_{t-1} + \cdots b_K x_{t-K} + a_1 r_{t-1} + \cdots + a_K r_{t-K} \qquad (9.11)$$

As in equation (9.8), the leading coefficient b_0 measures the immediate (or contemporaneous) impact of a trade on prices. That equation is extended by adding lagged return effects, allowing for a possible lagged response of prices to new information.

The second equation of the VAR models order-flow dynamics. Order flow tends to be serially correlated, i.e. orders tend to be followed by orders on the same side of the market, and there is also clustering of large orders. This produces serial correlation

---

[2] The proof is left as an exercise.
[3] For a more extensive introductory discussion of vector autoregressions, see the excellent textbooks of Lütkepohl (1993) and Hamilton (1994).

in the signed trade size variable x_t. Secondly, there may be feedback from the price process (returns) to trading. This causes a feedback effect from price returns to order flow. These effects are captured in the following equation:

$$x_t = d_1 x_{t-1} + \cdots d_K x_{t-K} + c_1 r_{t-1} + \cdots + c_K r_{t-K} \tag{9.12}$$

Notice that the equation for the order flow does not contain the current return r_t as an explanatory variable. This assumption is necessary to make the model econometrically identified. From an economic point of view, it means that order flow reacts only to previous price changes and not to the current return. This is a natural assumption in markets where trades are made at prices quoted by market-makers or at prices available in an electronic limit order book before the trade.

This model can be written compactly as a vector autoregression:

$$\begin{pmatrix} 1 & b_0 \\ 0 & 1 \end{pmatrix} \begin{pmatrix} r_t \\ x_t \end{pmatrix} = \sum_{k=1}^{K} \begin{pmatrix} a_k & b_k \\ c_k & d_k \end{pmatrix} \begin{pmatrix} r_{t-k} \\ x_{t-k} \end{pmatrix} + \begin{pmatrix} \varepsilon_{1t} \\ \varepsilon_{2t} \end{pmatrix} \tag{9.13}$$

Because of the presence of the contemporaneous order flow x_t in the equation for the returns, to identify the model one needs to assume that the error terms are uncorrelated:

$$E(\varepsilon_{1t}\varepsilon_{2t}) = 0. \tag{9.14}$$

Hasbrouck (1991) suggests using the long-run price impact of an unexpected trade as the measure of asymmetric information in the model. Precisely, the suggested measure is:

$$\alpha(\varepsilon_{2t}) = \lim_{H \to \infty} \sum_{h=0}^{H} E(r_{t+h}|\varepsilon_{2t}) \tag{9.15}$$

In the time-series literature, this measure is called the cumulative impulse response of the returns to a shock in the order-flow process. It can be calculated from the vector moving average (VMA) representation of the VAR model:[4]

$$\begin{pmatrix} r_t \\ x_t \end{pmatrix} = \sum_{k=0}^{K} \begin{pmatrix} a_k^* & b_k^* \\ c_k^* & d_k^* \end{pmatrix} \begin{pmatrix} \varepsilon_{1t} \\ \varepsilon_{2t} \end{pmatrix} \tag{9.16}$$

Spelling out the first equation for the prices gives an immediate generalization of equation (9.5):

$$r_t = a_0^* \varepsilon_{1t} + a_1^* \varepsilon_{1,t-1} + \cdots + b_0^* \varepsilon_{2t} + b_1^* \varepsilon_{2,t-1} + \cdots \tag{9.17}$$

---

[4] The technique for calculating the VMA coefficients and impulse responses is beyond the scope of this book, but the procedure is standard in time-series packages like Eviews.

Hence, the long-run effect of a trade shock ε_{2t} on prices is the sum of the coefficients b_i^*:

$$\alpha(\varepsilon_{2t}) = \sum_{i=0}^{\infty} b_i^* \qquad (9.18)$$

This measures the information effect of a trade on prices.

9.3   The efficient price

As the previous section has shown, some price effects of trading are temporary, and in an efficient market, in the long run, prices are expected to return to their fundamental values. However, the equilibrium price itself is not a fixed value, but moves with public news and information revealed by the trading process. In this section, we develop models that separate the equilibrium price dynamics from short-term price fluctuations around the equilibrium. Such models can be used, for example, to assess the speed of convergence to the equilibrium after a shock (e.g. a large transaction). The variance of the short-term deviations from the equilibrium price are a measure of market liquidity. Finally, in a setting where one asset is traded on several different markets (fragmented trading), the models can be used to assess how informative the trading process is in each market (the contribution to price discovery); this last topic will be dealt with in section 9.4.

First let us introduce the concept of the efficient price. This is the expectation of the future (terminal) value of the asset given all publicly available information:

$$p_t^* = E[F|\Omega_t] \qquad (9.19)$$

The information set Ω_t will contain public news, but also the publicly observable (aggregate) order flow, as in the Kyle (1985) and Glosten–Milgrom (1985) models discussed earlier. If the information available in the market is processed efficiently, the efficient price will be a martingale with respect to this information:[5]

$$p_t^* = p_{t-1}^* + \eta_t, \quad E_{t-1}[\eta_t] = 0 \qquad (9.20)$$

where $E_{t-1}[.]$ is shorthand notation for $E[.|\Omega_{t-1}]$. Due to microstructure frictions, the observed price p_t may deviate from the efficient price, but the deviations should be temporary:

$$p_t = p_t^* + s_t, \quad \lim_{h \to \infty} E[s_{t+h}|\Omega_t] = 0 \qquad (9.21)$$

The latter condition guarantees that in the long run prices will converge on their equilibrium level, although this equilibrium level itself (p_t^*) is not stationary and follows a martingale.

---

[5] A martingale is a process with the property that its increments have zero expectation, i.e. $E_{t-1}[p_t^*] = p_{t-1}^*$. The random walk is a special case of this, where the increments $\eta_t = p_t^* - p_{t-1}^*$ are independent and identically distributed.

This structure can be seen as a generalization of the model of Roll. Let the returns be defined by:

$$r_t = p_t - p_{t-1} \tag{9.22}$$

where p_t is the logarithm of the transaction price. Then the returns are given by:

$$r_t = p_t^* - p_{t-1}^* + s_t - s_{t-1} = \eta_t + \Delta s_t \tag{9.23}$$

which implies correlated transaction returns as long as s_t is not equal to zero. Hence, the prices observed are of the 'random walk plus noise' type, where the random walk is the efficient price and the noise is due to microstructure frictions. The 'noise' here can have complicated dynamics, but is stationary by assumption. In Roll's model, s_t is simply plus or minus half the bid–ask spread: $s_t = (S/2)Q_t$. The model introduced here allows for a richer dynamic structure of the microstructure frictions.

9.3.1 Inferring the efficient price

The efficient price is not directly observable. Hasbrouck (1993) discusses two ways of identifying it. The first method is based on prices only, and the suggestion is to estimate a reduced-form autoregressive model for the observed returns:

$$r_t = a_1 r_{t-1} + a_2 r_{t-2} + .. + a_K r_{t-K} + \epsilon_t \tag{9.24}$$

This autoregressive model can be inverted to a moving average (MA) representation (see Stock and Watson, 1988) of the form:

$$r_t = \epsilon_t + a_1^* \epsilon_{t-1} + \cdots = \sum_{k=0}^{\infty} a_k^* \epsilon_{t-k} \tag{9.25}$$

The sum of the MA coefficients in equation (9.25) then defines the change in the permanent component or the efficient price:

$$p_t^* - p_{t-1}^* = \left(\sum_{k=0}^{\infty} a_k^* \right) \epsilon_t \tag{9.26}$$

Hence, the efficient price conforms to a random walk:

$$p_t^* = p_{t-1}^* + \theta \epsilon_t \tag{9.27}$$

with $\theta = \sum_{k=0}^{\infty} a_k^*$.

Subtracting the efficient price innovation from the MA representation (9.25), we can decompose the returns into a shock to the efficient price and the changes in the transitory component:

$$r_t = \theta \epsilon_t + \Delta s_t \tag{9.28}$$

with:

$$s_t = \alpha_0 \epsilon_t + \alpha_1 \epsilon_{t-1} + \cdots = \sum_{k=0}^{\infty} \alpha_k \epsilon_{t-k} \tag{9.29}$$

and:

$$\alpha_k = - \sum_{i=k+1}^{\infty} a_i^* \tag{9.30}$$

This expression decomposes the return into a permanent component $(\theta \epsilon_t)$ and the first difference of the temporary component s_t. Notice that s_t can also be defined as the difference between the observed price and the constructed efficient price:

$$s_t = p_t - p_t^* \tag{9.31}$$

Hasbrouck (1993) suggests using the standard deviation of s_t as a measure of market quality. This measure can be seen as an extension of Roll's estimator, which was discussed in Chapter 6.

9.3.2 Structural models
In the decomposition described in the previous section, the innovations to the permanent and the transitory component are perfectly correlated, as both are linear functions of ϵ_t. However, this is not the only possible decomposition into permanent and transitory components. Another method of breaking the price down into an efficient price and a transitory component is by assuming that the permanent and transitory effects are mutually independent.

In the decomposition of the previous section, the innovations in the permanent and transitory component are perfectly correlated, as both are linear functions of ϵ_t. However, this is not the only possible decomposition into permanent and transitory components. Another way to decompose the price into an efficient price and a transitory component is by assuming that permanent and transitory effects are mutually independent. This 'structural' model is:

$$p_t = p_t^* + s_t \tag{9.32}$$
$$p_t^* = p_{t-1}^* + \eta_t \tag{9.33}$$
$$s_t = \beta(L)u_t \tag{9.34}$$

where η_t and u_t are uncorrelated at all lags. The dynamics for the prices are then:

$$\Delta p_t = \eta_t + \Delta s_t \tag{9.35}$$

Let us consider the simplest example, where $s_t = u_t$. Assume that $s_t = u_t$. The structural model for the returns is then:

$$r_t = \eta_t + \Delta u_t \tag{9.36}$$

with autocovariances:

$$\gamma_0 = Var(r_t) = \sigma_\eta^2 + 2\sigma_u^2 \tag{9.37}$$
$$\gamma_1 = Cov(r_t, r_{t-1}) = -\sigma_u^2 \tag{9.38}$$

Notice that this structure posits that $\gamma_1 < 0$, which is a typical feature of high-frequency returns. The variance of the transitory component, σ_u^2 can be estimated simply from the autocorrelation of the returns:

$$\sigma_u = \sqrt{-Cov(r_t, r_{t-1})} \tag{9.39}$$

which is Roll's estimator, introduced in Chapter 6.

This simple example also illustrates the difference between the structural model and the decomposition based on the moving average. The reduced-form moving average model for the returns is:

$$r_t = \epsilon_t - a\epsilon_{t-1}, \quad |a| < 1 \tag{9.40}$$

with $\gamma_0 = Var(r_t) = (1 + a^2)\sigma_\epsilon^2$ and $\gamma_1 = Cov(r_t, r_{t-1}) = -a\sigma_\epsilon^2$. We now show how to find the permanent–transitory decomposition in both models:

- The *permanent* component in the structural model is η_t, with variance $\sigma_\eta^2 = \gamma_0 + 2\gamma_1$. In the moving average model, the permanent component is $(1 - a)\epsilon_t$ with variance $(1 - a)^2\sigma_\epsilon^2 = \gamma_0 + 2\gamma_1$. Hence, the permanent components in both decompositions are the same.
- The *transitory* component in the structural model is u_t, with variance $\sigma_u^2 = -\gamma_1$. In the moving average model, the transitory component is $a\epsilon_t$ with variance $a^2\sigma_\epsilon^2 = -a\gamma_1$. Because $|a| < 1$, for $\gamma_1 < 0$ (which is typical for microstructure data) this variance is always smaller than σ_u^2.

Therefore, we can see that different assumptions about the underlying data-generating process result in different interpretations of the same correlations. One may wonder whether it is possible to combine the structural and the moving average models. For example, one could assume that η_t and u_t are contemporaneously correlated, with covariance $\sigma_{\eta u}$. This implies an autocorrelation structure $\gamma_0 = Var(r_t) = \sigma_\eta^2 + 2\sigma_u^2 + 2\sigma_{\eta u}$ and $\gamma_1 = Cov(r_t, r_{t-1}) = -\sigma_u^2 - \sigma_{\eta u}$. It is easily seen from these two equations that the three parameters σ_η, σ_u and $\sigma_{\eta u}$ cannot be identified separately. In fact, positing a correlation of zero between η_t and u_t gives the structural model, whereas positing a correlation of 1, i.e. $\sigma_{\eta u} = \sigma_\eta\sigma_u$, gives the same variance for s_t as the moving average decomposition.[6] This argument implies that the variance of s_t is not uniquely determined but depends on the identifying assumptions. As a general result, out of all possible decompositions, the moving average decomposition gives the *lowest* possible value for the variance of the transitory component, $Var(s_t)$. The intuition underlying this result is that in the moving average decomposition, the correlation between η_t and u_t is perfect and the variance of s_t attains its lower bound.

For further discussion of structural and reduced-form models for price discovery, see Hasbrouck (1993). De Jong and Schotman (2003) generalize the structural model to a multi-market setting.

---

[6] The proof is left as an exercise.

9.3.3 Prices and trades

In this subsection we extend the model for prices only to a model for both prices and trades. In the previous section, we argued that the vector autoregression is an adequate framework for modelling the joint dynamics of trades and prices. For convenience, we repeat the VAR equations here:

$$\begin{pmatrix} 1 & b_0 \\ 0 & 1 \end{pmatrix} \begin{pmatrix} r_t \\ x_t \end{pmatrix} = \sum_{k=1}^{K} \begin{pmatrix} a_k & b_k \\ c_k & d_k \end{pmatrix} \begin{pmatrix} r_{t-k} \\ x_{t-k} \end{pmatrix} + \begin{pmatrix} \varepsilon_{1t} \\ \varepsilon_{2t} \end{pmatrix} \tag{9.41}$$

For the analysis of permanent and transitory price effects, it is most convenient to invert the VAR to a vector moving average (VMA) model:

$$\begin{pmatrix} r_t \\ x_t \end{pmatrix} = \sum_{k=0}^{K} \begin{pmatrix} a_k^* & b_k^* \\ c_k^* & d_k^* \end{pmatrix} \begin{pmatrix} \varepsilon_{1t} \\ \varepsilon_{2t} \end{pmatrix} \tag{9.42}$$

Spelling out the first equation for the prices gives an immediate generalization of equation (9.25):

$$r_t = a_0^* \varepsilon_{1t} + a_1^* \varepsilon_{t-1} + \cdots + b_0^* \varepsilon_{2t} + b_1^* \varepsilon_{t-1} + \cdots \tag{9.43}$$

As in the univariate case, the return shocks can be decomposed into permanent and transitory effects:

$$r_t = \theta_1 \varepsilon_{1t} + \theta_2 \varepsilon_{2t} + \Delta s_t \tag{9.44}$$

with $\theta_1 = \sum_{i=0}^{\infty} a_i^*$ and $\theta_2 = \sum_{i=0}^{\infty} b_i^*$. The temporary component s_t is given by:

$$s_t = \alpha_0 \varepsilon_{1t} + \alpha_1 \varepsilon_{1,t-1} + \cdots + \beta_0 \varepsilon_{2t} + \beta_1 \varepsilon_{1,t-2} + \cdots \tag{9.45}$$

where α_k and β_k are defined by:

$$\alpha_k = -\sum_{i=k+1}^{\infty} a_i^*, \quad \beta_k = -\sum_{i=k+1}^{\infty} b_i^* \tag{9.46}$$

Hence, the efficient price innovation is again a random walk:

$$p_t^* = p_{t-1}^* + \theta_1 \varepsilon_{1t} + \theta_2 \varepsilon_{2t} \tag{9.47}$$

These equations are a straightforward generalization of the univariate model. They also allow us to calculate the relative contributions to price discovery of order flow and public information. For example, the relative contribution of order flow to the efficient price variance is:

$$R_x^2 = \frac{\theta_2^2 \sigma_{\varepsilon_2}^2}{\theta_1^2 \sigma_{\varepsilon_1}^2 + \theta_2^2 \sigma_{\varepsilon_2}^2} \tag{9.48}$$

where $\sigma_{\varepsilon_1}^2$ and $\sigma_{\varepsilon_2}^2$ are the variances of the price and order-flow innovations, respectively.

9.4 Price discovery in multiple markets

In this section we extend the dynamic model of prices to an asset that is traded on more than one market. Examples are European, Asian or Latin American stocks that are also listed on a US market, or US securities traded both on a central market (NYSE or NASDAQ) and on competing electronic communication networks (ECNs). This enables us to address the question of which market's price reflects the fundamental value most accurately, and which market contributes most to convergence on the equilibrium value.

We start from the idea that prices are given by the efficient price plus a stationary term. As before, the efficient price is a random walk:

$$p_t^* = p_{t-1}^* + \eta_t \tag{9.49}$$

The price on market i is:

$$p_{it} = p_t^* + s_{it}, \quad \lim_{h \to \infty} E_t \left[s_{i,t+h} \right] = 0 \tag{9.50}$$

Notice that the efficient price is *the same for each market*. Differences in prices between markets are due solely to temporary deviations from the efficient price. Hence, differences between prices are only temporary:

$$p_{it} - p_{jt} = s_{it} - s_{jt}, \quad \lim_{h \to \infty} E_t \left[s_{i,t+h} - s_{j,t+h} \right] = 0 \tag{9.51}$$

Prices are therefore *cointegrated* in the definition of Engle and Granger (1987): the price in any given market is non-stationary, but since all prices contain the same random walk component, the price difference is stationary.

9.4.1 Two markets

Hasbrouck (1995) suggests a reduced-form model for the prices in multiple markets (for clarity, we here present the model for two markets):

$$r_{1t} = \alpha_1(p_{2,t-1} - p_{1,t-1}) + \sum_{k=1}^{K} a_{11,k} r_{1,t-k} + \sum_{k=1}^{K} a_{12,k} r_{2,t-k} + \epsilon_{1t} \tag{9.52}$$

$$r_{2t} = \alpha_2(p_{2,t-1} - p_{1,t-1}) + \sum_{k=1}^{K} a_{21,k} r_{1,t-k} + \sum_{k=1}^{K} a_{22,k} r_{2,t-k} + \epsilon_{2t} \tag{9.53}$$

where the error terms ϵ_{1t} and ϵ_{2t} may be contemporaneously correlated. This is a so-called vector error correction model (VECM). It can be seen as a VAR model for the pair of returns $r_{1t} = p_{1t} - p_{1,t-1}$ and $r_{2t} = p_{2t} - p_{2,t-1}$, extended with an error correction term $p_{2,t-1} - p_{1,t-1}$. This term guarantees that in the long run, prices in the two markets return to the equilibrium relation of stationary difference between them.[7]

---

[7] A sufficient condition for this result is that $\alpha_1 \leq 0$ and $\alpha_2 \geq 0$ with at least one strict inequality.

The VECM allows decomposition of the observed prices as a function of current and lagged shocks to the price process (ϵ_{1t} and ϵ_{2t}). This is similar to the conversion to an infinite MA representation for the univariate model in section 9.3. The MA representation for p_{1t} is:

$$r_{1t} = \sum_{k=0}^{\infty} a_{11,k}^* \epsilon_{1t-k} + \sum_{k=0}^{\infty} a_{12}^* \epsilon_{2t-k} \tag{9.54}$$

This can be written, for the first market, as:

$$r_{1t} = \theta_1 \epsilon_{1t} + \theta_2 \epsilon_{2t} + \sum_{k=0}^{\infty} \alpha_{11,k} \Delta \epsilon_{1t-k} + \alpha_{12,k} \Delta \epsilon_{2t-k} \tag{9.55}$$

where $\theta_1 = \sum_{k=0}^{\infty} a_{i1,k}^*$ and $\theta_2 = \sum_{k=0}^{\infty} a_{i2,k}^*$. The coefficients θ_1 and θ_2 measure the permanent impact of a shock in the two-price processes. Likewise, for the second market we find:

$$r_{2t} = \theta_1 \epsilon_{1t} + \theta_2 \epsilon_{2t} + \sum_{k=0}^{\infty} \alpha_{21,k} \Delta \epsilon_{1t-k} + \alpha_{22,k} \Delta \epsilon_{2t-k} \tag{9.56}$$

Notice that θ_1 and θ_2 are the same for both markets; this is because the efficient price is identical.

The efficient-price dynamics can be written as:

$$p_t^* = p_{t-1}^* + \theta_1 \epsilon_{1t} + \theta_2 \epsilon_{2t} \tag{9.57}$$

Hence, the innovation in the efficient price can be attributed to the innovation in each observed price. This led Hasbrouck (1995) to suggest a measure of the contribution to the price discovery process, which he calls the *information share* (IS) of a market. His definition is:

$$IS_i = \frac{Var(\theta_i \epsilon_{it})}{Var(\theta_1 \epsilon_{1t} + \theta_2 \epsilon_{2t})} = \frac{\theta_i^2 Var(\epsilon_{it})}{\theta_1^2 Var(\epsilon_{1t}) + 2\theta_1 \theta_2 Cov(\epsilon_{1t}, \epsilon_{2t}) \theta_2^2 Var(\epsilon_{2t})} \tag{9.58}$$

These information shares do not necessarily add up to 1, since their sum depends on the covariance term in the denominator.

9.4.2 N markets

For more than two markets, the vector error correction model (VECM) is:

$$r_t = \alpha z_{t-1} + \sum_{k=1}^{K} A_k r_{t-k} + \epsilon_t \tag{9.59}$$

where $r_t = \Delta p_t$ is the vector of returns in the N markets. The $N \times N$ coefficient matrix A_k defines the impact of the lagged returns on contemporaneous returns; in the special case $N = 2$, the matrix A_k is:

$$A_k = \begin{pmatrix} a_{11,k} & a_{12,k} \\ a_{21,k} & a_{22,k} \end{pmatrix}$$

The cointegrating vector z_{t-1} has dimension $(N-1) \times 1$ with elements:

$$z_{i,t-1} = p_{i,t-1} - p_{N,t-1} \tag{9.60}$$

and α is an $N \times (N-1)$ matrix.

The inverted MA representation of the VECM (9.59) is:

$$\Delta p_t = C(L)\epsilon_t = C(1)\epsilon_t + \Delta C^*(L)\epsilon_t \tag{9.61}$$

Because the elements of p_t are cointegrated, they should have the same common permanent component. This puts restrictions on $C(1)$. Using the Granger representation theorem (Engle and Granger, 1987), De Jong (2002) shows that all the rows of $C(1)$ are the same and hence can be written as:

$$C(1) = \iota\theta' \tag{9.62}$$

where θ is an $N \times 1$ vector, and ι is an $N \times 1$ vector of ones. Because the linear combination of returns $\theta'r_t$ is non-stationary, pre-multiplying equation (9.59) by θ' shows that θ satisfies the $N-1$ restrictions:

$$\theta'\alpha = 0 \tag{9.63}$$

So the vector θ is easily derived from the VECM parameters.[8] With this restriction, we can write the MA representation of the VECM (9.59) as

$$\Delta p_t = \iota\theta'\epsilon_t + \Delta C^*(L)\epsilon_t \tag{9.64}$$

The efficient price in the multi-market setting is thus a random walk, whose innovations are a linear combination of the innovations of the VECM:

$$p_t^* = p_{t-1}^* + \theta'\epsilon_t \tag{9.65}$$

The price vector itself is:

$$p_t = \iota\theta' \sum_{s=0}^{t} \epsilon_s + C^*(L)\epsilon_t \tag{9.66}$$

It is straightforward to generalize all the other quantities and the information shares from two markets to the multi-market setting.

---

[8] One further restriction has to be imposed on θ to identify it fully. We return to this point later.

Full identification of θ   From the $N - 1$ dimensional restriction $\theta'\alpha = 0$, the vector θ can be identified only up to a scale factor. To determine the full solution, we need a bit more algebra. Firstly, we define a vector γ which satisfies both $\gamma'\alpha = 0$ and $\gamma'\iota = 1$ and is therefore uniquely identified. Then we define the $(N - 1) \times 1$ matrix β which defines the error correction terms $z_t = \beta' p_t$. Now consider a transformation of the data, in which p_t is pre-multiplied by β' and γ'. These parameters isolate the stationary (error correction) terms and the long-run component, respectively. This transformation is invertible and does not cause any loss of information. After this transformation the VECM reads:

$$\begin{pmatrix} \Delta\beta' p_t \\ \Delta\gamma' p_t \end{pmatrix} = \begin{pmatrix} (\beta'\alpha)\beta' p_t \\ 0 \end{pmatrix} + \begin{pmatrix} \beta' \\ \gamma' \end{pmatrix} \sum_{k=1}^{K} A_k \Delta p_{t-k} + \begin{pmatrix} \beta'\epsilon_t \\ \gamma'\epsilon_t \end{pmatrix} \qquad (9.67)$$

Notice that there is no error correction term for $\Delta\gamma' p_t$; this property will prove to be very useful. Substituting for $z_t = \beta' p_t$ and $m_t = \gamma' p_t$, the VECM can be written as:

$$\Delta z_t = (\beta'\alpha)z_{t-1} + A_{11}^*(L)\Delta z_{t-1} + A_{12}^*(L)\Delta m_{t-1} + \beta'\epsilon_t \qquad (9.68)$$
$$\Delta m_t = \qquad\qquad A_{21}^*(L)\Delta z_{t-1} + A_{22}^*(L)\Delta m_{t-1} + \gamma'\epsilon_t \qquad (9.69)$$

with $A^*(L)y_{t-1} = \sum_{k=1}^{K} A_k^* y_{t-k}$ and:

$$A_k^* = \begin{pmatrix} \beta' \\ \gamma' \end{pmatrix} A_k \begin{pmatrix} \beta' \\ \gamma' \end{pmatrix}^{-1} \qquad (9.70)$$

This system of equations can be rewritten to a stationary VAR in the vector $(z_t, \Delta m_t)'$:

$$a(L) \begin{pmatrix} z_t \\ \Delta m_t \end{pmatrix} = \begin{pmatrix} \beta' \\ \gamma' \end{pmatrix} \epsilon_t$$

where the sum of the VAR coefficients is:

$$a(1) = \begin{pmatrix} \beta'\alpha & A_{12}^*(1) \\ 0 & 1 - A_{22}^*(1) \end{pmatrix} \qquad (9.71)$$

By construction, this matrix is invertible.

Now, let us consider the VMA representation of the model:

$$\Delta p_t = C(L)\epsilon_t = \iota\theta'\epsilon_t + C^*(L)(1 - L)\epsilon_t \qquad (9.72)$$

Applying the same data transformations as before gives:

$$\Delta\beta' p_t = \beta' C^*(L)(1 - L)\epsilon_t \qquad (9.73)$$
$$\Delta\gamma' p_t = \theta'\epsilon_t + \gamma' C^*(L)(1 - L)\epsilon_t \qquad (9.74)$$

where we used the properties $\beta'\iota = 0$ and $\gamma'\iota = 1$. The first equation is overdifferenced (i.e. not invertible), and the invertible VMA representation for $(z_t, \Delta m_t)'$ is:

$$\begin{pmatrix} z_t \\ \Delta m_t \end{pmatrix} = \begin{pmatrix} \beta' C^*(L) \\ \theta' + \gamma' C^*(L)(1 - L) \end{pmatrix} \epsilon_t \qquad (9.75)$$

As the VAR representation (9.67) and the VMA representation (9.75) are equivalent, the sum of the VMA coefficients must equal the inverse of the sum of the VAR coefficients:

$$\begin{pmatrix} \beta'C^*(1) \\ \theta' \end{pmatrix} = \alpha(1)^{-1} \begin{pmatrix} \beta' \\ \gamma' \end{pmatrix} \tag{9.76}$$

Looking at the formula for the inverse of $\alpha(1)$ and selecting the last row of the matrix equality, we find:

$$\theta = \gamma(1 - A_{22}^*(1))^{-1} \tag{9.77}$$

Notice that the latter factor is a scalar, and from the definition of $A^*(L)$ we know that:

$$A_{22}^*(1) = \gamma'A(1)\bar{\gamma} \tag{9.78}$$

where $\bar{\gamma}$ is the last column of the inverse of the matrix $\begin{pmatrix} \beta' \\ \gamma' \end{pmatrix}$

Appendix: Lag polynomials

Definition   For the derivation of some results in this chapter it is often convenient to write the dynamic models using lag polynomials. A Kth order lag polynomial may be written as:

$$a(L)y_t = (1 + a_1L + a_2L^2 + \cdots + a_KL^K)y_t = y_t + a_1y_{t-1} + a_2y_{t-2} + \cdots + a_Ky_{t-K}$$

where $L^ky_t = y_{t-k}$. A frequently used lag polynomial is the first difference $\Delta = (1 - L)$:

$$\Delta y_t = (1 - L)y_t = y_t - y_{t-1}$$

Multiplication   Lag polynomials can be multiplied like ordinary polynomials. For example, let $\varphi(L) = (1 - \varphi L)$. Then:

$$(1-L)\varphi(L)y_t = (1-L)(1-\varphi L)y_t = (1-(1+\varphi)+\varphi L^2)y_t = y_t-(1+\varphi)y_{t-1}+\varphi y_{t-2}$$

The order of the polynomials in multiplication is interchangeable:

$$(1 - L)\varphi(L)y_t = \varphi(L)(1 - L)y_t$$

Inversion   An important operation is the inversion of lag polynomials. Let:

$$\varphi(L)y_t = \epsilon_t$$

which is a typical autoregressive (AR) model for y_t. Then:

$$y_t = \varphi(L)^{-1}\epsilon_t$$

with $\varphi(L)^{-1}\varphi(L) = 1$. For example, for the AR(1) polynomial $\varphi(L) = 1 - \varphi L$ we find:

$$\varphi(L)^{-1} = 1 + \varphi L + \varphi^2 L^2 + \cdots$$

Hence, the AR(1) model for y_t is:

$$y_t = \varphi y_{t-1} + \epsilon_t \quad \leftrightarrow \quad (1 - \varphi L)y_t = \epsilon_t$$

with moving average representation found by inversion of the AR polynomial:

$$y_t = (1 - \varphi L)^{-1}\epsilon_t = \epsilon_t + \varphi\epsilon_{t-1} + \varphi^2\epsilon_{t-2} + \cdots$$

More generally, for an autoregressive moving average (ARMA) model:

$$\varphi(L)y_t = \beta(L)\epsilon_t$$

with $\varphi(L) = 1 - \varphi_1 L - \cdots - \varphi_k L^K$, the infinite MA representation is:

$$y_t = \theta(L)\epsilon_t, \quad \theta(L) = \varphi(L)^{-1}\beta(L) \tag{9.79}$$

Sum of coefficients   The sum of the coefficients in an MA representation is often needed in order to determine the permanent effect of a shock. Let:

$$y_t = \sum_{i=0}^{\infty} \beta_i \epsilon_{t-i} = \beta(L)\epsilon_t$$

with:

$$\beta(L) = \beta_0 + \beta_1 L + \beta_2 L^2 + \cdots$$

The sum of the coefficients is therefore:

$$\sum_{i=0}^{\infty} \beta_i = \beta(1)$$

In the ARMA model (9.79), the sum of the coefficients is

$$\sum_{i=1}^{\infty} \theta_i = \theta(1) = \frac{\beta(1)}{\varphi(1)} = \frac{\beta_0 + \beta_1 + \cdots}{1 - \varphi_1 - \cdots - \varphi_K}$$

Exercises

Exercise 1
Show what restrictions the original Glosten–Harris model from Chapter 6 imposes on the VAR for r_t and x_t, as introduced in section 9.2.

Solution
The Glosten–Harris model is a regression of r_t on x_t and x_{t-1}. There is no feedback from returns to order flow. In the VAR, equation (9.13), this leaves only b_0 and b_1 as free parameters, all other coefficients being equal to zero.

Exercise 2

Consider the following model, which is a variant of that of Hasbrouck (1991). The efficient price is given by a random walk:

$$p_t^* = p_{t-1}^* + \lambda\varepsilon_t + \eta_t$$

where ε_t is the unexpected order flow and λ measures information effects. The quote midpoint equals the efficient price plus an effect of current and previous trades (possibly reflecting inventory control effects):

$$m_t = p_t^* + \beta_0 x_t + \cdots + \beta_L x_{t-L}$$

Finally, order flow is determined by:

$$x_t = -c(m_{t-1} - p_{t-1}^*) + \varepsilon_t$$

Derive the reduced-form VAR of this model and express the VAR coefficients in terms of the structural coefficients of the model.

Solution

Firstly, substitute $m_t - p_t^* = \beta(L)x_t$ from the second equation into the third equation, to find:

$$x_t = -c\beta(L)x_{t-1} + \varepsilon_t$$

In the VAR, this equation is:

$$x_t = d_1 x_{t-1} + \cdots + d_L x_{t-L} + \varepsilon_{2t}$$

with $d_i = -c\beta_i$ for $i = 1, \ldots, L$ and $\varepsilon_{2t} = \varepsilon_t$. The other coefficients, c_i, are zero.

Secondly, in the first equation replace p_t^* with $m_t - \beta(L)x_t$ and substitute:

$$\varepsilon_t = x_t + c\beta(L)x_{t-1}$$

This yields:

$$\Delta m_t = \beta(L)x_t - \beta(L)x_{t-1} + \lambda\left(x_t + c\beta(L)x_{t-1}\right) + \eta_t$$

or:

$$\Delta m_t = b_0 x_t + b_1 x_{t-1} + \cdots + b_{L+1} x_{t-L-1} + \eta_t$$

with $b_0 = \beta_0 + \lambda$, $b_i = \beta_i - (1 - \lambda c)\beta_{i-1}$ for $i = 1, \ldots, L$ and $b_{L+1} = -(1 - \lambda c)\beta_L$. Furthermore, $\varepsilon_{1t} = \eta_t$ and the other coefficients, a_i, are zero.

Exercise 3

A typical structure for high-frequency returns is a second-order moving average, or MA(2), with a strong negative first-order correlation and a small positive second-order correlation. A typical estimate would be:

$$r_t = \epsilon_t - 0.4\epsilon_{t-1} + 0.1\epsilon_{t-2}$$

Decompose the return into a permanent component and a temporary component.

Solution
The sum of the MA coefficients is $\theta = 1 - 0.4 + 0.1 = 0.7$. Hence, 70 per cent of the initial return shock will be included permanently in the prices. The remainder is temporary. The full permanent–transitory decomposition of the returns is:

$$r_t = 0.7\epsilon_t + \Delta s_t$$

with:

$$s_t = 0.3\epsilon_t - 0.1\epsilon_{t-1}$$

The variance of s_t is then $(0.3^2 + 0.1^2)\sigma_\epsilon^2 = 0.1\sigma_\epsilon^2$, which can be seen as a measure of microstructure frictions.

Exercise 4
Consider high-frequency return data, with variance $0.05 * 10^{-4}$ and a first-order serial correlation $\rho = -0.4$. With these data, calculate the volatility of the permanent and transitory components, using both the moving average and the structural model for price discovery.

Solution
In the moving average model, $r_t = \epsilon_t - a\epsilon_{t-1}$, the first-order serial correlation equals:

$$\rho = \frac{\gamma_1}{\gamma_0} = \frac{-a}{1 + a^2}$$

with solution $a = 0.5$ for $\rho = -0.4$. The variance of ϵ_t is obtained from $\gamma_0 = (1 + a^2)\sigma_\epsilon^2$, which gives $\sigma_\epsilon^2 = 0.04 * 10^{-4}$ or $\sigma_\epsilon = 0.2\%$. The variance of the permanent component is $\gamma_0 + 2\gamma_1 = \gamma_0(1 - 2\rho)$, which equals $0.01 * 10^{-4}$. Hence, the standard deviation of the permanent component is 0.01%. The transitory component equals $a\epsilon_t$ with standard deviation $0.5\sigma_\epsilon = 0.01\%$. The variance of the permanent component is the same in the structural model as in the MA model, but the variance of the transitory component differs. According to equation (9.38) the variance is $\sigma_u^2 = -\gamma_1 = -\rho\gamma_0 = 0.02 * 10^{-4}$. The standard deviation of the transitory component therefore equals 0.0142%. This is higher than in the moving average decomposition.

Exercise 5
In this exercise, you are asked to estimate the information shares using simulated market data, provided on the book's website. The data are generated from a model that was suggested in Hasbrouck (2002). There are two markets. The prices in market 1 are equal to the efficient price, p_t^* plus or minus half the bid–ask spread:

$$p_{1t} = p_t^* + \delta Q_t$$

The efficient price follows a random walk (without drift):

$$p_t^* = p_{t-1}^* + \eta_t$$

where the innovations η_t are IID normal with mean zero and variance σ_η^2. As in the Roll model, we assume that the bid–ask bounce is uncorrelated, i.e. $\Pr(Q_t = 1|\Omega_{t-1}) = 0.5$ and $\Pr(Q_t = -1|\Omega_{t-1}) = 0.5$. Prices in the second market have no bid–ask spread, but lag one period behind the market:

$$p_{2t} = p_{t-1}^*$$

For the time interval $(t-1, t)$, one should think of a short period such as a minute, or several minutes. The first market in this setting could represent a centralized order-driven trading platform like the NYSE or Euronext. The second could be a crossing network (like Posit or the NYSE After-Hours Trading Session) where orders are cleared at the central market's previously observed equilibrium price.

The data set provides a sample of 500 simulated data points. The parameters used for the simulation are $\delta = 0.001$, $\sigma_\eta = 0.005$ and $m_0 = 20$. Figure 9.1 shows the first 100 data points: the squares indicate the prices in market 1, and the solid line, the prices in market 2, which equal the lagged efficient price. Using these data, perform the following exercises:

(1) Construct the error correction term $z_t = p_{1t} - p_{2t}$ and the returns $r_{it} = p_{it} - p_{i,t-1}$ for $i = 1, 2$. Then, estimate a VECM model of the form:

$$r_{1t} = \alpha_1 z_{t-1} + \sum_{k=1}^{K} a_{11,k} r_{1,t-k} + \sum_{k=1}^{K} a_{12,k} r_{2,t-k} + \epsilon_{1t}$$

$$r_{2t} = \alpha_2 z_{t-1} + \sum_{k=1}^{K} a_{21,k} r_{1,t-k} + \sum_{k=1}^{K} a_{22,k} r_{2,t-k} + \epsilon_{2t}$$

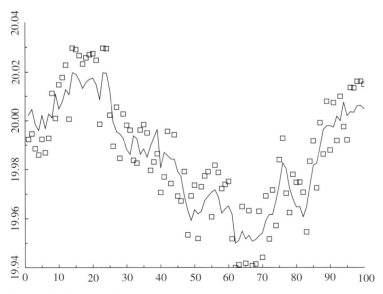

Figure 9.1. Intraday data.

(2) Calculate impulse responses for this VECM; a package like Eviews can do this automatically.
(3) Calculate the long-run impact coefficients, θ.
(4) Finally, calculate the information shares for market 1 and market 2.

Solution
(1) Using the simulated data, we obtain the following VECM estimates:

$$\alpha_1 = -0.6726; \ \alpha_2 = 0.1967; \ \sigma(\epsilon_1) = 0.0121; \ \sigma(\epsilon_2) = 0.0045; \ Corr(\epsilon_1, \epsilon_2)$$
$$= 0.3832$$

The number of lags, K, in the VAR is quite arbitrary, but $K = 5$ is the most commonly observed value in the empirical microstructure literature and this is used for these estimates. For brevity, the estimates of the lag coefficients, A_k, are not reported.

(2) The impulse responses are shown in Figure 9.2. It can be seen that the responses of both prices to a shock in p_1 converge to the same number, and likewise for a shock in p_2. These numbers give the values of θ_1 and θ_2 (to be calculated).

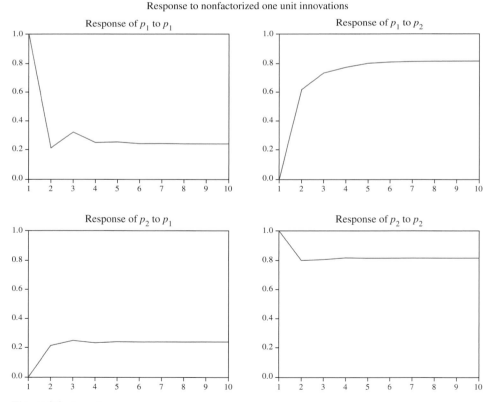

Figure 9.2. Impulse responses.

(3) From the parameter estimates we can estimate θ as follows. The condition $\alpha'\theta = 0$ implies:

$$\theta_2/\theta_1 = -\alpha_1/\alpha_2 = 0.6726/0.1967 = 3.42$$

As discussed in the text, θ can only be identified up to a scale factor, so we normalize θ such that $\theta_1 + \theta_2 = 1$. This gives $\theta_1 = 0.226$ and $\theta_2 = 0.774$.

(4) The information shares are calculated from:

$$IS_i = \frac{Var(\theta_i \epsilon_{it})}{Var(\theta_1 \epsilon_{1t} + \theta_2 \epsilon_{2t})} = \frac{\theta_i^2 Var(\epsilon_{it})}{\theta_1^2 Var(\epsilon_{1t}) + 2\theta_1 \theta_2 Cov(\epsilon_{1t}, \epsilon_{2t}) + \theta_2^2 Var(\epsilon_{2t})}$$

resulting in $IS_1 = 0.28$ and $IS_2 = 0.45$. These information shares add up to less than one, because the total variance is determined also by the covariance term, which cannot be attributed to a single market.

References

De Jong, F. 2002, 'Measures of contributions to price discovery: a comparison', *Journal of Financial Markets,* 5, 323–8.

De Jong, F. and P. Schotman, 2003, 'Price discovery in fragmented markets', Discussion Paper 3987, CEPR, London.

Engle, R. F. and C. W. J. Granger, 1987, 'Co-integration and error correction: representation, estimation and testing', *Econometrica,* 35, 251–76.

Glosten, L. and E. Harris, 1988, 'Estimating the component of the bid/ask spread', *Journal of Financial Economics*, 21, 123–42.

Glosten, L. and P. Milgrom, 1985, 'Bid, ask and transaction prices in a specialist market with heterogeneously informed traders', *Journal of Financial Economics*, 14, 71–100.

Hamilton, J. 1994 *Time Series Analysis*, Princeton University Press.

Hasbrouck, J. 1988, 'Trades, quotes, inventory and information', *Journal of Financial Economics,* 22, 229–52.

  1991, 'Measuring the information content of stock trades', *Journal of Finance,* 46, 179–207.

  1993, 'Assessing the quality of a security market: a new approach to transactions cost measurement', *Review of Financial Studies,* 6, 191–212.

  1995, 'One security, many markets: determining the contributions to price discovery', *Journal of Finance,* 50, 1175–99.

  2002, 'Stalking the "efficient price" in market microstructure specifications: an overview', *Journal of Financial Markets*, 5, 329–39.

Kyle, A. 1985, 'Continuous auctions and insider trading', *Econometrica*, 53, 1315–36.

Lütkepohl, H. 1993, *Introduction to Multiple Time Series Analysis*, 2nd edn, Berlin: Springer.

Stock, J. H., and M. W. Watson, 1988, 'Testing for common trends', *Journal of the American Statistical Association,* 83, 1097–107.

10 Policy issues in financial market structure

In the Introduction we observed that microstructure models are theoretical tools useful both in discussing market design and regulation and in explaining the empirical findings on market price dynamics. In this chapter we consider the issue of transparency, using the models of Kyle and of Grossman and Stiglitz to evaluate the effects of different types of information disclosure on market quality and traders' welfare. Further, we show how Kyle's model can be usefully extended to explain the intraday pattern of volume. Finally we show how liquidity can be crucial to understanding the forces that work for consolidation and for fragmentation.

10.1 Transparency

In this section we return to the transparency of financial markets, which was introduced in Chapter 1. The degree of transparency is relevant because it influences traders' strategies, hence the pricing process. However, given the great variety of aspects, assessing the effects of pre-trade transparency on market quality is complicated, so it is not surprising that the results offered by the literature differ significantly depending on the market structure considered and the type of information revealed. If one models transparency as the increased visibility of the liquidity suppliers' order flows, the effects of pre-trade transparency on market quality will show the benefits of the reduction in adverse selection costs for liquidity and uninformed traders' welfare. Clearly, when liquidity suppliers can screen informed and uninformed traders, they can also offer liquidity on better terms to the uninformed. If, however, pre-trade transparency is modelled as the visibility of traders' identification codes, the effects on market quality can differ, as has been shown by Foucault, Moinas and Theissen (2007) and Rindi (2008). Finally, an often-debated question is the relationship between clients and intermediaries, given that the latter enjoy privileged information on the motivation for their clients' trades and can exploit this by acting as a counterpart in the trades (dual capacity trading (Röell, 1990) or trading before the clients (front running)).

The empirical evidence on the effects of transparency, obtained both with field data and experimental works, is also mixed.[1] Madhavan, Porter and Weaver (2005) found that execution costs and volatility increased on the Toronto Stock Exchange when the real-time information on the limit order book was made public; Boehmer, Saar and Yu (2005), instead, reported the results of the OpenBook experiment conducted by the NYSE in January 2002, showing that when traders were allowed to observe the depth of the NYSE book in real time, execution costs decreased.

We now tackle these topics with the help of the models developed in Chapters 2 and 3, so that we can present the recent contributions to the discussion of transparency. As Chapter 1 shows, to model transparency it is necessary to specify what information can be obtained *ex ante* and who can get it. Recall from Figure 1.3 that information can involve order size and direction as well as traders' identity. Recall also that this information may involve all market participants or only some. Admati and Pfleiderer (1991) analyse the case in which the pre-announcement of orders reveals information on their size and the type of agent making the announcement. Röell (1990) discusses the case of dual trading, where the information on order size and agent type is accessible only to some intermediaries, and Foster and George (1992) and Madhavan (1996) discuss transparency in financial markets more generally. More recent contributions (Foucault, Moinas and Theissen, 2007; Rindi, 2008) take into account the role of market structure and show how greatly the effects of transparency on market quality can differ, depending on the type of information released. For instance, disclosure of the limit order book generally increases liquidity, whereas that of traders' identities may reduce it.

The next three subsections consider the public disclosure of the order size submitted by uninformed traders, namely 'sunshine trading'; then the case in which the same type of information is disclosed only to some market participants so broker-dealers can dual-trade; and finally the more complicated case of the public disclosure of all traders' identities. This will allow us to discuss the effects of anonymity on market quality and traders' welfare.

10.1.1   *Transparency with strategic informed agents*
In this subsection, transparency is analysed using the strategic trading models à la Kyle (1985) presented in Chapter 3.

Sunshine trading   We assume that information on the identity of some uninformed traders is made public or is known by the other market participants, and that their trading strategies are being pre-announced, which means that the size of the orders they will submit at a certain time in the near future is disclosed. The idea behind this practice is that by pre-announcing, uninformed traders should have

---

[1] For instance, Flood, Huisman, Koedijk and Mahieu (1999) find that pre-trade transparency increases liquidity, whereas Bloomfield and O'Hara (1999) and Perotti and Rindi (2006), taking an alternative approach, conclude that transparency can harm liquidity.

lower adverse selection costs; essentially, market-makers should reduce the costs for the orders that they recognize as uninformed. Admati and Pfleiderer (1991) call the pre-announcement of uninformed traders' orders 'sunshine trading'. They study the effects of pre-announcement, assuming a market similar to the competitive protocol of Grossman and Stiglitz (1980). Here, however, we analyse the efficacy of sunshine trading in the Kyle-type framework in which agents behave strategically; the Grossman–Stiglitz framework is left for the discussion of anonymity in section 10.1.2. The model used here differs from Kyle's standard model discussed in section 3.3.2 in that it has two types of liquidity trader: those who pre-announce orders and those who do not. By pre-announcing, liquidity traders disclose themselves as uninformed before trading starts; those who do not pre-announce do not reveal their type. The purpose of the model is to determine the effects of pre-announcement on market quality and traders' welfare. Which traders will take the other side of uninformed traders' pre-announced orders is also in question. The assumptions here are as follows:

- k risk-neutral informed agents maximize their expected end-of-period profit, i.e. $E[\tilde{\pi}_i|\delta + u, z_2]$, and submit the following orders to market-makers:

$$\tilde{x}_i = \beta_k \left(\tilde{\delta} + \tilde{u}\right) \qquad i = 1, \ldots, k$$

- a large number of competitive market-makers ensures semi-strong efficiency:

$$\tilde{p} = E(\tilde{F}|w)$$

- two groups of non-strategic liquidity traders submit orders such as:

$$\tilde{z}_1 \sim N\ (0, \sigma_{z1}^2), \quad \text{for those who do not pre-announce}$$
$$\tilde{z}_2 \sim N\ (0, \sigma_{z2}^2), \quad \text{for those who do pre-announce.}$$

For the solution to the model without pre-announcement, we can use our earlier results; in fact, by substituting the sum of the parameters σ_{z1}^2 and σ_{z2}^2 for parameter σ_z^2 in (3.24) we obtain:

$$\lambda_k = \frac{\sqrt{k}}{(k+1)\sqrt{1+\sigma_u^2}\sqrt{\sigma_{z1}^2 + \sigma_{z2}^2}} \quad \text{and} \quad \beta_k = \frac{\sqrt{\sigma_{z1}^2 + \sigma_{z2}^2}}{\sqrt{(1+\sigma_u^2)\,k}} \tag{10.1}$$

It is now possible to solve the model with pre-announcement, starting from the following hypothesis:

- the strategies of the k informed agents are:

$$\tilde{x}_i = \alpha z_2 + \beta_k \left(\tilde{\delta} + \tilde{u}\right) \qquad \forall\, i = 1, ..., K$$

Notice that z_2 enters the insiders' strategies. A priori, in fact, insiders might have an incentive to accommodate part of the pre-announced orders.

- The net flow of orders that market-makers observe is:

$$\widetilde{w}' = k\beta_k \left(\widetilde{\delta} + \widetilde{u}\right) + k\alpha z_2 + z_2 + z_1,$$

- the market-makers' pricing rule is therefore:

$$\widetilde{p} = \eta + \lambda'_k \widetilde{w}'.$$

This strategy can be derived as follows:

$$\widetilde{p} = E(\widetilde{F}|w') = E(\overline{F} + \widetilde{\delta}| \, k \, \beta_k(\delta + u) + k \, \alpha \, z_2 + z_2 + \widetilde{z}_1)$$
$$= \overline{F} - \lambda'_k \, (k \, \alpha + 1) \, z_2 + \lambda'_k \widetilde{w}' = \eta + \lambda'_k \widetilde{w}'$$

with:

$$\eta = \overline{F} - \lambda'_k \, (k \, \alpha + 1) \, z_2 \quad \text{and} \quad \lambda'_k = \frac{k\beta_k}{k^2\beta_k^2 \left(1 + \sigma_u^2\right) + \sigma_{z_1}^2}.$$

As before, each informed agent maximizes expected profits:

$$E[\widetilde{\pi}_i|\delta + u] = E[x_i(\widetilde{F} - p)|\delta + u] = E\left[x_i\left(\widetilde{F} - \eta - \lambda'_k\widetilde{w}''\right)\right]$$

with:

$$\widetilde{w}'' = (k - 1)\,\beta_k\left(\widetilde{\delta} + \widetilde{u}\right) + (k - 1)\alpha\,z_2 + \widetilde{z}_1 + z_2 + x_i$$

and from first-order conditions we obtain:

$$\widetilde{x}_i = \frac{1 - (k-1)\beta_k(1 + \sigma_u^2)\lambda'_k}{2\lambda'_k(1 + \sigma_u^2)}(\widetilde{\delta} + \widetilde{u}) + \frac{\alpha}{2}z_2$$

and consequently:

$$\beta_k = \frac{1}{(1 + \sigma_u^2)(1 + k)\,\lambda'_k} \quad \text{and} \quad \alpha = 0$$

This result shows that, if everybody knows z_2, speculators will ignore z_2 and condition their trade only on z_1.

Having found that $\alpha = 0$, it is straightforward to derive the market-makers' price function:

$$\widetilde{p} = \eta + \lambda'_k \widetilde{w}' = \overline{F} - \lambda'_k \, (k \, \alpha + 1) \, z_2 + \lambda'_k \left(k \, \beta_k(\widetilde{\delta} + \widetilde{u}) + k \, \alpha \, z_2 + z_2 + \widetilde{z}_1\right)$$
$$= \overline{F} + \lambda'_k \widetilde{w}$$

As before, the equilibrium values of λ'_k and β_k can be obtained by equating conjectures and realizations:

$$\lambda'_k = \frac{\sqrt{k}}{(k + 1)\sqrt{1 + \sigma_u^2}\,\sigma_{z_1}} \quad \text{and} \quad \beta_k = \frac{\sigma_z}{\sqrt{(1 + \sigma_u^2)\,k}} \qquad (10.2)$$

Comparing these values of β_k and λ'_k to those without pre-announcement, we observe that pre-announcement is equivalent to a reduction in the variance of the noise trades; hence the effects of pre-announcement can be evaluated in terms of changes of σ_z:

(1) $\partial\lambda_k/\partial\sigma_z^2 > 0$: following pre-announcement, adverse selection costs for unannounced orders increase; this explains why λ_k increases and liquidity decreases;

(2) $\partial Q/\partial\sigma_z^2 = 0$, where $Q = 1 + k/[1 + (1+k)\sigma_u^2]$ (3.25); a reduction in noise trading has two mutually offsetting effects on price efficiency: it reduces the noise produced by uninformed trading but concurrently increases informed traders' aggressiveness, β_k.

(3) $\partial Var(P)/\partial\sigma_z^2 = 0$: noise variance does not change price volatility ($Var(p) = (1 + \sigma_u^2)(1 + 1/k)$ (3.27));

(4) $\partial E(\pi_I)/\partial\sigma_z^2 < 0$: a reduction in noise trading reduces informed agents' welfare ($E(\widetilde{\pi}_i) = \sigma_z/\left[(k+1)\sqrt{k}\sqrt{1+\sigma_u^2}\right]$ (3.28));

(5) $\partial E(\pi_{z1})/\partial\sigma_z^2 < 0$: a reduction in noise trading increases the expected costs of liquidity traders[2] who do not pre-announce, thus reducing their welfare ($E(\widetilde{\pi}_i) = -\sigma_z\sqrt{k} /\left[(k+1)\sqrt{1+\sigma_u^2}\right]$ (3.29));

(6) $\partial E(\pi_{z2})/\partial\sigma_z > 0$: the expected costs of pre-announcers fall to zero after pre-announcement, so their welfare increases.

In conclusion, under this model's assumptions, the effects of pre-announcement are positive in terms of welfare and liquidity only for those uninformed traders who pre-announce. It would be interesting to verify, using Spiegel and Subrahmanyam (1992), whether pre-announcement is still an equilibrium strategy when uninformed traders behave strategically (Rindi, 1994).

10.1.2   Dual trading

Let us now assume that the information on z_2 can be communicated only to a broker-dealer or to an uninformed strategic agent. An example from financial markets is the access that broker-dealers normally have to their customers' order flow. This situation could induce some intermediaries to practise dual trading by acting as both brokers, who bring clients' orders to the market, and dealers, trading on their own account.

Let us consider how the model changes when we allow for dual trading:

- as previously, k informed agents maximize their expected profit, $E(x_i(F-p)|\delta+u)$ and submit $\widetilde{x}_i = \beta\left(\widetilde{\delta} + \widetilde{u}\right)$;
- a fraction, $\widetilde{z}_1$, of liquidity traders' orders remains anonymous whereas z_2 is known to a strategic broker-dealer who submits $y = -\alpha z_2$ to the market. This is the only privileged information this risk-neutral agent holds;

---

[2] Liquidity traders are assumed not to be optimizing agents; however, following the early literature on market microstructure (e.g. Admati and Pfleiderer, 1988), here we compute liquidity traders' costs as the difference between what they pay for the asset and its expected value.

- after observing the following order flow:

$$\widetilde{w} = k\beta_k(\widetilde{\delta} + \widetilde{u}) + (1 - \alpha) z_2 + \widetilde{z}_1$$

market-makers quote a price function equal to:

$$\widetilde{p} = \overline{F} + \frac{k\beta_k}{k^2\beta_k^2(1 + \sigma_u^2) + (1 - \alpha)^2\sigma_{\widetilde{z}2}^2 + \sigma_{\widetilde{z}1}^2}\widetilde{w}$$

which as before guarantees semi-strong efficiency.

The broker-dealer does not know the asset's liquidation value but, due to his privileged information on z_2, he still has an incentive to trade; he maximizes the end-of-period profits conditional on z_2 and trades y. The broker-dealer's objective function is:

$$\text{Max}_{y} \; E(\widetilde{\pi}_y | z_2) = E(y\left[\widetilde{\delta} - \lambda_k(k\beta_k(\widetilde{\delta} + \widetilde{u}) + y + \widetilde{z}_2 + \widetilde{z}_1)\right] | z_2)$$

$$\text{with} \quad \widetilde{\pi}_y = y[\widetilde{\delta} - \lambda_k(k\beta_k(\widetilde{\delta} + \widetilde{u}) + y + \widetilde{z}_2 + \widetilde{z}_1)].$$

From the first-order condition we obtain:

$$-\lambda_k z_2 = 2\lambda_k y \qquad y = -\frac{z_2}{2} \quad \text{and therefore} \quad \alpha = 1/2$$

and the equilibrium parameters are:

$$\lambda_k = \frac{\sqrt{k}}{\sqrt{1 + \sigma_u^2(k + 1)}\sqrt{(1 - \alpha)^2\sigma_{\widetilde{z}2}^2 + \sigma_{\widetilde{z}1}^2}} \tag{10.3}$$

$$\beta_k = \frac{\sqrt{(1 - \alpha)^2\sigma_{\widetilde{z}2}^2 + \sigma_{\widetilde{z}1}^2}}{\sqrt{k(1 + \sigma_u^2)}} \quad \text{and} \quad \alpha = 1/2 \tag{10.4}$$

This result shows that the broker-dealer will be prepared to fill half the uninformed trader's order ($\alpha = 1/2$) that he observes from his own portfolio. This is a special case of Röell's (1990) model. By suitably extending the analytical framework presented above, one can also discuss other problems related to dual trading and front running (Danthine and Moresi, 1998).

Let us now comment on the value obtained for α. Note that the broker who gets the information (e.g. a buy order from a liquidity trader) knows that it does not come from an insider. If this order were fully transferred to the market, the price would rise, since unlike broker-dealers the other agents do not know that it comes from a liquidity trader and thus revise their price estimates upwards. The broker-dealer takes advantage of this discrepancy between the market price and his own best estimate, filling the client's order in part out of his own portfolio. He is aware that the sale will lower the price, which is why he does not fill the whole order, for if he did so, this would perfectly offset the client's demand and the final price would be unchanged. Thus the broker-dealer behaves like a monopolist facing a linear demand curve, and offers half the quantity demanded, so that the price is driven below the marginal cost.

The following example illustrates the broker-dealer's behaviour. Let us assume that when the price is €100, the broker-dealer receives a buy order for a hundred shares. The strategy he adopts is to supply half that amount from his own portfolio and buy the remaining fifty shares from the market at a price of €101 (supposing the price rises by 1 per cent with the buy order). At this price, the dealer resells all the shares ordered and the price goes back down to €100. The profit comes from selling at €101 the fifty shares he already had in his portfolio at €100.

10.1.3   Identity disclosure and rational liquidity provision

We now tackle the issue of anonymity by extending the rational expectations model set out in Chapter 2 to a regime of full transparency. Under those assumptions, participants observed only the market price and thus traded under the regime with anonymity. We now compare that case with a regime of full pre-trade transparency in which the identity of both informed and uninformed traders is disclosed and agents can consequently tell whether their counterparts are informed or uninformed.

Competitive equilibrium   Under pre-trade transparency, the model can be solved with the same procedure as for anonymity, except that now the uninformed agents use not only the information contained in the market price, but also that contained in the insiders' orders, X_I. In addition, when traders know the insiders' identities, they can discover the signal S by simply observing their demands, and the system becomes fully revealing; this is the reason why, under full pre-trade transparency, an equilibrium may not exist. To avoid this, we must assume that at the beginning of the trading game, insiders receive an endowment shock equal to $\tilde{I} \sim N(0, \sigma_I^2)$. This being so, each uninformed agent's conjecture about the demand functions of the insiders and the other uninformed participants is as follows:[3]

$$\tilde{X}_I = \frac{\tilde{S} - p^T}{A\sigma_\varepsilon^2} - I \tag{10.5}$$

$$\tilde{X} = \frac{E(\tilde{F} \mid p^T, X_I) - p^T}{A \ Var \ (\tilde{F} \mid p^T, X_I)} = -H^T p^T + \Omega X_I \tag{10.6}$$

$$\tilde{x} \sim N\left(0, \sigma_x^2\right) \tag{10.7}$$

It is easily shown that $E\left(\tilde{F} \mid p^T, X_I\right) = E\left(\tilde{F} \mid X_I\right)$, which is tantamount to demonstrating that $\tilde{X}_I$ is a sufficient statistic of the market price, and that the information that uninformed agents get from the insiders' orders already contains the information transmitted by the market price. Notice that, observing $\tilde{X}_I = \frac{\tilde{S} - p^T}{A\sigma_\varepsilon^2} - \tilde{I}$, uninformed agents extract the signal:

---

[3] The insiders' demand function does not change from the regime of anonymity, as in both cases they receive the same signal S.

$$\widetilde{\Theta}' = \widetilde{S} - A\sigma_\varepsilon^2 \widetilde{I} = A\sigma_\varepsilon^2 X_I + p^T = \Theta'$$

In fact, uninformed agents observe X_I and p^T, but do not know $\widetilde{S}$ and $\widetilde{I}$.[4] As before, they use the signal $\widetilde{\Theta}'$ to update their estimate of the future value of the asset, thus obtaining:

$$E\left(\widetilde{F}|\Theta'\right) = \delta\left(X_I A\sigma_\varepsilon^2 + p^T\right)$$

with:

$$\delta = \frac{\sigma_S^2}{\sigma_S^2 + \sigma_I^2 A^2 \sigma_\varepsilon^4}$$

and:

$$Var\left(\widetilde{F}|\Theta'\right) = \sigma_S^2 + \sigma_\varepsilon^2 - \frac{\sigma_S^4}{\sigma_S^2 + \sigma_I^2 A^2 \sigma_\varepsilon^4}$$

Substitution of $E\left(\widetilde{F}|\Theta'\right)$ and $Var\left(\widetilde{F}|\Theta'\right)$ into (10.6), allows us to derive the uninformed traders' demand:

$$X_U = \left(\frac{\delta A\sigma_\varepsilon^2}{A \ Var\ (\widetilde{F} \mid \Theta')}\right) X_I - \left(\frac{1 - \delta}{A \ Var\ (\widetilde{F} \mid \Theta')}\right) p^T$$

Equating the parameters obtained here with those from traders' conjectures on X, i.e. $X = -H^T p^T + \Omega X_I$, we derive the equilibrium values for the parameters H^T and Ω, namely $H^{T*} = 1 - \delta/[A \ Var(\widetilde{F} \mid \Theta')]$ and $\Omega^* = \delta a\sigma_\varepsilon^2/[A \ Var(\widetilde{F} \mid \Theta')]$

We can now determine the *equilibrium price* under the regime with transparency by plugging X and X_U back into the market-clearing condition (2.43):

$$\widetilde{p}^T = \left[\frac{N}{A\sigma_\varepsilon^2} + MH^{T*}\right]^{-1} \left[\left(\frac{N + M\Omega^*}{A\sigma_\varepsilon^2}\right)\widetilde{S} - \left(N + M\Omega^*\right)\widetilde{I} + Z\widetilde{x}\right] \qquad (10.8)$$

As under anonymity, we can now calculate the indicators of liquidity, volatility and informational efficiency under the new regime:

$$LT = \left|\frac{dp^T}{dx}\right|^{-1} = \left[\frac{N}{A\sigma_\varepsilon^2} + MH^{T*}\right] = \left[\frac{N}{A\sigma_\varepsilon^2} + \frac{M}{A \ Var\ (F \mid \Theta')}\right] \qquad (10.9)$$

$$Var\left(p^T\right) = (LT)^{-2}\left[\left(\frac{N + M\Omega^*}{A\sigma_\varepsilon^2}\right)^2 \sigma_S^2 + \left(N + M\Omega^*\right)^2 \sigma_I^2 + Z^2\sigma_x^2\right] \qquad (10.10)$$

$$IET = \left(Var\left(\widetilde{F} \mid \Theta'\right)\right)^{-1} = \left(\sigma_S^2 + \sigma_\varepsilon^2 - \frac{\sigma_S^4}{\sigma_S^2 + \sigma_I^2 A^2 \sigma_\varepsilon^4}\right)^{-1} \qquad (10.11)$$

---

[4] Uninformed agents turn into 'quasi-insiders', since they see a signal $\widetilde{\Theta}' = \widetilde{S} - A\sigma_\varepsilon^2 \widetilde{I}$, which is equal to the insiders' signal, $\widetilde{S}$, plus some noise due to $\widetilde{I}$.

Comparing these indicators of market quality under anonymity and transparency, we draw the following conclusions:

$$L - LT < 0 \tag{10.12}$$

$$Var\left(p^*\right) - Var\left(p^T\right) \lessgtr 0 \tag{10.13}$$

$$IE < IET \tag{10.14}$$

Liquidity and informational efficiency are superior under transparency, while relative volatility depends on the parameter values.

These results hold when the number of market participants is exogenous. If we make the equilibrium number of insiders, N, endogenous, the conclusions concerning the two regimes change. It can be shown (Rindi, 2008) that under transparency liquidity is less (not greater) than under anonymity. This is because with transparency the better-informed agents have less incentive to enter the market and sustain a cost in order to obtain information; the market price itself provides a free signal quite similar to the one they obtain, permitting free-riding by other agents who lack the insiders' information. Since insiders are the best liquidity suppliers in a market-place organized as an open order book, liquidity will decrease if they withdraw. Both the empirical evidence on the Paris Bourse (Foucault, Moinas and Theissen, 2007) and the Italian secondary market for treasury bonds (Scalia and Vacca, 1999), and the experimental findings (Perotti and Rindi, 2006), are consistent with this result.

Imperfect competition   So far, we have considered the Grossman and Stiglitz protocol (1980), in which agents behave competitively. In the spirit of Kyle (1989), let us now take a model in which agents behave strategically and see how transparency affects liquidity under imperfect competition.

Under transparency, the informed trader submits $X_I^S = S - p^{ST} - A\sigma_\varepsilon^2 I / [A\sigma_\varepsilon^2 + \lambda_I^T] = D^T(S - p^{ST}) - G^T I$ with $D^T = 1/[A\sigma_\varepsilon^2 + \lambda_I^T]$ and $G^T = A\sigma_\varepsilon^2/[A\sigma_\varepsilon^2 + \lambda_I^T]$. This demand is derived from the first-order conditions: $S - p^{ST} - (\partial p^{ST})/(\partial X_I)X_I^S - (A/2)[2(X_I^S + I)]\sigma_\varepsilon^2 = 0$ with $\lambda_I^T = \partial p^{ST}/\partial X_I^S = [(N-1)D^T + MH^{ST} + M\Omega^{ST}D^T]^{-1}$. Each uninformed trader places a net demand equal to:

$$X^{ST} = \frac{E(\widetilde{F}|\Theta'_{ST}) - p^{ST}}{A \, Var\,(\widetilde{F}|\Theta'_{ST}) + \lambda_U^T} = -H^{ST}p^{ST} + \Omega^{ST}X_I^S \tag{10.15}$$

where:

$$H^{ST} = \left(1 - \frac{Cov(\widetilde{F}, \Theta'_{ST})}{Var(\widetilde{\Theta}'_{ST})}\right) \Bigg/ (A \, Var\,(\widetilde{F}|\Theta'_{ST}) + \lambda_U^T)$$

$$\Omega^{ST} = \left[\frac{Cov(\widetilde{F}, \widetilde{\Theta}'_{ST})}{Var(\widetilde{\Theta}'_{ST})}(A\sigma_\varepsilon^2 + \lambda_I^T)\right] \Bigg/ [A \, Var\,(\widetilde{F}|\Theta'_{ST}) + \lambda_U^T]$$

$$\lambda_U^T = [ND^T + (M-1)H^{ST} + (M-1)\Omega^{ST}D^T]^{-1}$$

The parameters λ_I^T and λ_U^T can be obtained by solving for p the informed and unin-formed traders' conjectured market-clearing conditions, which are equal to $(N-1)$ $[D^T(S-p^{ST})-G^T I]-M[H^{ST}p^{ST}-\Omega^{ST}X_I^S]+Z\widetilde{x}+X_I^S=0$ and $N[D^T(S-p^{ST})-G^T I]-(M-1)[H^{ST}p^{ST}-\Omega^{ST}X_I^S]+Z\widetilde{x}+X^{ST}=0$ respectively. Notice that uninformed traders use the signal $\widetilde{\Theta}_{ST}'$ to update their expectations on $\widetilde{F}$. As we saw earlier, it is straightforward to show that uninformed traders will discard the signal from the market price and update their beliefs on $\widetilde{F}$ by observing X_I^S and extracting $\widetilde{\Theta}_{ST}'=\widetilde{S}-A\sigma_\varepsilon^2\widetilde{I}=p^{ST}+(A\sigma_\varepsilon^2+\lambda_I^T)X_I^S$. This is because the signal that they can extract from the informed traders' demands is less noisy than the market price. Solving the system with four equations and four unknowns, H^{ST}, Ω^{ST}, λ_U^T and λ_I^T, yields the following results:

$$\widetilde{p}^{ST}=[LST]^{-1}[(ND^T+M\Omega^{ST}D^T)\widetilde{S}-(NG+M\Omega^{ST})\widetilde{I}+Z\widetilde{x}] \qquad (10.16)$$

and

$$LST=[ND^T+MH^{ST}+M\Omega^{ST}D^T]=\left[\frac{N}{A\sigma_\varepsilon^2+\lambda_I^T}+\frac{M}{A\,Var\,(F|\Theta_{ST},\Theta_{ST}')+\lambda_U^T}\right]$$
$$(10.17)$$

Using the expression for the equilibrium price one can run numerical simulations to provide comparisons with the anonymous regime.

10.2 Concentration of volume and volatility

As mentioned in the Introduction to this book, the availability of high-frequency data has allowed researchers to analyse patterns of volumes and liquidity over the trading day. One of the most common pieces of empirical evidence in intraday analysis is that volume and liquidity cluster at the beginning and at the end of the day.

Admati and Pfleiderer (1988) use a Kyle-type framework to explain this result. Their model is similar to the one outlined in section 3.2 in every respect except that they consider two categories of liquidity trader rather than one: discretionary traders who decide the time of the day when they enter the market and whose aggregate order flow is equal to $\sum\widetilde{y}_j$ and non-discretionary traders, who submit random orders equal to $\widetilde{z}$ as previously.

To summarize, the model consists of:

- k informed agents submitting market orders equal to:

$$\widetilde{x}_i=\beta_k(\widetilde{\delta}+\widetilde{u})$$

- a group of competitive market-makers who post the price function:

$$\widetilde{p}=\overline{F}+\lambda_k\,\widetilde{w}$$

- two groups of liquidity traders with the following aggregate demand:

$$\sum \widetilde{y}_j + \widetilde{z} \sim N\ (0, \eta)$$

As before, the values of the parameters λ_k and β_k that are compatible with the equilibrium in linear strategies are:

$$\beta_k = \frac{\sqrt{\eta}}{\sqrt{(1 + \sigma_u^2)\ k}} \qquad \text{and} \qquad \lambda_k = \frac{\sqrt{k}}{(k+1)\sqrt{(1 + \sigma_u^2)\ \eta}} \qquad (10.18)$$

with:

$$\widetilde{w} = k\ \beta_k(\widetilde{\delta} + \widetilde{u}) + \sum_{j=1}^{M} \widetilde{y}_j + \widetilde{z}$$

The equilibrium parameters λ_k and β_k differ from the previous results (3.24) only in the variance of the liquidity traders' net demand.

The discretionary liquidity trader will enter the market when his costs are lowest. These costs are equal to:

$$E[(\widetilde{p} - \widetilde{F})y_j | y_j] = \lambda_k y_j^2$$

and they are lowest at the point where the value of λ_k is the lowest and, consequently, where liquidity is greatest. Discretionary liquidity traders therefore concentrate at the moment when the market is most liquid. Admati and Pfleiderer show that concentration of trading affects volume. In other words, volume is greater when trades are concentrated, because of the increase in volume offered by both liquidity traders and informed agents. In their demonstration, Admati and Pfleiderer proxy trading volume by a measure of turnover that, in addition to the volume intermediated by the market-makers (V^M), also includes the trades of informed agents (V^I) and liquidity traders (V^L):

$$V^I = \sqrt{Var\left(\sum_{i=1}^{K} \widetilde{x}_i\right)} = \sqrt{Var(k\beta_k(\widetilde{\delta} + \widetilde{u}))},$$

$$V^L = \sum_{j=1}^{M} \sqrt{Var\left(\widetilde{y}_j\right)} + \sqrt{Var(\widetilde{z})},$$

$$V^M = \sqrt{Var(\widetilde{w})}$$

Admati and Pfleiderer further demonstrate that liquidity traders will choose to trade at time t^* which is also the time when the informed traders' and the market-makers' volume will be greatest. Hence the equilibrium time t^* will be characterized by:

(1) $V_{t^*}^L > V_t^L, \forall t \neq t^*$
(2) $V_{t^*}^I > V_t^I$
(3) $V_{t^*}^M > V_t^M$

Point 2 can be demonstrated by considering that:

$$V^I = \sqrt{Var\left[k\,\beta_k\,\left(\widetilde{\delta} + \widetilde{u}\right)\right]} = \sqrt{k\,\eta}$$

Concentration of liquidity traders' activity at time t^* increases trading volumes both directly by increasing the variance of liquidity traders' demands, and indirectly by inducing insiders to trade at the same time.

If fixed entry costs are introduced, this phenomenon is reinforced. As we saw in the previous model, informed agents' expected profits are equal to:

$$E(\widetilde{\pi}_i) = E[\widetilde{x}_i(\widetilde{F} - \widetilde{p})] = \frac{\sqrt{\eta}}{\sqrt{k}(k+1)\sqrt{1 + \sigma_u^2}}$$

where $\sigma_z = \sqrt{\eta}$. Hence the informed traders' entry condition is:

$$\frac{\sqrt{\eta}}{\sqrt{k}(k+1)\sqrt{1 + \sigma_u^2}} - C$$

and according to the implicit function theorem we obtain

$$\frac{\partial k}{\partial \eta} = 2\frac{k\,(k+1)}{\sqrt{\eta}(3k+1)} > 0 \tag{10.19}$$

Thus, when η increases, informed traders' expected profits also increase, and this induces at least one informed agent to enter the market. Given that λ_k diminishes as k increases, the entry of an informed agent increases liquidity and thereby reduces expected costs for liquidity traders. This intensifies the concentration of trading. This result depends on λ_k being an inverse function of k. As a matter of fact, when agents receive homogeneous signals an increase in their number increases competition, and hence liquidity. If the signals are heterogeneous, however, these results can change.

10.3 Consolidation and fragmentation

Real-world examples of financial markets show that there are forces both for consolidation and for fragmentation. Concentration of trading appears desirable in terms of liquidity and traders' welfare, but different types of investor (retail v. institutional, patient v. impatient) or specific constraints can induce cross-listing in more than one trading venue; under some circumstances fragmentation too can foster market competition.

In this section we build an example in the spirit of Admati and Pfleiderer (1998) that we can use to discuss how liquidity can affect the process of convergence on a consolidated or a fragmented market equilibrium. Concentration may be explained by economies of scale. As investors place their orders in markets with the lowest transaction costs, they bolster a virtuous circle by increasing the number of investors in those markets. Yet some traders may still have an incentive to fragment their orders, so as to reduce the price impact.

Let us assume that there are two possible markets, A and B. Further assume that each market consists of one informed and one discretionary liquidity trader who can choose their trading venue, and a group of noise traders who cannot choose and submit $\tilde{z}_A \sim N(0, \sigma_A^2)$ and $\tilde{z}_B \sim N(0, \sigma_B^2)$ on markets A and B respectively. The informed trader trades to speculate on his private information and submits either $\tilde{x}_A$ on market A, or $\tilde{x}_B$ on market B, whilst the discretionary liquidity trader submits either $\tilde{y}_A$ on market A, or $\tilde{y}_B$ on market B with $\tilde{y} \sim N(0, \sigma_y^2)$, and σ_y^2 the size of the trade. It follows that the order flows in the two markets are equal to:

$$\tilde{w}_A = \tilde{x}_A + \tilde{y}_A + \tilde{z}_A \tag{10.20}$$
$$\tilde{w}_B = \tilde{x}_B + \tilde{y}_B + \tilde{z}_B$$

Using a Kyle-type model, we can show that if agents on one market cannot observe the order flow of the other market, volume tends to be concentrated in the market where the volume of noise trading (σ_A^2 or σ_B^2) is larger.

Assuming that traders conjecture the following price function for the specialist trading on the two markets:

$$p(\tilde{w}_A) = \overline{F} + \lambda_A \tilde{w}_A \tag{10.21}$$
$$p(\tilde{w}_B) = \overline{F} + \lambda_B \tilde{w}_B$$

Assuming further that the best response of the discretionary liquidity trader to these pricing functions is:

$$\text{Min} \left[E(C_A| y_A) + E(C_B| y_B) \right] \tag{10.22}$$

$$\text{s.t.} \quad \tilde{y}_A + \tilde{y}_B = \tilde{y} \tag{10.23}$$

with:

$$C_A = (p(\tilde{w}_A) - F)\, \tilde{y}_A \tag{10.24}$$
$$C_B = (p(\tilde{w}_B) - F)\, \tilde{y}_B$$

Substituting expressions (10.24) into (10.22), the discretionary liquidity trader's objective function becomes:

$$\underset{y_A, y_B}{\text{Min}} \left[E(C_A| y_A) + E(C_B| y_B) \right] = \lambda_A\, \tilde{y}_A^2 + \lambda_B\, \tilde{y}_B^2 = \lambda_A\, \tilde{y}_A^2 + \lambda_B\, (\tilde{y} - \tilde{y}_B)^2 \tag{10.25}$$

and from the first-order conditions we can derive:

$$\tilde{y}_A = \frac{\lambda_B}{\lambda_A + \lambda_B}\, \tilde{y} \tag{10.26}$$

$$\tilde{y}_B = \frac{\lambda_A}{\lambda_A + \lambda_B}\, \tilde{y}$$

Considering that:

$$\frac{\tilde{y}_A}{\tilde{y}_B} = \frac{\lambda_B}{\lambda_A} \tag{10.27}$$

we can conclude that the deeper the market, the larger the discretionary liquidity trader's order:

$$\sigma_A > \sigma_B \quad \text{if} \quad \lambda_B > \lambda_A$$

The next step is to determine the best response of the informed trader who maximizes end-of-period expected profits:

$$\operatorname*{Max}_{x_A, x_B} [E(\tilde{\pi}_A|F) + E(\tilde{\pi}_B|F)] = \tilde{x}_A(\tilde{F} - \overline{F} - \lambda_A \tilde{x}_A) + \tilde{x}_B(\tilde{F} - \overline{F} - \lambda_B \tilde{x}_B) \quad (10.28)$$

where $\tilde{\pi}_A = \tilde{x}_A(\tilde{F} - p(\tilde{w}_A))$ and $\tilde{\pi}_B = \tilde{x}_B(\tilde{F} - p(\tilde{w}_B))$, and submits:

$$\tilde{x}_A = \frac{\tilde{F} - \overline{F}}{2\lambda_A} \tag{10.29}$$

$$\tilde{x}_B = \frac{\tilde{F} - \overline{F}}{2\lambda_B}$$

Notice that the deeper the market, the larger the informed trader's order. The equilibrium values of λ_B and λ_A can be obtained by imposing the semi-strong efficiency condition and equating previous conjectures on the specialists' pricing function to the realizations of the function itself:

$$p(\tilde{w}_A) = E(\tilde{F}|w_A = \tilde{x}_A + \tilde{y}_A + \tilde{z}_A) \tag{10.30}$$
$$p(\tilde{w}_B) = E(\tilde{F}|w_B = \tilde{x}_B + \tilde{y}_B + \tilde{z}_B)$$

and therefore:

$$p(\tilde{w}_A) = \overline{F} + \frac{Cov(\tilde{F}, \tilde{w}_A)}{Var(\tilde{w}_A)} \tilde{w}_A \tag{10.31}$$

With $Cov(\tilde{F}, \tilde{w}_A) = (\sigma_F^2/2\lambda_A)$ and $Var(\tilde{w}_A) = \sigma_A^2 + (\lambda_B/(\lambda_A + \lambda_B))^2 \sigma_y^2 + (\sigma_F^2/4\lambda_A^2)$, we obtain:

$$\lambda_A = \frac{\dfrac{\sigma_F^2}{2\lambda_A}}{\sigma_A^2 + \left(\dfrac{\lambda_B}{\lambda_A + \lambda_B}\right)^2 \sigma_y^2 + \dfrac{\sigma_F^2}{4\lambda_A^2}} \tag{10.32}$$

Expression (10.32) shows that the liquidity of market A is affected by the liquidity of market B and vice versa.

By symmetry, the value of λ_B can also be derived:

$$\lambda_B = \frac{\dfrac{\sigma_F^2}{2\lambda_B}}{\sigma_B^2 + \left(\dfrac{\lambda_A}{\lambda_A + \lambda_B}\right)^2 \sigma_y^2 + \dfrac{\sigma_F^2}{4\lambda_B^2}} \tag{10.33}$$

The equilibrium values of λ_A and λ_B can be obtained if we recall that, given that $\lambda_A/\lambda_B = \sigma_B/\sigma_A$, we can use $\lambda_B/(\lambda_A + \lambda_B) = \sigma_A/(\sigma_A + \sigma_B)$ to solve the system of the two equations (10.32) and (10.33):

$$\lambda_A = \frac{1}{2}\sqrt{\frac{\sigma_F^2}{\sigma_A^2 + \frac{\sigma_A^2}{(\sigma_A + \sigma_B)^2} + \sigma_y^2}}$$

$$\lambda_B = \frac{1}{2}\sqrt{\frac{\sigma_F^2}{\sigma_B^2 + \frac{\sigma_B^2}{(\sigma_A + \sigma_B)^2} + \sigma_y^2}}$$

(10.34)

Notice that if $\sigma_B < \sigma_A$, then $\lambda_A > \lambda_B$, confirming the previous conjecture: the market with larger volume is the one with greater liquidity. Notice also that if market A is larger than market B, i.e. $\sigma_A > \sigma_B$, both the informed and the discretionary liquidity traders will have an incentive to trade on this market, which will induce a virtuous circle. Notice also that as σ_B becomes smaller than σ_A, λ_B tends to increase and market B becomes illiquid. The next question to ask is whether fragmented markets are desirable and how it is possible for two markets to consolidate. Two markets can consolidate either by merger or if there is a change in post-trade transparency; in terms of the model presented so far, it can be shown how two markets are consolidated as soon as traders on market A are allowed to observe the order flow submitted to market B. Following the expressions (3.5) to (3.7), it is straightforward to show that when the two markets merge, the price function and the informed trader's demand can be written as:

$$p(\widetilde{w}_A + \widetilde{w}_B) = \overline{F} + \lambda_A(\widetilde{w}_A + \widetilde{w}_B)$$
$$= E(\widetilde{F}|\widetilde{w}_A + \widetilde{w}_B)$$

(10.35)

$$\widetilde{x} = \frac{\widetilde{F} - \overline{F}}{2\lambda}$$

(10.36)

with:

$$\lambda = \frac{1}{2}\sqrt{\frac{\sigma_F^2}{\sigma_B^2 + \sigma_A^2 + \sigma_y^2}}$$

(10.37)

The discretionary liquidity trader, instead, submits $\widetilde{y} \sim N(0, \sigma_y^2)$.

If we introduce a change in market transparency whereby agents can observe both markets' order flows simultaneously, the price function is still equal to (10.35) and the discretionary liquidity trader is indifferent between the two markets as he minimizes:

$$\underset{y_A, y_B}{\text{Min}} [E(C_A| y_A, y_B) + E(C_B| y_B, y_A)] = \widetilde{y}_A(\lambda(\widetilde{y}_A + \widetilde{y}_B)) + \widetilde{y}_B(\lambda(\widetilde{y}_A + \widetilde{y}_B))$$

$$= \lambda(\widetilde{y}_A + \widetilde{y}_B)^2 = \lambda \widetilde{y}^2$$

(10.38)

There is an impact on liquidity, however, as the consolidation of the markets increases their liquidity; it is easy to prove that:

$$\lambda < \text{Min}\ (\lambda_A, \lambda_B) \tag{10.39}$$

Let us assume, for example, that $\sigma_A^2 > \sigma_B^2$, and $\lambda_A < \lambda_B$; it follows that if $\lambda < \lambda_A$, then (10.39) holds and comparison between λ and λ_A ((10.37) and (10.34)) shows that:

$$\frac{1}{2}\sqrt{\frac{\sigma_F^2}{\sigma_B^2 + \sigma_A^2 + \sigma_y^2}} < \frac{1}{2}\sqrt{\frac{\sigma_F^2}{\sigma_B^2 + \frac{\sigma_B^2}{(\sigma_A + \sigma_B)^2} + \sigma_y^2}}$$

It can be concluded that consolidation enhances liquidity and consequently reduces noise traders' trading costs. However, it can increase discretionary liquidity traders' transaction costs.[5] If, for example, $\sigma_A^2 = \sigma_B^2$ and hence $\lambda_A = \lambda_B$, when markets are fragmented the discretionary liquidity traders' costs are equal to:

$$\lambda_A\ \tilde{y}_A^2 + \lambda_B\ \tilde{y}_B^2 = \lambda_A \left(\frac{\lambda_B}{\lambda_A + \lambda_B}\ \tilde{y} \right)^2 + \lambda_B \left(\frac{\lambda_A}{\lambda_A + \lambda_B}\ \tilde{y} \right)^2$$

$$= \lambda_A \left(\frac{\sigma_B}{\sigma_A + \sigma_B}\ \tilde{y} \right)^2 + \lambda_B \left(\frac{\sigma_A}{\sigma_A + \sigma_B}\ \tilde{y} \right)^2$$

$$= \lambda_A \frac{1}{4}\tilde{y}^2 + \lambda_B \frac{1}{4}\tilde{y}^2 = \lambda_A \frac{1}{2}\tilde{y}^2$$

whereas when markets are consolidated, total costs are equal to λy^2; we know that $\lambda < \lambda_A$, but it can be shown that with $\sigma_A^2 = \sigma_B^2$, $\lambda > \lambda_A/2$.

The policy implication of this simple exercise is that the liquidity gains of concentrating order flow in one trading venue have to be weighed against the potential benefits of competition between market-places in terms of low handling fees and other costs.

References

Admati, A. and P. Pfleiderer, 1988, 'A theory of intraday patterns: volume and price variability', *Review of Financial Studies*, 1, 3–40.

1991, 'Sunshine trading and financial market equilibrium', *Review of Financial Studies*, 4, 443–81.

Bloomfield, R. and M. O'Hara, 1999, 'Market transparency: who wins and who loses?', *Review of Financial Studies*, 12, 5–35.

Boehmer, E., G. Saar and L. Yu, 2005, 'Lifting the veil: an analysis of pre-trade transparency at the NYSE', *Journal of Finance*, 60, 783–815.

Danthine, J. P. and S. Moresi, 1998, 'Front-running by mutual fund managers: a mixed bag', *European Finance Review*, 2, 29–56.

Flood, M., R. Huisman, K. G. Koedijk and R. Mahieu, 1999, 'Quote disclosure and price discovery in multiple dealer financial markets', *Review of Financial Studies*, 12, 37–59.

---

[5] On this point see Madhavan (1992) where the impact of trade disclosure on market fragmentation is analysed in a model in the spirit of Glosten and Milgrom (1985).

Foster, M. M. and T. J. George, 1992, 'Anonymity in securities markets',*Journal of Financial Intermediation,* 2, 168–206.

Foucault, T., S. Moinas and E. Theissen, 2007, 'Does anonymity matter in electronic limit order markets?', *Review of Financial Studies*, 20, 1707–47.

Glosten, L. and P. Milgrom, 1985, 'Bid, ask and transaction prices in a specialist market with heterogeneously informed traders', *Journal of Financial Economics*, 14, 71–100.

Grossman, S. and J. Stiglitz, 1980, 'On the impossibility of informationally efficient markets', *American Economic Review*, 70, 393–408.

Kyle, A. 1985, 'Continuous auctions and insider trading', *Econometrica*, 53, 1315–35.

1989, 'Informed speculation with imperfect competition', *Review of Economic Studies*, 56, 317–56.

Madhavan, A. 1992, 'Consolidation, fragmentation, and the disclosure of trading information', 3, 579–603.

1996, 'Security prices and market transparency', *Journal of Financial Intermediation*, 5, 255–83.

Madhavan, A., D. Porter and D. Weaver, 2005, 'Should securities markets be transparent?', *Journal of Financial Markets*, 8, 265–87.

Perotti, P. and B. Rindi, 2006, 'Market for information and identity disclosure in an experimental open limit order book', *Economic Notes*, 1, 95–116.

Rindi, B. 1994, 'Sunshine trading revisited: a model with strategic liquidity traders', Working Paper 94.10, University of Venice.

2008, 'Informed traders as liquidity providers: anonymity, liquidity and price formation', *Review of Finance*, 12, 497–532.

Röell, A. 1990, 'Dual capacity trading and the quality of the market', *Journal of Financial Intermediation*, 1, 105–24.

Scalia, A. and V. Vacca, 1999, 'Does market transparency matter? A case study', Working Paper 359, Research Department, Bank of Italy.

Spiegel, M. and A. Subrahmanyam, 1992, 'Informed speculation and hedging in a noncompetitive securities market', *Review of Financial Studies*, 5, 307–29.

Index